The Theatre of Richard Maxwell and the New York City Players

Routledge Advances in Theatre and Performance Studies

1 Theatre and Postcolonial Desires
Awam Amkpa

2 Brecht and Critical Theory
Dialectics and Contemporary
Aesthetics
Sean Carney

3 Science and the Stanislavsky
Tradition of Acting
Jonathan Pitches

4 Performance and Cognition
Theatre Studies and
the Cognitive Turn
*Edited by Bruce McConachie
and F. Elizabeth Hart*

5 Theatre and Performance
in Digital Culture
From Simulation to
Embeddedness
Matthew Causey

6 The Politics of New
Media Theatre
Life®™
Gabriella Giannachi

7 Ritual and Event
Interdisciplinary Perspectives
Edited by Mark Franko

8 Memory, Allegory, and Testimony
in South American Theater
Upstaging Dictatorship
Ana Elena Puga

9 Crossing Cultural Borders
Through the Actor's Work
Foreign Bodies of Knowledge
Cláudia Tatinge Nascimento

10 Movement Training
for the Modern Actor
Mark Evans

11 The Politics of American
Actor Training
*Edited by Ellen Margolis and
Lissa Tyler Renaud*

12 Performing Embodiment in
Samuel Beckett's Drama
Anna McMullan

13 The Provocation of the Senses
in Contemporary Theatre
Stephen Di Benedetto

14 Ecology and Environment in
European Drama
Downing Cless

15 Global Ibsen
Performing Multiple Modernities
*Edited by Erika Fischer-Lichte,
Barbara Gronau, Christel Weiler*

16 The Theatre of the Bauhaus
The Modern and Postmodern
Stage of Oskar Schlemmer
Melissa Trimingham

17 **Feminist Visions and Queer**
   Futures in Postcolonial Drama
   Community, Kinship, and
   Citizenship
   Kanika Batra

18 **Nineteenth-Century Theatre and**
   the Imperial Encounter
   Marty Gould

19 **The Theatre of Richard Maxwell**
   and the New York City Players
   Sarah Gorman

The Theatre of Richard Maxwell and the New York City Players

Sarah Gorman

Routledge
Taylor & Francis Group
NEW YORK   LONDON

First published 2011
by Routledge
711 Third Ave, New York, NY 10017

Simultaneously published in the UK
by Routledge
2 Park Square, Milton Park, Abingdon, Oxon OX14 4RN

*Routledge is an imprint of the Taylor & Francis Group,
an informa business*

Typeset in Sabon by IBT Global.

Library of Congress Cataloging-in-Publication Data
Gorman, Sarah, 1969-
    The theatre of Richard Maxwell and the New York City Players / by
Sarah Gorman.
        p. cm.—(Routledge advances in theatre & performance studies ; no. 19)
        Includes bibliographical references and index.
    1.   Maxwell, Richard, 1967– 2.   Dramatists, American—20th
century—Biography. 3.   Theatrical producers and directors—United
States—Biography. 4.   Experimental theater—United States. 5.   New
York City Players (Theater troupe) I. Title.
        PS3613.A93Z68 2011
        792.09747'1—dc22
        2010053784

ISBN13: 978-0-415-99092-9 (hbk)
ISBN13: 978-0-203-81025-5 (ebk)

For Marjorie and Jeff

Contents

List of Figures   xi
Preface   xiii
Acknowledgments   xix

1   **Introduction: Opportunity Knocks**   1

2   **Bad Acting *on Purpose*:**
    Practising Intelligibility and Legitimacy on Stage   30

3   **Passionate Indifference: Cook County Theater Department**   50

4   **'I Got Balls, See?' A Study of Working-Class Masculinity in**
    the Plays of Richard Maxwell and the New York City Players   69

5   **Concert Hall Slash Sports Facility:**
    The Anthropological Space of Richard Maxwell's Theatre   91

6   **Conclusion: Inscrutability, Irony and Binary Assignations**   117

Notes   131
Bibliography   139
Index   147

Figures

1.1 Rosemary Allen and Kevin Hurley use dining tables
     to stand in for their bed. (Photo: Michael Schmelling.)   19
2.1 Ellen LeCompte and Pete Simpson play mother and
     son in *Drummer Wanted*. (Photo: Michael Schmelling.)   40
2.2 Jim Fletcher as King Henry IV. (Photo: Michael Schmelling.)   45
2.3 Thomas Bradshaw, Alex Delinois, Sibyl Kempson
     and Jim Fletcher fight in *The End of Reality*.
     (Photo: Michael Schmelling.)   46
3.1 Rebecca Rossen, Roberto Argentina, Chris Sullivan and
     Vicky Walden in *Minutes and Seconds*. (Photo: Lara Furniss.)   58
3.2 Roberto Argentina, Gary Wilmes and Vicky Walden
     in *Minutes and Seconds* (Photo: Lara Furniss.)   60
3.3 Gary Wilmes and Vicky Walden in *Tosca*.
     (Photo: Lara Furniss.)   63
4.1 Brian Mendes in *The End of Reality*.
     (Photo: Michael Schmelling.)   79
4.2 Jim Fletcher and Greg Mehrten in *Ode to
     the Man Who Kneels*. (Photo: Michael Schmelling.)   85
5.1 Jim Fletcher in Showcase. (Photo: Unknown.)   106
5.2 Brian Mendes, Anna Kohler, Jim Fletcher and
     Greg Mehrten in *Ode to the Man Who Kneels*.
     (Photo Michael Schmelling.)   113

Preface

During a period of research leave in 2006 I identified some quiet time to work on my research at a writer's retreat in Wengen, Switzerland. Unfortunately my sense of inner peace and well being was short-lived as I was forced back to the real-world demands of university life by the news that funding to extend my study leave depended upon my securing consent from the University ethics committee. I had failed to ask Richard Maxwell, and other members of the New York City Players to sign official consent letters to state clearly that they understood that I would be drawing upon opinions expressed during interview in my research. After a heated telephone exchange with the chair of our Ethics committee, I agreed to forward all the emails between myself and company members, so that each informal exchange (in which we agreed to a discussion) could stand-in for the absent formal pro-forma letter. Whilst frustrating at the time, the issue of 'ethics' and the disparity between my and the university's understanding of an ethical relationship between researcher and artist, came to prey upon my mind a great deal. What has become clear to me, over the past nine years of my interest in NYCP, is how the theorising and fixing of ideas associated with conventional academic writing can often undermine the nuanced complexity of what actually takes place in the rehearsal room and on stage. I have been repeatedly surprised, during my period of questioning, by answers that contradict my expectations and reveal the company's preoccupations to have been located in an entirely different set of concerns to my own.

In January 2006 I sat in on rehearsals for *The End of Reality* and completed a chapter for Jen Harvie and Andy Lavender's *Making Contemporary Theatre: International Rehearsal Processes*. My experience of rehearsal observation was fascinating, but also unsettling as it revealed the importance of shared understanding and intuition in the company's work, a feature I found that I had to all but explain away when sitting down to provide a theory and rationale for the activities I witnessed. As part of my work on *The End of Reality* rehearsals I refer to Sara Ahmed's warning that in attempting to 'translate' what the observer sees, anthropological study regularly 'de-terms' its 'strangeness' and so robs it of its radical potential. Ahmed's suspicion of the inevitable transfer of value-sets from observer to the observed has provided a sobering reminder to strive for a visible sense of self-reflexivity in a culture which, despite its supposed reinvention after poststructuralism, continues to revere the objective, masterful voice. Reflecting upon past experiences of presenting this work, I realise how little control I have over how my observations are received. Sections of rehearsal room conversation I have been convinced would remain funny lost some of their humour 'in translation' and came to appear potentially dogmatic or strident when deprived of the ironic context of their utterance. Mendes and Maxwell responded to a draft of my chapter saying that they appreciated its 'honesty', but I came away perhaps feeling that perhaps I had not done the company justice. This sense of ambivalence about writing, when one has come to identify so closely with the object of study, must be familiar to many, however the necessity to strike a balance between critical distance and personal dialogue renders the process more difficult than one would initially imagine. Company dynamics are inevitably tied up with friendships; the tone of interviews and exchanges are informed by a sense of mutual trust and respect; differences of opinion on occasion must be tempered in order to avoid an unproductive rift; fascinating, yet sensitive confessions must be used with tact. All of these limitations characterise (and yet humanise) the task of putting together a book project about a practitioner or group of artists.

During the course of a particularly fruitful research trip to Bonn I met Natalie Alvarez, a Canadian academic also conducting research into NYCP. We were both due to see *The Frame* (2006) at Halle Beuel. After the evening's performance we exchanged ideas about the experience of researching Maxwell's work and academic research in general. One issue we discussed was Maxwell's approachability and willingness to discuss his work. He operates an 'open rehearsal' policy and has accommodated Alvarez, myself and countless other critics and academics on numerous occasions in order to respond to enquiries about his plays and directorial methodology. Alvarez confessed that she found him a reluctant, but 'natural intellectual', a description I found apt, but unusual given that Maxwell has openly admitted that he is 'resistant to talking about work in an intellectual way'[1]. Although he may not respond enthusiastically to such an idea, it is clear that within his work Maxwell is constantly revisiting and testing received ideas about theatre, culture and acting. A survey of references to points of inspiration reveal an eclectic range of starting points: Naomi Klein's *No Logo*, Khalil Gibran's *The Prophet*, the work of Forced Entertainment and Goat Island; Heavy Metal documentaries, coming of age films and disaster movies. What is also curious about Alvarez's description is that Maxwell clearly finds it difficult and challenging to discuss his work. Conversations and interviews are regularly punctuated by long pauses as he searches for the most appropriate vocabulary to express his thoughts. I believe that what emerges from Alvarez's description and Maxwell's resistance to intellectualising is a sublimated suspicion of verbal articulation which I believe provides fruitful and productive material for contemplation. Although I do not want to make any easy equivocations between Maxwell as a person and his work, the issues of language, feeling, articulation and communication clearly hold a great deal of significance for him and have subsequently had a tremendous impact upon his work. It is the repeated staging and dramatisation of the strenuous task of articulation which I have found so compelling and which has led me, throughout the project of book writing, to return to these ideas as central whether explored through spatial metaphor, gender, anti-Humanism or social geography. Regardless as to whether Maxwell feels comfortable with the moniker of intellectual, his work stands up to the most rigorous scrutiny and offers up a significant amount of material revealing original and insightful approaches to contemporary Western society.

Being located in the UK, I did not encounter Maxwell's work until 2001 when The Barbican, London programmed *Boxing 2000* and *Drummer Wanted* into its studio theatre, The Pit. I was fascinated by the work's generic oddity and the hypermasculine world of the plays. I became more emotionally involved with Maxwell's work when, in October 2003 I attended Maxwell's production of *Henry IV Part 1* at the Brooklyn Academy of Music before the cancellation of its London run in The Barbican main house. In an early telephone interview Maxwell confessed that he had been shaken by the response to *Henry IV* and after developing 'a thick skin really quickly' found himself wondering whether the show was 'radical or just really bad?'

Prior to our discussion, I had composed a letter of complaint to the Barbican about the cancellation, and received a response from Artistic Director Graham Sheffield. He revealed that he deeply regretted the decision as he, too had found 'much to admire within the concept' but went on to disclose that, 'as we move towards finding our own "Shakespearean and classic voice" in the post RSC era at the Barbican, we feel [Maxwell's production] was simply too far away from where the majority of our audience currently is!" [2] The Barbican have continued to support Maxwell's work, to a certain extent, programming pieces such as *Joe* (2002), *Showcase* (2003) and *The End of Reality* (2006), however much of his post 2006 work has enjoyed greater exposure in mainland Europe, appearing in cities including Geneva, Bonn, Graz, Groningen, Cardiff and Dublin. Phillipa Wehle has wondered at Maxwell's European appeal, writing that he is 'beloved of the French and other Europeans, but so uniquely American?' (Wehle 2007:165). After the Barbican cancellation my interest in Maxwell's work expanded to include a fascination with his representation of a middle-American masculine identity, which manifests itself here within my chapter about gender and masculinity. Maxwell was generous enough to read through various drafts of my writing and engage in a challenging and stimulating exchange. For example, whilst apologising for being 'one of those annoying "living playwrights"' he confessed that 'I can't resist commenting on what you've written, and that's partly because I'm intrigued by your insights.'[3]

I have also come to realise that my interest in Maxwell's work arose out of a fascination with the kind of 'rough' or unfinished theatre I was introduced to at Lancaster University as part of my MA in 1992 and then during my time working at the University's Nuffield Theatre. Artists such as Forced Entertainment, Goat Island, Graeme Miller, desperate optimists, Stan's Cafe and Reckless Sleepers regularly visited Lancaster, and came to influence teaching on both BA and MA programmes. As part of my time at Lancaster I was granted my own unique opportunity to 'fail' onstage in a production entitled *Dying I Come*, in which I played a Judy Garland impersonator. My performance included a terrible; if well-intentioned rendition of *Smile*, [4] a performance which perplexed audience members, who, after the event admitted to be unsure as to whether it was 'really bad' or a well-honed performance of a bad impersonation. In retrospect I realise I should have been flattered at their ambiguity, instead I felt rather humiliated and resolved to direct my energies into other aspects of theatre production. My own experience of exposing a lack of training has fuelled my interest in watching artists and companies who attempt to strip away layers of rehearsal and finesse in order to expose a vulnerable (and extremely nervous) performer.

On reflection, I also came to realise that I was drawn to the dramatisation of gruff male inarticulacy in Maxwell's work as it resonated with my sense of the romanticisation or celebration of this kind of inarticulacy in British northern working class males. Completing an Art Foundation course in Wakefield, West Yorkshire, I experienced a very male-dominated culture, which prized expression through painting and sculpture over verbal articulacy. Those capable of applying themselves with a quiet determination, and yet without appearing to take themselves too seriously, were deemed to have the most integrity. In addition, I realise that my own family members have always eschewed 'fuss', with the dictum 'least said soonest mended' navigating us through even the most emotionally gruelling times. Finally, I have always found Forced Entertainment's predilection for the fictional worlds of those affected by decisions, rather than decision-makers, very moving, and see this objective repeated across many of Maxwell's productions (Etchells 1999:32). Ultimately, the appeal of Maxwell's work, then, appears to lie in his critical yet fond depiction of vulnerable working-class people who strain to articulate their inner thoughts. As Sara Jane Bailes has suggested in her recent book *Performance Theatre and the Poetics of Failure*, in this performance of awkwardness it is 'unclear who or what is failing whom' (Bailes 2011: 156); characters in failing performances appear caught in the thrall of forces beyond their control and reliant upon the diminished resources available to them. The plight of subjects coming to terms with their own lack of agency appears particularly pertinent to me as a product of a particular type of northern British upbringing, but also to a postmodern or postcolonial critique of a late capitalist world caught up in the competitive thrust of global market forces.

Influenced, as I am by poststructuralist poetics, I would be reluctant to imply that some interpretations of Maxwell's work are more authoritative than others. I have been working with cognisance of Barthes' "Death of the Author" and this has tempered my inclusion of Maxwell's attempts to explain approaches to his work. Whilst I have found material garnered from interviews to be illuminating and invaluable, with Barthes in mind I am reluctant to defer back to Maxwell's viewpoint as necessarily the most persuasive. Contexts of viewing have also inevitably played a part in my reception of his work. I have travelled to see two of Maxwell's pieces in New York, but have seen the remainder in Europe, in: London, Cardiff, Paris, Groningen, Santarcangelo, Bonn, Brussels and Geneva.[5] The make-up of the theatre audience always plays a key part in shaping one's experience of watching Maxwell's work; the response of the audience differs, for example, according to the accuracy of the translation used for the sur or sub-titles and the number of fluent English speakers present. Whilst watching the work in England or America I have noticed how the enthusiastic laughter from some quarters appears a little forced, as if theatre enthusiasts are keen to perform the fact that they 'get' what the work is about. Critics of *Henry IV Part 1* observed this phenomenon during the Brooklyn Academy of Music production and I would concur that it does appear to be a repeated feature of audience behaviour for some of his plays.

The issue of a definitive or authoritative interpretation is important to Maxwell because he resists providing easy answers and incorporates elements that introduce a certain degree of ambiguity about his intention. He has gone out of his way to state that he 'prefers to let the audience project onto what it is they're seeing' (Wehle 2001: 4). It strikes me that Maxwell is uneasy about the excavation of the potential meaning and processes behind his work. Part of this resistance may be to do with his suspicion of esoteric intellectual discourse, or more simply to do with privacy, however, I feel it is important to clarify that, although he is open to dialogue Maxwell does not want to explain away the complexities of the work. For him, once a 'shorthand' theory has been attached then it loses its magic. He confesses, 'that's the thing I don't like about shorthand is that once it's identifiable . . . the magic has gone. Now it's a novelty, it's a gimmick' (Gorman 2007: 241). By agreeing to suspend their suspicions about academics and those keen to explain away mystique Maxwell and other NYCP members have been of great assistance to my research. I have been responsible for determining the detailed content of the chapters and although they have always informed fruitful exchange, Maxwell has held back from suggesting whether my interpretations ring true or false.

As I approach the end of a significant research process the activities of introducing and rounding-up my findings have forced me to revise my own journeys and attitudes towards the work over the past decade. Current research plans involve returning to the feminist performance and theory I felt inspired by as an MA student in the mid-90s and along with a number of other academics I find myself compelled to revisit the subject of feminist theatre and performance in our supposedly post-feminist, post-ironic, post-emotional, post-racial age. Attending a recent symposium about post-structuralism and feminism [6] I found statements from Anita Biressi about the fall from favour of class studies and Jen Coates' reminder that 'we have lost sight of the fact that we still live in a patriarchy' strangely reassuring, as if they were returning to agenda items which appeared to have been forgotten. The symposium explored the use-value of poststructuralism in popularising a drive to celebrate pluralism and to see ideology as created in and perpetuated through language. However, a consensus also appeared to emerge, which proposed that poststructuralism had somehow robbed class and gender politics of their clout by suggesting that they relate to two subaltern experiences among many. Indeed, however marginalised an educated white woman may feel in a patriarchal Western society it is difficult to see how it presents as urgent a political message as the plight of an educated Afghan woman living under the Taliban.

This symposium caused me to question why, given my longstanding feminist concerns, I had found myself writing my first book about a male American playwright. It is possibly because gender did appear, at one point, to be off the political and academic agenda. However, my interest in Maxwell's work remains informed by an ongoing interest in both class and gender, and I have found a significant amount of stimulating material, both within the plays and the wider contextual reading which has expanded my understanding. Although the archetypical men and women of his most recent work (*Ode to the Man Who Kneels*, 2007, *People Without History*, 2008, *Das Maedchen* 2010) do not lend themselves quite as readily to pro-feminist critique, I have remained interested in the way that Maxwell's work deconstructs received assumptions about a number of topics close to my heart. I have found much to write about his approach to a range of subjects, including: theatrical realism; Method-driven approaches to acting; vernacular, language, class, masculinity, social mobility and failure. His work is also provocative in its engagement with representations of American culture and landscape and the anti-Humanist bias evident in his characterisation speaks eloquently of the end of America's 'victory culture' and the demise of the American Dream (Agnew and Sharp 2002: 95). The aim of this book is to share a wealth of knowledge about Maxwell's work with as wide a readership as possible and to situate his work in the context of social, cultural and aesthetic preoccupations informing a late 20th and early 21st century Western landscape. My interpretation will inevitably be shaped by my own cultural and gendered perspective and I realise that many more interrogative frameworks remain to be applied: I look forward to being part of an ongoing discussion about the relevance of the work of Richard Maxwell and the New York City Players as an increasing number of scholars and critics take note of his work.

Acknowledgments

I would like to extend my gratitude to colleagues at Roehampton University, both past and present, who have supported my research directly and indirectly. I would like to thank Jo Clegg, Veronika Wilson, Josh Abrams, Lis Austin, Simon Bayly, Xavier Briche, Trevor Dean, Debbie Hall, Sophie Hills, Adrian Heathfield, Victoria Lewis, Joe Kelleher, Emily Orley, Terry O'Connor, Jen Parker-Starbuck, Ioana Szeman, Fiona Wilkie, Jonathan Wilson, Graham White, Lee White, Pa Skantze, Ernst Fischer, Susanne Greenhalgh, Susan Painter, Jen Harvie, Sophie Nield, Gianna Bouchard, Alan Read, Adrian Kear, Peter Majer and Peter Reynolds. I would also like to thank the many Roehampton students who have provided insights into the work of the New York City Players through their explorations in the Advanced Theatre Practices, Thinking Through Theatre and Performing Failure modules.

I would also like to thank old colleagues at De Montfort University, Royal Holloway University of London and Lancaster University. In particular I would like to thank Geraldine Harris, Andrew Quick, Keith Sturgess, Margaret Eddershaw and Rob Clow for the support and encouragement they have provided over the years. I am also very grateful to colleagues in the wider academic community who have invited me to speak about the New York City Players and have provided invaluable feedback: Mary Richards, Fiona Templeton, Helen Paris, Sara Jane Bailes, Gretchen Schiller, Steve Blandford, Dan Rebellato, Theron Schmidt, Nick Ridout, Aoife Monks, Helen Freshwater, Andy Lavender, Trish Reid.

I would like to thank: Julie Rainey, Graham White, Sophie Nield, Emma Govan-Brodzinski, Lara Furniss, Justin Hayford, Natalie Alvarez and Siobhan Glennon for reading through drafts of the various chapters and providing insightful advice and comments. I would also like to thank Liz Levine and her colleagues at Routledge and IBT Global for helping process and prepare the manuscript. Very special thanks to friends and family who have been very patient and understanding about my absence from family activities as I have worked to complete the manuscript.

Finally, I would like to express my gratitude to Richard Maxwell himself and all members of the New York City Players who have generously given their time in talking over ideas and granting me time in the rehearsal room. In particular I would like to thank Brian Mendes, Sibyl Kempson and Jim Fletcher, who have patiently fielded my questions in theatre bars across the globe. Thanks too to Nicholas Elliott, Jerimee Bloemeke, Scott Sherratt, Christina Masciotti, Justin Hayford, Gary Wilmes, Kate Gleason, Tory Vazquez, Vicky Walden, Michael Schmelling, Stephanie Shaw and all at the Santarcangelo 2009 festival. Thanks in particular to Michael Schmelling and Lara Furniss for their generosity in giving permission to use their photographs.

I would like to acknowledge the support of the Arts and Humanities Research Council who supported my research through the Research Leave Scheme. Finally, I would like to express my extreme gratitude to Paul and Emily Lansley whose love and affection buoys me up day after day.

1 Introduction
Opportunity Knocks

The work of Richard Maxwell and the New York City Players has received significant international recognition over the past ten years: the company was invited to perform as part of the Venice Biennale's thirty-seventh theatre festival (2005) and has received three OBIEs, for *House* (1999), *Drummer Wanted* (2002) and *Good Samaritans* (2005).[1] Many of Maxwell's plays have been published in journals or by Theatre Communications Group in the collection *Plays, 1996–2000: Richard Maxwell*. He has been commissioned to write material by venues in the United States, the United Kingdom, Germany, Austria, the Netherlands, France and Ireland. In 2010 Maxwell was awarded a Guggenheim Fellowship and at the time of publishing, was preparing work for Brussels' Kunsten Festival. Although a number of scholars have discussed his work, and his productions always generate numerous reviews, there is comparatively limited material available for those wishing to study his work in greater depth. The aim of this volume is to fill this gap and provide a critical survey of Maxwell's work since 1992, including his early participation in Cook County Theater Department. In addition to performing close readings of his plays I also interrogate the choices Maxwell has made as a director in mounting productions of his own work. I refer to my project as an analysis of both the intra- and extra-diegetic worlds of the plays—that is to say I scrutinise the plays as representations of coherent fictional worlds as well as paying attention to the context of production in order to examine how choices relating to casting, lighting, blocking and set design affect the signification of the production as a whole. The socio-political concerns that emerge throughout the book signify that Maxwell's work is necessarily situated in the context of contemporary American culture. Similarly, his experimentations with language, casting and scenography call for a contextual analysis of the practitioners and theatre companies influencing his work. In addition to introductory and concluding chapters, the book comprises four chapters, each considering the work from a clearly identified viewpoint (Method Acting and Humanism; the problem of historiographical research; constructions of masculinity; the representation of space). Each chapter introduces and contextualises the nominated critical framework and provides detailed textual analysis from a range of relevant performances. My approach is informed by a desire to identify and focus upon repeated themes emerging from Maxwell's work, but also to situate his ideas more generally in relation to a burgeoning culture of theatre activity. It is my hope that this format will enable those reading the whole book to gain a rounded understanding of a range of aspects of the work, and for others wishing to use the book for discrete chapters, to gain a perspective on a particular pre-defined approach.

Maxwell's work is perhaps unusual in terms of a tradition of 'downtown' New York theatre-making as it borrows a metatheatrical and deconstructive bias from fellow New York theatre-makers such as Richard Foreman and The Wooster Group, whilst also paying homage to a history and tradition of realist playwriting and actor training. In making a distinction between these companies, I would argue that The Wooster Group and Richard Foreman, whilst interrogating the ontological significance of theatre, borrow their methodologies from performance-art, Happenings or postmodern dance. Maxwell, on the other hand, retains a fascination with theatre, but borrows his frame of reference from a tradition of mainstream *and* alternative theatre. It is interesting to note that Maxwell's work is cited as an example of 'postdramatic theatre' in Hans Thies Lehmann's eponymous text as Lehmann cites the 'blurred boundary between theatre and forms of practice such as performance art' as one of the features characterising this new genre of postdramatic theatre'.[2] Maxwell's work can be distinguished from performance work because he identifies as the sole author of the work and as the 'director' of the piece, working practices customarily regarded as 'hegemonic' and 'theological' in the performance discourse (Vanden Heuvel 1991, MacDonald 1993); he also writes plays which feature teleological narratives and constructs ostensibly coherent characters, who are portrayed by actors who remain in role for the duration of the performance. However, in other aspects, Maxwell's work is very much in keeping with avant-garde performance work. Like Foreman he recruits both professional and non-professional actors, and as in the case of The Wooster Group and UK ensemble Forced Entertainment, he incorporates signs of the 'amateur' into his performances. The emotionally restrained mode of delivery his actors customarily demonstrate suggests that they are not pursuing a psychologically-motivated method of characterisation and the (broadly) linear flow of the narrative is regularly punctuated, or interrupted by soft rock ballads and clumsy fight sequences. The approach to acting and direction, in particular, suggests that Maxwell is heavily influenced by Brechtian *Verfremdungseffekt* and his recruitment of untrained performers indicates that he is interested in capitalising on their lack of experience in disguising nerves and stage-fright and so exploiting some aspect of their 'real' or 'authentic' physiology, a feature more commonly associated with performance-art. Maxwell's work has also been compared to Beckett, another canonical master, with one reviewer writing that his plays are about, 'the dead, numbed center of everyday life, about a Beckettian existential despair' (Sandman 2009).

Maxwell was born in Fargo, North Dakota in 1967 and moved to Niles, Illinois when he was thirteen. He studied acting at Illinois State University (including a year abroad in the UK at Brighton Polytechnic) and won a fellowship to work with Steppenwolf Theatre Company in Chicago between 1991 and 1992. Whilst at Steppenwolf he met Brian Mendes and Kate Gleason and founded Cook County Theater Department (CCTD) along with high school friend Gary Wilmes, and a number of other local artists. Maxwell worked with CCTD until 1994 when he moved to New York, started writing plays and took up internships with The Wooster Group and worked as Resident Artist at the Ontological Theater. After leaving Chicago Maxwell wrote and directed *Burlesque* (1995) before starting work with The New York City Players (NYCP) with *Billings* in 1996. Maxwell continues to live in New York and regularly works with artists and collaborators from CCTD.

In response to Wehle's question in my preface about why NYCP enjoys such popularity in France, I would propose that it is perhaps Maxwell's fondness for, yet critical relationship to, contemporary America which underpins his European appeal. Work considered critical of American politics and culture will inevitably enjoy support from audiences already suspicious of the creep of cultural imperialism. Discussing his perception of a sense of European cultural superiority with Bonnie Marranca in 2002, Maxwell stated that he sensed a resistance to his work in Europe. His suspicions are perhaps fuelled by a perceived sense of disquiet about American culture, particularly by Northern European countries such as France and England who bemoan the effects of cultural imperialism upon their own sense of cultural identity. Agnew supports Maxwell's suspicions when he reveals:

> Many in the European elites were and have remained largely dismissive of the American experiment. Most, though have failed to examine it on its own terms, as an exercise in political organization of space, and have preferred to make supercilious claims about its cultural vulgarity, compared to posh and sophisticated European drawing room culture . . . (Agnew 2002: 2)

Although Maxwell is critical of many American values in his work he also writes with a profound affection for American people and the American cultural landscape. He told Marranca, 'I can criticise because I live here. I don't have any problem with America, *per se*. I like living here. But I have a problem with the current [Bush] administration.' Indeed, a survey of his work over the past fifteen years demonstrates a repeated desire to return to the subjects of contemporary American attitudes to work, individualism, social mobility, class and multiculturalism. As with contemplations around emotional disclosure and masculine vulnerability, his attitude does not fit easily into any single ideological faction. His appreciation for the 'honest' American value of 'gumption' is perhaps more customarily aligned with a conservative politics, as is his apparent nostalgia for an America unspoilt by multinational capitalism.[3] However, his repeated dramatisation of the disparity between, what C. W. E Bigsby has termed, 'a utopian rhetoric and a diminished and flawed experience' and his celebration of blue-collar labour, places him at the more progressive, liberal end of the political spectrum (Bigsby 2000: xii). Richard Sennett has written that it has become a 'journalistic cliché to divide America into red and blue states', however the levels of disquiet caused by the contrasting Republican and Democrat strongholds do clearly provide more scope for investigation than Sennett would allow as Maxwell's characters repeatedly mine ideological schisms and play out the tensions arising from the contradictions and ambiguities inherent in either camp (Sennett 2004). Maxwell has admitted that he is reluctant to produce issue-based plays and suspects that, 'political theatre doesn't work by and large'; however it is impossible to view his work without registering his ambivalence about fundamental American myths of freedom and individualism (Bomb Magazine 2010). The presence of multiracial blue-collar workers in his plays is also testament to an interest in class and the illusion of social mobility. His references to churches being demolished to accommodate luxury flats and the prevalence of coexisting liquor stores and churches in suburban outposts also points to an interest in what Una Chaudhuri has called the 'erasure of spatial particularity' as one of the 'hallmarks of postmodernism represented in drama (and elsewhere) through the figure of America' (Chaudhuri 1995: 4). Maxwell's oeuvre articulates many of the contradictions and complexities about the changing American social and political landscape without providing easily palatable solutions.

As I have established, social-mobility plays a key role in Maxwell's oeuvre. In Chapter 2 I discuss the illusion of agency and free will as belonging to a Humanist ethos. Throughout the book I argue that although Maxwell's politics are not always readily identifiable, there is ample evidence of a drive to de-mystify Humanist ideology, particularly in relation to contemporary American attitudes towards social mobility and freedom. Myths of freedom and individualism underpin the popular conception of the American Dream, a philosophy characterising the sense of limitless optimism experienced by generations of American immigrants and settlers. Along with a significant body of American playwrights such as Miller, Shepard, Albee and Mamet, Maxwell questions fundamental values underpinning American national identity. These values are fundamental because, according to John Agnew, 'the Declaration of Independence and the United States Constitution are usually taken to enshrine an ideology of individual success and personal improvement often labelled in the Twentieth Century as the American Dream' (Agnew 2002: 3). The importance of an ideology of individualism is central to Maxwell's work, at times it appears as if his characters are unable to communicate effectively because their individual agenda occludes any concern or empathy for others.

A piece such as *The Frame* (2006) concerns itself most obviously with the myth of America as a place offering new opportunities and new beginnings. The Mentis family are forced to leave Germany after Father Mentis has been executed for murder. Upon their arrival the characters describe the land as 'beautiful'. They meet an English character who tells them, 'those who preceded us, they founded everything that you can see around you!' She confesses to having been saved by 'generous benefactors' who 'came in out of the blue and saved me'[4]. As what Jeffrey D. Mason has termed 'the object of hope' America has fed the aspirations of generations of migrants seeking a better life. Although Maxwell's work is largely set in the present, plays such as *Cowboys and Indians* (1998) and *Ode to the Man Who Kneels* (2007), look back to an era of western expansion and settlement across the continent. Once again, aspiration and social mobility are key themes developed, as characters experience the disparity between the promise and reality of freedom. America's symbolic presence as a utopian land of plenty provides a fascinating context in which to locate a more general sense of dissatisfaction with Enlightenment values.

Mason describes America's promise as conferring a 'special status', which 'carries a unique burden':

> For more than two centuries, the United States has offered itself as the realization of the aspirations of multitudes, appropriating the halo of freedom and righteousness in spite of what seems, . . . to be a growing chorus of resentful, accusatory and critical voices. As the object of hope, "America" becomes a concept that transcends mere nationality, a symbol belonging not only to its citizens, but to those who yearn, no matter from what cultural tradition they might spring. (Mason1999: 2)

The promise of freedom, equality and choice in reward for hard work has made America into the Land of Opportunity for many. The repetition of this promise through political rhetoric, multinational advertising and corporate sponsorship has resulted in America taking on a symbolic, even mythological status, which, as Mason suggests, touches individuals across the world regardless of location. However, a closer analysis of the myth reveals it to be informed by the very prejudices and hierarchies early settlers sought to leave behind. Contemporary social commentators characterise the period between the 1990s and 2010 as the most financially segregated for centuries, with the gulf between rich and poor widening considerably (Duncan and Goddard 2009: 132). In addition, the reality of the 'freedom' of Americans can be seen to have been bought at a cost. More recent Columbus Day celebrations have included rituals and events acknowledging the loss of lives by Native Americans and slaves brought over to America to provide labour for Southern landowners (Zinn 1996: 613). The idea of limitless social mobility enshrined in the ideology of the American Dream has come under threat, as Duncan and Goddard observe, '[i]n 2009, with America more unequal than at any time since World War Two, poor children have limited opportunities to move up the social ladder; [whilst] middle class kids still have a fighting chance' (Duncan and Goddard 2009: 132). Indeed, many commentators observe that America is entering a significant period of change. Faith in the foundational values of the United States constitution has been destabilised by the ramifications of the Vietnam War and the Watergate scandal, both of which significantly undermined public trust in authority. Further controversy about insider-dealing on Wall Street, aggressive foreign policy and a re-emergence of neo-conservative values have fuelled what is lamented by many as a shift away from the liberal, inclusive values which supposedly characterise a utopian American ideology. Although I have mentioned his evident affection for his country, Maxwell can also be seen to be joining the likes of Miller and Shepard in dismantling assumptions underpinning the myth of America as a utopian land of freedom.

In addition to employing idiosyncrasies of American slang, Maxwell makes reference to recognisable features of American consumer life. Characters refer to baseball diamonds, burger restaurants, baseball mascots, computer games, Nike trainers and Xboxes. These references function primarily to ground his characters within a certain socio-cultural locale; however they also lend an insight into the playwrights' perception of the importance of consumption upon the national psyche. Interestingly, for such a diverse population, advertising has played a crucial role in shaping a sense of national identity. Frances Alice Keller is attributed with 'recognising the potential to use advertising to assimilate people in the face of subcultural pluralisms' (Duncan and Goddard 2009: 196). Duncan and Goddard write:

> . . . it is possible to locate a single, dominant American culture, were this not so, we would hardly hear the multitude of fearful voices arguing that American cultural imperialism is neo-colonialism, making all the world's languages subservient to the linguistic debasement of American English and all the world's people conform to cheap and transient American tastes. (Duncan and Goddard 2009: 193)

Maxwell does not incorporate references to consumer goods in order to critique cultural imperialism, but rather to ground his plays in the present moment and provide what could be considered to be a well-observed, authentic insight into 'what matters' to working and middle class Americans. In *Burger King* (1997) it is difficult to discern a critical attitude towards fast-food outlets, or the market domination of fast food giants such as Burger King or McDonalds. Instead, Maxwell creates an unusually philanthropic restaurant manager, whose honesty and desire to 'nourish the community' provide an amusing counterpoint to the actuality of low-status fast-food employment. Donald, the highly motivated manager of Maxwell's play finds his position threatened by mutinous staff unhappy with their lot, and consequently his own Puritan work ethic is undermined. Sherry brings the difficult topic of cheap labour to light when she asks, 'Where is there a place where someone can't always do our jobs for lower pay? Name one. They start at $5.15. You don't want to work for that? That's okay. We'll pay $4.75. And they will. And people will work for it. Mexicans or whatever' (Maxwell 2004b: 63). Sherry's speech demonstrates the power of global market forces such as Burger King or McDonalds to undercut the value of labour. Within this climate, it is not difficult to see why a contented, motivated workforce becomes something of an unattainable dream.

Critics of the homogenising power of global commerce regularly employ the bastardized verb 'to McDonaldize' to describe a dumbing-down of corporate, if not all principled thought. Stjepan G. Meštrović has borrowed George Ritzer's thesis about the 'McDonaldization of Society' to argue that the drive to efficiency and rationalisation, which characterises the success of the fast-food giant, now exemplifies attitudes towards Western emotion. For Meštrović, McDonaldized emotions are, 'bite-size, pre-packaged, rationally manufactured emotions—a "happy meal" of emotions . . . consumed by the masses' (Meštrović 1997: xi). Duncan and Goddard refer to 'McCulture' as the popularly adopted term for the homogenising influence of American consumer capitalism. Agnew and Sharp consider McDonaldization as part of a 'mission to spread American values', evidence of a sense of American enterprise galvanised by the need to keep the frontier 'open' and to continue conquering new territories (Agnew and Sharp 2002: 79). A sense of apprehension about the pernicious influence of corporate advertising has also informed one of Maxwell's more recent pieces, *Ads* (2010) a performance event employing pre-recorded footage of New Yorkers describing both ad hoc and orthodox belief systems. Maxwell revealed that

> The idea started when I read Naomi Klein's *No Logo*. In that book she talks about a really well articulated critique of the branding economy we exist in. She talks about space being usurped by private interests, being crowded by advertisers. We are wearing them but also letting that represent or shape our identity. (Arts Beat 2010)

Attitudes towards liberal capitalism are invariably entwined with attitudes towards labour and productivity. Puritan values, including a strong work ethic are considered to be 'essential to American individualism' (Duncan and Goddard 2009: 7). However the changing cultural landscape of America is thought to include a move away from self-application and hard work towards, as I mentioned previously, towards a more therapeutic culture which prioritises self-knowledge and awareness. As part of America's transition into a postmodern era, Robert M. Collins identified a 'therapeutic attitude' as an influential force 'which ran through American culture in the 80s and early 90s' (Collins 2007: 148). As part of a continuing development from a materialist to a post-materialist culture Americans could be seen throughout the twentieth century to be gradually 'giving priority to physical sustenance and safety towards a new emphasis on self-expression, self-esteem, self-realization and the quality of life' (Collins 2007: 153). For Collins, 'feelings were the coin of the realm in the new therapeutic cultural regime' and the change marked a shift towards an 'increasingly solipsistic quality of American culture' (Collins 2007: 154). Critics of Maxwell's work have repeatedly commented upon his 'emotional disconnect' (Wehle 2007: 161) so it is fortuitous to situate his work within the context of both a therapeutic discourse and Meštrović's 'bite-size', 'pre-packaged' emotions. Male characters in his earlier plays appear boorish and inarticulate when compared to the self-aware characters of contemporary American TV and Hollywood films. As I have discussed, Maxwell is clearly working through ideas about feelings, emotion and confession. The speech patterns of *Boxing 2000* and *Drummer Wanted* are very different to those in *Ode to the Man Who Kneels*, *Ads* and *The End of Reality* (2006). Sublimated sentiment gives way to anxiety articulated through verse, song and quasi- religious prose. In later plays participants are given longer speeches and the opportunity to articulate feelings verbally rather than largely through song. Ironically, in either model, the characters appear no better off for articulating their vulnerability, if anything they are left at a disadvantage, having revealed the innermost workings of their soul rather than taking refuge behind a stoic, inscrutable façade. Much of the humour and irony of Maxwell's work can be seen to arise from its being seen by audiences capable of measuring it against the dominant therapeutic discourse, however there does not appear to be one consistent message about contemporary American values, apart from to say that regardless of class, race, socio-economic status; regardless of their living in comparative comfort, figures in Maxwell's plays are tortured by self-doubt and rejection in way that can never easily be explained away or moderated through language.

Recent changes in government administration suggest that contemporary America is changing. The political shift to the right experienced post-Reagan, and even under the patronage of Clinton, could be seen, with the inauguration of President Obama, to be moving tentatively back towards the left.[5] For Duncan and Goddard, Barack Obama, America's first black president, 'represented what might be possible, still, in America, and the world—a coming together, a new beginning, a redefinition' (Duncan and Goddard 2009: 2). However, the 'homeland security' rhetoric popularised by George W. Bush still holds an importance place in contemporary understandings of what it means to be American. At the time of writing New York Mayor, Michael R. Bloomberg is publicly supporting the proposed development of a Muslim community centre in Park Place, a location two blocks away from the site of the destroyed World Trade Centre. The proposed development has provoked heated national debate and opposition from Christian and Jewish religious groups. The American Center for Law and Justice, founded by Reverend Pat Robertson has filed a lawsuit against the City Landmarks Preservation Commission, arguing that it acted too hastily in agreeing to build the community centre on the site of a church destroyed in the September 11 attack. Abdul Rauf's vision was for a centre to encourage inter-faith dialogue and interaction, but this vision, although ratified by the Preservation Commission, has come to appear idealistic in the light of the recent furore (Barbaro 2010). As Barbara Ozieblo has pointed out, '[t]he notion of "Americanness" has undoubtedly been complicated by 9/11 and the war in Iraq; the very concept of the "alien" has been re-examined and the permeability of borders and frontiers questioned' (Ozieblo 2006:12). Many critics interpreted *The End of Reality* as a commentary upon 9/11, interpreting the security guards and monologues about fear as a realisation of larger societal fears. Maxwell has not shared his intention for the piece, beyond revealing that 'underneath all of this banal dialogue there was a real existential struggle happening within the minds of the characters' (Kelsey 2008); however his choice of career for these blue-collar workers does appear to have been timely. As Naomi Klein observed, 'the uncontested heroes of September 11 were the blue-collar first responders—the New York fire fighters, police and rescue workers, 403 of whom lost their lives as they tried to evacuate the towers and aid the victims. Suddenly, America was in love with its men and women in all kinds of uniforms . . . ' (Klein 2007).

In redefining what it means to be American and reviewing the past Americans can be seen to be taking account of what it means to live in a postcolonial, postmodern world. The emergence of multiculturalism as a powerful discourse has provided a challenge to the largely white, Euro-centric values of a previous age, and has enabled the voices of Native and African Americans to be heard. However, as Sennett points out, the separation of America into Democratic and Republican states endures, resulting in a quarrelsome political climate in which left and right wing factions debate almost every new government policy in the public glare of the media. As I have suggested previously, Maxwell's work does not fit easily into either political camp, although his preoccupation with subaltern subjects and the pertinence of a post-Humanist reading to his work suggests that his sympathies lie largely with the left. What is clear from a survey of his work is his profound engagement with and sympathy for everyday American people, he is interested in their belief systems and the minutiae of their quotidian concerns. The crisis of identity characterising postmodern, postcolonial, post 9/11 America provides a background context in which his plays are situated but his fundamental concerns return to issues of faith; family; father-son relationships, male-female relationships and the psychological harm visited upon the hypermasculine, archetypal American male.

An appraisal of Maxwell's work between 1996 and 2010 reveals changing interests and preoccupations. Although much of his theatre work has
continued to occupy the ambiguous territory between deconstructive performance, musical and theatrical realism, recent projects such as, *The Darkness of This Reading* (2005), *The Feud Other* (2009), *Ads, Das Maedchen*
(2010) and *Neutral Hero* (2010) reveal Maxwell's desire to experiment with
new forms and media. Maxwell has repeatedly emphasised the fact that he
does not aspire towards a single 'style', but is continually experimenting
with fresh ideas and approaches in order to keep him 'new' (Gorman 2007:
237). In 2006 Maxwell told John O'Mahony that: 'the exploration (in *The
End of Reality*) is going somewhere you don't know. I guess that is probably
why I've always had a hard time with the word "style". It implies a kind
of finishedness, having an answer before you've got there. I would quit if I
knew before what I was trying to find' (O'Mahony 2006). He provided a
further insight into the challenge of new approaches during an interview
with Elizabeth LeCompte in 2009:

> . . . part of the mission of New York City Players is to try to work with
> new people all the time. It's a way of staying in touch with what you're
> doing by running it by people who aren't obliged to agree. (LeCompte
> 2009: 73)

Despite his protestations, a large proportion of literature available about
Maxwell's work tends to focus upon one particular aspect of his work.
Critics and academics most commonly discuss his approach to direction,
and the apparently neutral acting style his actors adopt. His use of language
and emotion also comes under scrutiny, with critics often appreciatively
assessing his ability to capture the cadences and particularities of contemporary urban American speech. Brian Walsh describes Maxwell's 'signature
style' as a 'uniform flatness' (Walsh 2004: 102); Robin Pogrebin states that
Maxwell's characters speak in 'flat tones . . . without inflection' (Pogrebin
2000); Lyn Gardner describes the work as 'deadpan with no reflection,
no emotion' (Gardner 2005); and Kieran Quirke perceived a 'consistently
deadpan acting style' with 'no vocal inflection and no movement' (Quirke
2005). Sarah Hemming has suggested that Maxwell's characters performed
with 'a complete lack of expression, as if reading a station announcement
about a delayed train' (Hemming 2005). Phillipa Wehle has described Maxwell's work as manifesting 'an anti-theatrical approach to directing that
favours poker-faced delivery and stiff unnatural movements that contradict
his texts'. For her, 'gestures are limited and language is mechanical not
jovial. Maxwell's "*ha, ha, has*", delivered loudly but without emotion, have
become legend' (Wehle 2007: 158). Alexis Soloski sees the deconstructive
potential of this supposedly neutral attitude when she writes, 'Maxwell's
oeuvre comprises a series of negations that questions how people speak,
move and behave onstage by stripping away the most theatrical trappings'

(Soloski 2010) and in *Ads*, Charles Isherwood sees 'the flat, sometimes awkwardly inflected readings' to resemble 'the scripted performances given by the (sometimes non-professional or untrained) actors'. He suggests that, '*Ads* reflects Mr. Maxwell's abiding fascination with the poetry in speech that has not been manicured into smooth stage dialogue, and his conviction that exploring truths about experience in art often benefits from a level of artlessness' (Isherwood 2010). Although 'style' is perhaps too crude a term, it is clear that a familiar set of issues, themes and preoccupations repeat themselves throughout Maxwell's work; some features, such as his interest in poetry and vernacular, reach back to his work with Cook County Theater Department. I discuss the use of the term 'deadpan' at length in Chapter 2, noting how Maxwell takes issue with the term as a kind of dismissive 'shorthand' to the very focused, committed work he invites his actors to do.

Despite the degree of attention his approach to intonation attracts, Maxwell is not the first to work with deadpan, or to address the notion of neutrality. A broader cultural survey brings to light other film-makers and theatre practitioners ostensibly working with a 'deadpan' aesthetic. The work of film-maker, Hal Hartley has repeatedly been described in these terms and John Jesurun's actors, in early pieces such as *Shatterhand Massacre* (1985) and *Everything that Rises must Converge* (1990) could also be seen to be experimenting with a style of vocal inflection which confuses the meaning of actors' lines. NYCP collaborator Brian Mendes recalls that comparisons were made between the work of Cook County Theater Department and the work of Hal Hartley as early as 1994. Dialogue delivered onstage by actors in the Wooster Group, Forced Entertainment and Richard Foreman performances could also be seen to evidence a similar kind of emotional distance as performers address the audience directly and moments of heightened emotion are presented as instances of contrivance, performed with commitment, but with a clear distinction retained between actor and character. The work could indeed be characterised as post-Brechtian, manifesting, as it does, a desire to keep the object of both the actors and audience's engagement (the mounting of the performance) at the forefront of the activity.

Before I move on to consider the many theatre-makers and playwrights informing, and aligned with Maxwell's approach, I would like to spend some time considering the particular overlap between the work of Maxwell and Hal Hartley, an American film-maker producing work since 1984[6]. Although I would not suggest that Maxwell's work necessarily resembles that of Hartley, there does appear to be some congruence in approach to line delivery, masculinity and emotion. Sophie Wise has assessed Hartley's work using a vocabulary remarkably similar to those of Maxwell's critics. She cites Hartley's 'trademark deadpan dialogue' and a 'signature style' that comprises of 'static, restrained gestures and emotionless delivery'. Wise suggests that the 'restrained, unemotional line delivery . . . reminds us of the inherent performativity of words' and argues that the distance between words and intention reveal how language creates and interpellates the subject rather than the subject being in command of his or her words:

> Hartley's manipulation of the performance style emphasises that the subject of speech requires an agent (actor) to speak that subject. In other words, a character depends as much on the performativity of the script as on an actor's performance of that script. The films demonstrate that the subject is the result of a word rather than the opposite. Words literally construct the characters, hold them up, and propel them through the narrative. The subject is not preformed but literally per-formed, formed through the film. In these films, characters effectively speak themselves into being. (Wise1999: 256)

Wise found Hartley's 'artificiality' paradoxically 'satisfying' and 'natural' and refers to words as performative 'utterances'. She argues that because emotions or actions are 'contained within words', the words render gesture unnecessary: 'a physical outward display of emotion would seem tautological'. Wise provides a fascinating thesis to apply to Maxwell's work. If we accept that there exists a similar distance between gesture and dialogue in the work of Hartley and Maxwell, then Wise's notion of action as 'tautological' does indeed seem appropriate and we can conclude that Maxwell's characters remain still because to perform physically and perform linguistically amounts to an excess of unnecessary signification. Ironically, the stillness of Maxwell's actors can be understood as an example of observation; an attempt at 'realism' rather than conjecture. As with many of the critics who admire Maxwell's direction, Wise feels that the economy of physical gesture and verbal intonation in Hartley's work, can act productively to 'enhance the emotion of a scene through its alienation' (Wise 1999: 259). She implies that by creating a discernible distance between what actors say and how they say it, Hartley's actors make visible the poststructuralist concern that language and linguistic value systems shape the individual.

My own findings about Maxwell's untrained actors are sympathetic to those of Wise. Hartley and Maxwell have both endowed their characters (and possibly encouraged their actors to hone) an evident lack of virtuosity. As discussed previously, their lack of competence in emotional disclosure reveals the presence of 'schooling' in attaining a skill largely held to be natural. However, the drawing back from virtuosity, or the exploration of 'artlessness', has caused disagreement between critics as to whether it results in emotional estrangement for the audience, or a means of accessing emotional authenticity. For Matthew Leyland, Hartley's 'deadpan delivery' is 'too self-conscious to provide much emotional engagement' and yet for Wise, it can 'enhance the emotion of a scene' (Leyland 2004, Wise 1999). Ben Brantley suggests that Maxwell's uninflected lines, 'seem to magnify and dissect what is spoken' and 'perversely makes the fear more credible [as if it were] a fact of life rather than a moment of self-dramatisation'

(Brantley 2006). Ironically, then for a practitioner whose project works alongside those of The Wooster Group and Richard Foreman, Maxwell has been charged with being a 'new realist'; his attenuation of emotion has been received as 'authentic' rather than a technique of estrangement. He has described himself as a 'realist' in interview, and states that he often copies down snippets of overheard conversation 'like a legal transcript'.[7] Hartley and Maxwell represent something of a conundrum, for some their marked emotional restraint is 'hyper-realistic' for others it is unproductive and alienating. For me, their most interesting work draws attention to social practices and discourses shaping the individual. As Tim Etchells has suggested, 'a force bears upon you from society and culture, a violent force by which you are subjected to its economies, pressed into its limits, framed and made by its language' (Etchells 2003). The potential harm of conflicting social forces is made visible if we interpret inarticulate male characters as 'pressed into' society's limits rather than as reluctant participants.

Mac Wellman has pointed to the resurgence in popularity of realism in the work of new downtown playwrights, stating, 'I would make the argument that there is more new, truly original work in this vein, what I am tempted to call the theater of the normal parareal and hypernormal, than ever before in our history' (Wellman 2006: vii). Maxwell has admitted that there are times when he does identify as a 'realist'. However, 'it's a new realism. It's real because we are acknowledging the artificiality of it, and that's what makes it real. There is no real effort (on the part of the actors) to create another "reality" that the story is creating' (Marranca 2002). The perception of his work as emotionally withdrawn, perhaps also has something to do with Maxwell's upbringing in Illinois. Midwesterners are considered to be 'honest' and to exemplify a 'down to earth directness'. Their speech patterns are described as 'flat' and 'they view themselves as liberals who conserve American values' (Duncan and Goddard 2009: 57). Maxwell's sense of authentic language is inevitably coloured by the environment of his upbringing, and it is ironic to consider that speech patterns that for him signify as 'natural' sound so unconventional to a theatre audience. He has admitted that, 'I do know that the comments I've gotten which gratify me are things like, "I felt like while I was watching it I couldn't tell whether what I was seeing was real or fake". Like a switch was being flicked on and off, like a constant toggling between "this is reality" and "this is artificiality"' (Moore 2003).

The experimentation evident in the work of NYCP suggests that Maxwell's heritage extends through the line of experimental American theatre customarily referred to as 'downtown New York'. Indeed, as mentioned above Maxwell has worked with The Wooster Group and Richard Foreman, and regularly collaborates with other downtown regulars such as Radiohole, Sibyl Kempson and Thomas Bradshaw.[8] His work enjoys airings alongside contemporaries such as Elevator Repair Service, Young Jean Lee, Mac Wellman, Will Eno, Nature Theatre of Oklahoma, Madelyn

Kent, Builder's Association, Barbara Cassidy, and the Cannon Company. Wellman has described examples of this work as containing, 'recognizable American types [who] speak our language as though it were as foreign to them as it is to most of those who live far from these shores' (Wellman 2006: iiv). However, Maxwell is also indebted to a strong tradition of more canonical playwrights such as Sam Shepard, David Mamet, Richard Nelson, Emily Mann and Harold Pinter all of whom 'contrast dreams with a reality of dreary small towns, shabby hotels, loveless isolated lives, self-deception and violence' (King 1991: 10).

Maxwell's work has been compared to that of David Mamet by critics identifying a resemblance between subject matter and language. Both use contemporary patterns of local speech and dramatise a particularly male struggle to harness the resources a limited vocabulary has to offer. David Savran proposes that 'the most radical aspect of Mamet's dramaturgy remains his mobilisation of a poetry for the theatre based not on eloquence but on the disjunction between language and desire, on the failure of speech to articulate need' (Savran 1991: 72). He also situates Mamet's interest as depicting 'the crisis of contemporary masculinity, torn by the demands of fierce rivalry in the commercial sphere and sensitivity and generosity in the personal one' (Savran 1991: 71). In *Sexual Perversity in Chicago* (1974) Mamet draws upon (then) contemporary rhythms of working-class Chicago speech to dramatise a breakdown in communication between characters. The character of Bernie's speech is 'torn by redundancies, contradictions, ellipses, clichés, false starts and changes in grammatical subject' (Savran 1991: 68). Developing a similar argument to Wise, Savran contends that 'rather than dramatize the subject's mastery of language, the new realists demonstrate how the subject is articulated by a discourse over which he or she has little control' (Savran 1991: 65).

Critics have also recognised similarities between the work of Sam Shepard and Maxwell, indeed Maxwell himself has said, 'I like Sam Shepard, he's been a big influence'. Given a collection of Shepard plays by his father when he was fourteen, Maxwell became fascinated by his use of 'raw, irreverent, honest' language. The ubiquity of Shepard's work in the 1990s put him off his work for a time, and he 'distanced himself in the hope of finding something new'. He said, 'when I was in my twenties I resisted all kinds of comparisons and similarities, but now I have relaxed a bit' (Marranca 2002). A survey of criticism about Shepard readily reveals why such comparisons may have been so forthcoming. For example, following a similar pattern to Maxwell, Shepard's plays incorporate language 'drawn from American popular culture' (Bottoms 1998: 4). Furthermore, his plays have been described as examples of 'superrealism'; Shepard has also directed many of his own plays, (developing a relationship with Magic Theatre, San Francisco); he also incorporates popular music. Finally, he can be seen to dramatise a stoicism and lack of 'self-pity' associated with the American Midwest, and offers 'few opportunities for intellectual analysis of character' (McTeague 1994: 110–111). Like Maxwell, in addition to playwriting and directing work Shepard has worked as an actor and musician. Shepard has drawn upon images of the archetypal cowboy and the untamed west; a feature that appears to have intertextually, if not directly informed Maxwell's own Western plays. Significantly, Bottoms has identified an anti-Humanist drive in Shepard's work, akin to that proposed by Wise and Savran in relation to Hartley and Mamet. Bottoms identifies a need for Shepard's characters to '[P]erform themselves into existence . . . they seem trapped within a distinctly limited range of potential options, victims of deterministic influences which, try as they might, they cannot shake off' (Bottoms 1998: 15). Bottoms further argues that Shepard is preoccupied by the question of what it means to 'be an American male', and suggests that the 'posturing "heroism"' of the 'cowboys and rock stars; fathers and sons' represents a 'violent and arrogant machismo, which is implicitly located as the source of America's tendency towards personal and societal self-destruction':

> Through their dramatization of tycoons, gunfighters, drifters, visionary artists, and modern day Fausts, the plays suggest that the still prevalent frontier myth of the heroic "rugged" individual, demanding independence at all costs, lies at the very root of the ruthless, self-aggrandizement which still holds sway at every level of American culture. (Bottoms 1998: 16)

However, in contrast to Shepard, Maxwell tends to work within structured, rather than fragmented narratives (Bottoms 1998: 3) and his controlled characters tend to sublimate emotion rather than allow it to erupt in violent outbursts. Furthermore, it would appear that the frustration apparent in Shepard's work is driven by the notion that an essential 'authentic' self is buried deep beneath layers of social etiquette and convention. Bottoms suggests that:

> The urge towards full self-expression is predicated on the assumption that there is indeed an authentic inner self to find expression, as distinct from the exterior, socially conditioned personality. By his own admission, Shepard's work periodically appeals to an almost religious sense of some inner essence which one has to discover by stripping away the artificial layers of the everyday persona, or perhaps (in the Jungian formulation) by "individuating" the fractured part of the mind in the whole. (Bottoms 1998: 13)

No such split would appear to exist for Maxwell's characters, each of whom tends to reveal deeply held beliefs without too much provocation. Although his characters struggle to communicate we are not necessarily given the sense that this is due to a conflict between a deeper, suppressed psyche and a more authentic inner self. Comparisons with Mamet, Hartley and Shepard draw out particular aspects of Maxwell's work, in particular those of language, representations of masculinity and references to the Frontier. The repetition of themes across the work of these artists suggests that they contribute to a national preoccupation or manifest a drive to cope with, or temper changes to a shared value system. Maxwell's conscious and intertextual influences clearly extend beyond the practitioners cited here, however it seems useful to draw out the peculiarities of Hartley, Mamet and Shepard in order to discover what other artists' approaches might tell us about the choices Maxwell has made. What is particular about Maxwell's work is his very basic theatre aesthetic and his tendency to focus in upon the quotidian and the mundane.

As I have established, Maxwell's work occupies a marginal position between a more traditional theatre discourse and experimental or avantgarde practice. In addition to the (possibly unconscious) influence of the work of figures such as Shepard, Mamet and Hartley, his work demonstrates a familiarity with theatre of the American and European avantgarde. Along with contemporaries such as Young Jean Lee, Elevator Repair Service, Radiohole and Nature Theatre of Oklahoma, Maxwell demonstrates a suspicion of issue-based theatre and eschews the type of didactic political message characterising much New York performance of the 1980s and 1990s. Whilst admitting her own frustrations about representations of race, Young Jean Lee has spoken of her distaste for an overtly political theatre. She states that, 'I do have a bee in my bonnet about race, and nobody wants to hear a person of colour ranting about race and how unfair the world is to them' (Bomb Magazine 2010). For Maxwell, 'political theatre doesn't work. It's just something about the live medium and putting across a message in the work or by the play that does not seem well suited to theatre' (Bomb Magazine 2010). Maxwell and Lee are perhaps typical of a recent generation of downtown New York theatre-makers whose work remains socially engaged but who choose not to produce issue-based work. This generation can be seen as being influenced by avant-garde practitioners such as The Wooster Group and Richard Foreman, theatre-makers who have disrupted conventional narrative-based theatre in order to draw attention to unquestioned conventions and latent value-systems at work. Foreman has largely created his own pieces, whilst The Wooster Group has drawn upon a rich tradition of literary classics in order to interrogate, amongst other things, the white, conservative, Eurocentric bias of the American dramatic canon. Although Michael Vanden Heuvel has argued that The Wooster Group have moved away from deconstruction, and that deconstruction, along with postmodern theory, 'has had its day', it is still worth pursuing the extent to which the group's work might constitute a poststructuralist or postmodern poetics. The Wooster Group's oeuvre has obviously undergone change over the past thirty years. Vanden Heuvel provides an overview of an early era typified by 'ritual-based, anthropological research' towards a 'cooler, more detached and heavily mediated exploration of fragmentation, discontinuity and deconstructed textuality' (Vanden Heuvel 2004: 73). The anti-humanist ethos of poststructuralist theory, developed in the work of Derrida, Barthes, Lacan, Foucault and Cixous, questions the accepted ideological transparency of realist forms and calls for vigilance in pursuing and identifying the 'hidden teleologies' at work in hegemonic discourse (Norris 1995: 237). By juxtaposing and integrating more than one text into their work, The Wooster Group enable repeated assumptions about nation, race and gender to become visible. The chaotic, fragmentary nature of much of their work resists the closure of meaning and taming of ambiguity customarily associated with realist theatre and so remains 'political' in so far as it challenges hegemonic discourse, it also avoids delivering a direct 'political message' of the kind Maxwell suggests is antithetical to theatre. This work is political in the way that it 'exposes' ideology. David Román suggests that, 'hegemony's performance forces its subjects to a conversion into its alleged neutrality; its claims to be true and real . . . Political performers expose the coercive attempts' (Román 2005: 39). Given Lee and Maxwell's avowed suspicion of theatre with a 'message', I would argue that the type of deconstructive politics associated with The Wooster Group has come to motivate much of the work done by contemporary downtown theatremakers. Citing 'The City's Best (And not so Best)' progressive theatre companies, Tom Sellar conducts a survey of New York companies presenting experimental work since 2000. Those he considers worthy of note include: Young Jean Lee; Thomas Bradshaw, Richard Maxwell; National Theatre of the United States of America; Temporary Distortion; Witness Relocation; Big Art Group, Sibyl Kempson and Mike Iveson; Elevator Repair Service; Nature Theatre of Oklahoma and Radiohole (Sellar 2010). However, Sellar is doubtful about the potential political impact of some of this work. He writes:

> Even during a decade of deep social transformation and political upheaval, most American performance groups showed few signs of dissent or engagement. The emphasis remains firmly on cool eclecticism and irony, formalism and fragmentation—perhaps reflecting a downtown theater culture dominated by (mostly white) MFA aesthetes. (Sellar 2010)

It is interesting that Sellar cites 'fragmentation' and 'irony'; both deemed characteristics of postmodern theatre. Perhaps Sellar's contention that this work is not politically engaged emanates from a preference for issue-based rather than deconstructive political theatre.

In addition to downtown contemporaries and New York avant-garde influences, Maxwell's work also sits comfortably in the context of wider American and European experimental theatre. Goat Island, Forced Entertainment, Lone Twin, Jerome Bel, Victoria and Rimini Protokoll could all be seen to be working against an aesthetics of virtuosity in order to question the humanist drive for 'presence and authenticity' (Vanden Heuvel 2004:

73). Many of the practitioners cited have been discussed in relation to an aesthetics of failure or 'heightened amateurism', demonstrating that Maxwell is very much working with, and responding to, contemporary social and aesthetic concerns. For Nicholas Ridout theatre is 'most itself [when] it goes wrong, falls short of grace . . . Failure then is constitutive, that there is something wrong with theatre is the sign that it is theatre' (Ridout 2006: 33). Sara Jane Bailes is similarly interested in the anti-mimetic properties of theatrical 'awkwardness', she argues that: '[r]egardless of its emphatic presence and authenticity, then, live performance (re)produces its own fundamental, provisional and often spectacular ineptitude. It makes failure occur just as failure enables its occurrence' (Bailes 2011: 7). Although Ridout sees the risk of failure in all theatre practice, it is clear that Maxwell is situated amongst a particular group of avant-garde practitioners who actively heighten the risk of failure by co-opting the signs of rehearsal, shoddiness, bad acting, nervousness, stage fright and leaving certain elements up to chance. Bailes has discussed how the visual style of Elevator Repair Service, borrows elements of this approach:

> The group takes inspiration from an aesthetics marked by imperfection, the provisional nature of temporary and sometimes inappropriate circumstances, and the invention that recycling space, materials and dialogue can reveal. . . . Costumes usually look borrowed or informal (even if they are not), and the visual style they manufacture is often intentionally "slightly off", hovering between tacky, trendy and absurd. (Bailes 2010: 87)

I discuss my perception of 'roughness' in Maxwell's work in terms of a 'rehearsal aesthetic', which works to make visible the labour behind rehearsing, mounting and building a performance. However, it is also beneficial to explore recent writing about performance and failure in order to understand how Maxwell's work both departs from and ameliorates this area of concern. In terms of Maxwell's directorial style and use of space Richard Foreman appears to have been a notable influence. Maxwell's 'rehearsal aesthetic' manifests itself, in part, by appropriating rough props and furniture that would appear more at home in the rehearsal room rather than on stage in production. Actors regularly make use of the final stage set in an anti-illusionistic manner. In *Good Samaritans*, for example, Rose and Kevin make love on the tables used moments before to designate a communal dining area; in *Drummer Wanted* Frank and his mother use two chairs to stand in for a car. Aronson has identified a 'homemade' quality to Foreman's sets enabling us to identify a possible overlap between Maxwell and Foreman's approach (see figure 1.1). Aronson recalls that in Foreman's work, 'set pieces and especially the scenic painting purposely subvert the slick, polished look of commercial theatre in which even dirt and decay is carefully and beautifully designed' (Aronson 2005: 162).

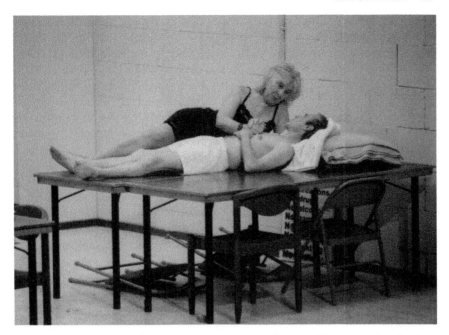

Figure 1.1 Rosemary Allen and Kevin Hurley use dining tables to stand in for their bed. (Photo: Michael Schmelling).

Foreman's influence can also be seen to extend into Maxwell's direction. Foreman has spoken of his desire to keep both his actors and his audiences 'off-balance' to prevent them from falling back on conventional patterns of reading or behaving. For Bigsby, Foreman's work is, 'an anti-illusionist theatre in which empathy is deliberately inhibited' (Bigsby 2000: 256). Juliana Francis, a performer with the Ontological Hysteric Theater has described this as 'a kind of oscillation that he wants you to arrive at, so you never really are in a kind of state that makes you feel secure. It's always this unsettled feeling, instead of landing things, and nailing things, and confidently fulfilling something (quoted in Swettenham 2008: 68). Like Maxwell, Foreman makes use of amateur and non-trained actors in an attempt to find an unconventional authenticity:

> When I started producing plays I was interested in seeing people on stage. I felt I'd never seen people appear on stage, I'd only seen actors onstage, and an actor acting is a special kind of person, one who bears little resemblance to my experience of people in real life. . . . What interested me was taking people from real life, non actors, and putting them onstage to allow their real personalities to have a defiant impact on the conventional audience. (Foreman 1992: 32)

Foreman's attraction to non-trained actors is predicated upon an assumption that it is possible for 'real' personalities to signify onstage. This attitude is potentially at odds with Maxwell who appears to hold that it is the risk, or the attempt to 'be brave' in the precarious event of performance which signifies most prominently, rather than an authentic inner self. A desire to retain traces of tension about the actor's body also characterise both Foreman and Maxwell's work, both motivated by the desire to make visible the training which would customarily work to suppress or erase these signs. Foreman has observed:

> [t]he basic Stanislavski method, as it has been taught in America, trains an actor to find a way to be relaxed during performance, even within a highly emotional scene. Most Twentieth century art however is not about being relaxed. Ours is an era of stress, and serious art reflects that stress, even if it wants to establish an alternative. (Quoted in Swettenham 2008: 72)

Maxwell agrees that acting or rather 'industry standard' Method acting, taught in American drama schools dedicates much time to:

> [h]elping actors deal with the fear of performance . . . it's telling them not to let the anxiety show. People who don't have acting training have coping mechanisms but they have them from life. I'm interested in the different ways that the people cope with the thing I'm asking them to do. (Quoted in Ellis 2005)

The depiction of acting as a kind of 'coping mechanism' is in keeping with a post-Humanist, deconstructive politics, 'exposing', as it does the coercive drive of hegemonic culture to compel the subject to conform to an ideal state of being. Risks associated with failure to conform include humiliation and a sense of disenfranchisement. Companies such as Goat Island and Forced Entertainment share Maxwell's interest in failure. Goat Island's performers are not trained dancers, and yet the company devise and choreograph complex dances, which the performers repeat with intense concentration. Forced Entertainment experiment with failure, most obviously in their durational performances, calling for an ensemble of performers to repeat a set of pre-defined tasks over a prolonged period of time. Such tasks might include dressing and undressing; storytelling; interrupting stories and asking/responding to direct questions, over a seven to twelve hour period. In the work of Goat Island Steve Bottoms has identified, 'a parallel with Jerzy Grotowski's notion of a "poor theatre" in which the actor performs a kind of physical sacrifice for the audience's benefit'. Although their work may show no obvious resemblance it is possible to see how the repetition of set tasks over time in a Forced Entertainment piece might amount to a similar kind of physical sacrifice. Bottoms writes that in Goat Island's 'impossible dances' he sees:

Bodies perpetually and inevitably failing in their attempts to execute the prescribed movements. . . . Where conventional choreography asks the body to soar, to express its capabilities as beautifully and seamlessly as possible, Goat Island's performers are subjected to a kind of strategic humiliation, exposing their awkwardness, their vulnerability, their limits. (Bottoms 2007: 77)

Representations of failure within Forced Entertainment's work can also be found in the performer's attempts to execute a task or an attempt to relay a tale. Tim Etchells has spoken of the live medium of theatre as an 'economy of humiliation' in which, 'you betray yourself, you show more than you wish to, you stumble, you slip. It's simple: you stand there and you fail' (Etchells 2003). The deliberate staging of failure found in the work of Goat Island, Forced Entertainment and NYCP represents a moving and pertinent way of drawing attention to the social forces which compel the human subject to strive to realise certain, often unconscious goals. As Steve Bottoms has written, '[w]e live, we are sometimes told, in a posthumanist age. Man is not the independent, self-realising entity that liberal humanism imagined him to be' (Bottoms 2007: 75).

Maxwell's work perhaps differs from his contemporaries in that he finds different strategies with which to render both established actors and non-trained actors vulnerable onstage. Established actors are challenged to 'shed their training' and non-trained actors are invited to test their commitment to the project by questioning what it is they want from the experience of performing. Journalist John Kelsey volunteered to be directed by Maxwell as an alternative way of interviewing the director for *Bomb Magazine* in 2008. After working through a pre-learned monologue a number of times Kelsey put a series of questions to Maxwell about how he should proceed. Eventually he asked, 'so, it's just a question of work and paying attention to the work that you are doing?' to which Maxwell responded, 'It goes deeper than that. When you repeat something over and over, when you rehearse something over time and you're meeting together . . . that requires a huge amount of courage and willingness to expose yourself. I think that it can go pretty deep—your reasons for doing what you are doing' (Kelsey 2008). This questioning of the actor's commitment to the present reality of *the attempt to perform* is what prevents the performance from becoming 'fixed'. In Maxwell's view, if the actors are committed to the event of performance, then their response to the text, and their reasons for wanting to be on stage, will differ each night.

With a similar aim to Maxwell, Forced Entertainment work with strategies of improvisation and task-based work during a prolonged rehearsal and devising process. Their priority is to retain something of the risk and spontaneity of the first performance. As Alex Mermikides writes, '[t]he emphasis is on the "liveness" of the performance situation—defined by Peggy Phelan as "representation without representation"—the "reality" of the audience, performer and their meeting in real time' (Mermikides 2010: 104). Etchells has admitted that, 'in the theatre works we set up a dynamic where apparently what is happening is all very amateur, but we are controlling that very (let's say, very) well. It's like you invoke certain kinds of failure or certain kinds of inadequacies because they suit your purpose in a way' (Etchells 2003). He has also described how a kind of 'stage managed' failure is 'clearer' in their durational works, suggesting that the staged failure is 'doubled by a kind of real set of things like that . . . it is impossible to fully stage manage and fake your way through six hours of scrutiny' (Etchells 2003).

The question of controlled or accidental failure was thrown into relief during a collaborative performance between NYCP and Forced Entertainment at the Künstlerhaus Mousonturm, Frankfurt in 2003. As part of a short performance festival to celebrate 20 years of Forced Entertainment's work the company had organised a series of collaborations with a variety of artists and academics. Alongside *Marathon Lexicon* (2003), a twelve-hour durational piece, the company performed songs for *Portrait* (2003) part of an event co-written by Maxwell and Etchells and accompanied by members of NYCP. NYCP performers reciprocated by delivering a series of monologues written by Etchells. Given both companies interest in failure and bad acting, I was interested to hear from Maxwell that he felt the stakes were high for this event, as if, 'there's room for failing in the rehearsal room, but here, there's no room for failure'.[9] The performance itself was fascinating, most notably perhaps because, whilst singing Maxwell's songs, several of Forced Entertainment's performers manifested the signs of fear trained actors are customarily taught to suppress. Their voices appeared strained as they attempted to sing and occasionally broke as they attempted to negotiate the higher notes. Having followed the company since 1992 I was intrigued by the experience of watching them perform Maxwell's songs. I felt as if this was the first time I had really seen the actors exposed onstage; the first time I had really seen them 'fail'. Watching *Marathon Lexicon* the next day I witnessed again, how adept the performers are at dealing with certain types of performance challenges (wading through densely rhetorical academic prose; coping with a lack of food and rest) but Forced Entertainment's largely verbal mode of communication, means that they have not become inured to the stress imposed by singing. The revelation of the performing body as 'brave' was pronounced on this occasion and provided a fascinating insight into coping mechanisms the performers drew upon to get them through.

Drawing upon the arguments of Wise, Savran and Bottoms, I explore the theme of failure in several chapters, most markedly as a way of drawing attention to the post-Humanist challenge I perceive in Maxwell's work. My investigation has led me to consider failure in relation to class and gender performativity; the American Dream and to scrutinise American models of Method Acting as embodying Humanist values. My interrogation of received models of Method Acting produced a substantial amount of material pointing to the Humanist illusion of agency at the heart of Method ideology and a wealth of post or anti-Method writing lamenting its influence, and until recently, dominance, across American actor training. NYCP do not deliberately set out to refuse the influence of Method training but they do eschew the illusion of control and self-possession taught in most actor-training institutions. Despite wanting to evade accusations about 'style', longstanding NYCP collaborators Jim Fletcher and Brian Mendes both have insightful ways of describing the nature of their approach to acting, and in particular the approach they adopt for NYCP productions. Mendes has admitted that, 'it's taken a while to let go as an actor of the tendency to want to be good: to want to make something of this, to want to make it interesting'. He experiences the difficulty in reigning in his instinct to 'do more':

> I get caught feeling I should do more, so it was a constant reminder to try to do less. And I don't mean that just 'less is more' but I mean that as a meditative state. Get on stage. Look here. Say this. Move here. That is worthy enough. It needn't be embellished. (Maxwell and Mendes 2006: 350)

Fletcher has referred to the work he does with NYCP as 'industrial acting' a, description which suggests he considers the holding back from emotion as a type of almost utilitarian measure, a way of measuring how economical it is possible to be with the merest hint at emotion. He has also stated that he believes acting conjoins with faith. He has stated, '[t]hat's what's acting is about anyway—what do you believe?'[10] Both Mendes and Fletcher's comments provide interesting disclosures about the experience of working with, and acting for Maxwell. References to faith and meditation suggest a deep emotional and spiritual engagement with the process; acting for them is neither a mode of self-expression nor an invitation to retreat into a fictional psychological state. These terms of embodiment repeat, to a certain extent, the findings of Phillip B. Zarrilli's work on psychophysical acting. Zarrilli argues that by disciplined psychophysical training the actor can learn to generate emotion from, what we might describe, in Maxwell's terms, a 'commitment' to the task: '[t]he feeling is generated by the actor's fully embodied attention to and awareness of the task, while keeping an open kinaesthetic awareness (Zarrilli 2009: 108). [11] The free play of concentration and sensual reception across cognitive and somatic zones enables a more nuanced and substantial response to the task in hand. Critical of the Humanist ethos of much Western actor training, Zarrilli states that ' . . . the problem of Western dualistic thinking creates problems for the actor. Acting is either too easily or over-intellectualized or becomes overly subjective. This is due to our compartmentalization of mind, body and emotion' (Zarrilli 2009: 76).

Although Maxwell's actors do not collectively or consciously train in Asian martial and meditative arts in order to inform their practice, it is useful to conceive of his approach as psychophysical. Maxwell insists upon intense commitment and concentration from his actors, so that they are acutely aware of their experience of the present moment. Although Maxwell does not instruct actors to undertake a specific type of training, conversations with long-term collaborators suggest that they have found meditative practice and participation in sports in general useful resources to draw upon. Sitting in on rehearsals for *The End of Reality* I saw the company use yoga and Tae Kwon Do exercises as warm-up exercises. Sibyl Kempson practiced yoga as a way of preparing her mind and body for performance and Brian Mendes drew parallels between the type of concentration he had when playing sports and when performing with colleagues on stage.

As an artist, Maxwell can be seen to be responding to contemporary global concerns, although his worldview remains uncompromisingly American. His work is situated within both a performance and theatre context, demonstrating a deep and prolonged engagement with contemporary theatre practice and playwriting. The presence of songs in his work evidences the further influence of American rock and country music. His songs enjoy a life beyond his plays, having been released on CDs such as *Showtunes*—sung by the original artists (1999) and *I'm Feeling So Emotional* (2002). The songs tend to function as a form of emotional release for otherwise reserved characters. Monosyllabic characters occasionally find themselves granted the temporary gift of articulation, as if they are suddenly enthused to communicate, rationalise and conjugate through song. Bailes has described Maxwell's songs as, 'hyperbolic yet earnest ballads' (Bailes 2011: 155). Sublimated tensions are often rendered tangible when set to music, for example in *Drummer Wanted*, Frank and his mother both deliver songs, ostensibly at a karaoke bar, expressing anxiety at losing a loved one. The content of the songs contrasts with the largely hectoring and hostile tone characterising their exchanges at other points in the play. As Wessendorf has suggested, 'since the protagonists cannot express their emotions directly, they have to take recourse to prefabricated songs to indicate their feelings and create the semblance of an inner life' (Wessendorf 2003). Music enables NYCP to explore the skill of articulation through both dialogue and song. Characters are shown to embody different skills as they attempt to execute different tasks. Lyrics are rarely complex, and often deal with quotidian, unromantic subjects, however much of their rhetoric appears indebted to contemporary pop or folk music, containing references to dreams, aspirations and hidden desire. Although actors' voices may crack under the strain to reach a high note, in contrast to the often halting patterns of speech the song lyrics are usually delivered in a fluent, melodic manner. Furthermore, musical accompaniment is provided by professional musicians who play expertly written melodies. Maxwell has stated that he, 'like[s] opening up the experience of song to all kinds of emotions including very prosaic, quotidian feelings. Why not have a mild transcendence or a mild moment, and a song come out of that?' (quoted in Moore 2003). The presence of songs in Maxwell's work alludes to the profound influence of popular music, and popular culture in general, upon working class and middle class American families. Although a reliance upon 'popular' rather than 'high' culture could be seen by some to signal some kind of aesthetic crisis, representative of a kind of 'dumbing down', I do not believe that Maxwell intends this interpretation for his characters. As I have suggested previously, Maxwell appears respectful of working class values, and celebrates allegiances to popular belief systems and the fleeting pleasures of consumption as a way of dramatising a determination, against all odds, to believe in *something*.

In terms of the structure of the overall book Chapter 2 sets out to examine Maxwell's directorial approach to acting, and in particular the much vaunted suggestion that his actors employ a 'deadpan' style. In addition to being resistant to the idea that he employs a recognisable style at all, Maxwell has been vocal about his disdain for deadpan as a 'shorthand' description for his actors' work. He has stated that this term, 'gives the impression that I'm asking actors to "play a negative" which is a phrase that gets bandied about in acting classes that I actually agree with. I'm careful when I speak to actors that I do not want them to feel any pressure to emote, which is different than saying, "don't emote" or "don't feel."'[12] Within this chapter I purse the idea of 'deadpan' as a putative 'theory'; explore what it might mean to ask actors to 'draw back from characterizing emotion'[13] and consider how this might signify for an audience accustomed to realist theatre conventions. I propose that the economy of the actors' gestures might signify as 'bad' or 'failed' acting and employ theories by Bailes, Etchells and Alvarez questioning the radical potential of 'professional amateurism' (Kear 2005). One of my main findings is that the directorial decision to foreground acting as a task enables an audience to glimpse a subject in thrall to the societal compulsion to perform appropriately. The amateur actor's inability to convincingly achieve 'otherness' makes visible the role of training and education in helping the actor achieve a level of neutrality on stage. I argue that training and education are customarily only accessible to privileged classes and that the suppression of signs of education and training work to create a false illusion of equal access for all.

Chapter 3 takes the form of a historiographical project to identify traces of Cook County Theater Department's (CCTD) past and to make visible the problems associated with my attempt to draw meaning from archival material. Piecing together archives of shows such as *Fable* (1993); *Minutes and Seconds* (1994); *Nothing and Advertising* (1994) and *Clowns Plus Wrestlers* (1994) I attempt to make sense of CCTD's associative and visually sophisticated approach to theatre making. Drawing upon interviews with founder members I scrutinise the visual and oral material for signs of a definitive aesthetic or methodological 'break' or continuity. Although I find many aspects of the aesthetic style to be different, it is possible to glimpse an anti-intellectual attitude and a mode of delivery which continues on in Maxwell's work with NYCP.

Chapter 4 scrutinises the construction of masculinity with Maxwell's work. Bob Vorlicky has proposed that the theatrical space has come to be associated with emotional disclosure and subsequently endowed with 'feminine' qualities, as 'men are not supposed to speak too personally, or so dictates the myth of male behaviour in America' (Vorlicky 1999: 198). I use Vorlicky's proposition to analyse the presence of amateur actors on stage in Maxwell's work. I argue that where the trained actor 'succeeds' in emoting in a convincing manner for a conventional theatre audience, he concomitantly 'fails' to perform heteronormative masculinity as he is succeeding in a feminine arena. Correspondingly, when the amateur actor fails to achieve an illusion of preparedness for the stage, he refuses to be assimilated into a feminine space and so retains a sense of embodying a successful, hypermasculine male. I test this proposition against a number of specific performances and productions before shifting my attention to the fictional worlds of *Showcase* (2003), *Billings* (1996), *Boxing 2000* and *House* to perform an analysis of language and hypermasculine patterns of speech. I scrutinize Maxwell's use of contemporary urban American vernacular and cadences associated with inarticulate two-dimensional characters such as Bill and Ted of *Bill and Ted's Excellent Adventure* and Beavis and Butthead[14]. Drawing upon the linguistic work of Jen Coates I identify how these language patterns are customarily associated with a reluctance to disclose personal or emotional information. Coates refers to the phrase to 'mask up', a notion introduced to her by a colleague working in male prisons, which interviewees had employed to identify the reserved, distancing techniques men would deliberately employ in prison to disguise vulnerability. I associate Maxwell's early interest in 'neutral' acting exercises and his use of Lecoq's neutrality exercises with this very masculine drive to reign-in emotional disclosure. Moving on from an analysis of language, I explore examples of work from 2006 and 2007 in which central male characters are given prolonged monologues dealing with emotional revelation. The character of Tom in *The End of Reality* and The Kneeling Man in *Ode to the Man Who Kneels* are both shown to be tortured respectively by a challenge to faith and a broken heart. These plays do not, as one might expect, begin to characterise emotionally communicative characters as better adjusted or equipped to deal with a hostile world. Instead of finding emotional disclosure therapeutic they continue to experience crisis and mourn the intractable nature of their predicament. This development reveals that Maxwell does not pursue any simplistic claims about emotional disclosure, indeed both restrained and open characters work to undermine the dominance of popular therapeutic discourses circulating in contemporary America which would hold that the widespread adoption of the 'Californian' self and rejection of the 'New England' self proves emotional disclosure precipitates self-knowledge and contentment (Collins 2007: 153). As Antony Easthope has argued, 'the masculine myth has always tried to perpetuate its power by feigning invisibility. As soon as masculinity can be seen as masculinity, its power is challenged and it is called into question (Easthope 1986: 167). Maxwell's inclusion of patterns of speech which signify as both 'inappropriate' to the realist stage and 'appropriate' to hypermasculine vernacular amounts to a dramatisation and questioning of masculine behaviour. Furthermore, Maxwell's use of argot renders visible the role of class in perpetuating the myth of the generic male subject. Erving Goffman observed the following back in 1963:

> In an important sense there is only one complete unblushing male in America: a young, married, white, urban, northern, heterosexual Protestant father; college educated, fully employed, of good complexion, weight and height, and a recent record in sports. Every American male tends to look out at the world from this perspective, this constituting one sense in which one can speak of a common value system in America. Any male who fails to qualify in any one of these ways is likely to view himself—during moments at least—as unworthy, incomplete and inferior. (128)

Maxwell's dramatisation of male patterns of speech and behaviour, and his directing work with both trained and untrained actors, enables audiences to glimpse a performative equivalent of the 'blushes' Goffman would have appear for any male not adhering to the idealised myth of generic American masculinity.

Chapter 5 features an extended consideration of the use and representation of space within Maxwell's work. In a similar approach to the chapter on masculinity, I start by considering how Maxwell's direction destabilises modes of reception associated with theatrical realism. I argue that he ruptures the closed hermeneutic world customarily associated with the realist play by making signs of labour and rehearsal visible to the spectator. Influenced by Marc Augé's theory of supermodernity and space, I argue that Maxwell invests in the idea of theatre as an 'anthropological place', that is, 'a place in which the social is 'engendered' and in which 'journeys have to be made' (Augé 1995:81). In addition, I contend that he mourns the loss of such 'organic', 'social' spaces by citing and exploring 'non-places' within the fictional world of his plays. For Augé a non-place is one which is akin to 'the airports and railway stations, hotel chains, leisure parks and large retail outlets', spaces that for Augé, 'cannot be defined as relational or historical, or concerned with identity' (Augé 1995: 77). I argue that Maxwell bolsters a sense of identity crisis by dramatising his characters' relationships with an alienating, homogenous environment. Although Augé does not specify an American landscape when he discusses non-places, it is clear that he is influenced by the work of Baudrillard who has written about contemporary America as 'a giant hologram' (Baudrillard 1986:29). I discuss the features of supermodernity as they appear in Maxwell's plays and identify how non-places are associated with environments which prove to hold few opportunities for their characters. The depersonalised spaces occupied by the salesman in *Showcase*; the security guards in *The End of Reality* and the family in *House* contribute to a sense of constriction, as if they prevent, rather than promote opportunities for social interaction and community involvement. Having considered the representation of non-spaces, I move on to analyse the construction of images of the Frontier and the West, as featured in *Ode to the Man Who Kneels*, *Cowboys and Indians* [15] and *The Frame*. Drawing upon work by John Agnew, Joanne Sharp and Jonathan Smith, I consider how Maxwell's invocation of the West fits into a long tradition of literature about Frontier imagery and The American Dream. Identifying The American Dream as one 'of equal opportunity and progress for all' Agnew and Sharp reiterate the importance of the illusion of the frontier as 'open' to a sense of American exceptionalism (Agnew and Sharp 2002: 95). Frederick Jackson Turner's thesis that 'as of the 1890s the historical American frontier was settled' caused anxiety for a population accustomed to thinking of themselves as progressive, adventurous and continually expanding (Mogen, Busby and Bryant 1989:28). My analysis of Maxwell's representation of Frontier life reveals individuals who, in contrast to the customary myth of the inscrutable, self-possessed cowboy, fail to achieve self-realisation as a result of their adventures in a rugged, primitive landscape. In Maxwell's plays the Westfarers remain trapped by insecurity and repeat the follies and petty crimes of their forefathers.

In my concluding chapter I take the opportunity to pursue some unexplored avenues of thought and consider what Maxwell's most recent work might suggest for the future. I interrogate the suggestion that Maxwell's work can be understood purely in terms of the 'irony' Sellars suggests pervades much contemporary American experimental theatre. I also return to the presence of the subaltern in Maxwell's work, performing an analysis of his construction of female characters. I go on to examine the values of 'honesty' repeated in *People Without History* (2008) and *Das Maedchen: The Girl Torn Between the Days* and consider how the ambiguity of intention behind this term opens up a space for an 'ironic' *and* potentially conservative reading of his work.

The book is structured around several different approaches, most notably: acting, social geography, historiography, feminist and gender analysis. These approaches arose out of a sense of the themes crucial to Maxwell; they represent the preoccupations he repeats and foregrounds in his writing and approach to direction. His post-Brechtian techniques of keeping the house lights illuminated and retaining the marks of rehearsal point to a desire to frame his work as a form of critical engagement with the function of theatre in normalising learned forms of behaviour. His emphasis on the mundane experiences of blue-collar workers, for example, allows him to refer to a range of often convoluted social practices and events which have become normalised within mainstream American culture and Western liberal capitalist societies in general. He repeatedly creates characters in thrall to the illusion of agency bestowed by the myth of America as the Land of Opportunity and the rewards of a Puritan work ethic. His characters refer to the insidious creep of multinational capitalism; a sense of growing apprehension about public safety; the transferral of consumer values into the realm of education, culture and art. His characters experiment with therapeutic speech and attempt to reach out to other members of their community but ultimately are left to fend for themselves, to rely on their own impoverished resources to 'get ahead'. Maxwell's overarching interest in inarticulate lower class characters evidences a critique of hegemonic Humanist values throughout his work.

Maxwell is deeply influenced by the social milieu and cultural practices surrounding him, and as a result I have worked to locate his work within the context of contemporary American culture and international theatre practice. Ultimately it is impossible to generalise about where his work should be located politically or generically. Politically, he courts controversy by having his characters voice 'honest' opinions which are antagonistic to a liberal audience; generically he works to undermine theatrical illusion whilst borrowing strategies from both mainstream and experimental theatre. By citing the conventional in an unconventional way he opens an aperture for audiences to glimpse contradictions inherent within received bodies of knowledge about ontology and the role of the individual within Western capitalist society. Maxwell is an important figure in contemporary international theatre, combining insightful social commentary with a belief in the theatre as a space for meaningful social engagement. He presents an affectionate, yet critical image of America which has endeared him to theatre-goers across the globe and repeatedly identifies new challenges to keep testing his own assumptions and methodologies. It is his ambiguous and unstable relationship to hegemonic American culture and mainstream theatre practice which makes his theatre such an interesting medium to use to explore how social forces come to bear upon the individual.

2 Bad Acting *on Purpose*
Practising Intelligibility
and Legitimacy on Stage

A survey of Maxwell's plays over the past thirteen years reveals his preoccupation with the lives of blue-collar workers. A significant proportion of his plays feature characters who, albeit in monosyllabic prose, mull over questions of fate, faith and opportunity in a competitive and aspirational culture. Plays such as *House* (1998), *Boxing 2000*, (2000); *Drummer Wanted* (2001); and *The End of Reality* (2006) dramatise the confusion caused by an illusion of freedom and autonomy and allude to the different ways that race, economic stability, geographical location and class impinge upon each character's sense of opportunity and freedom. Ironically, critics rarely pick up on this aspect of Maxwell's work; a survey of critical and journalistic writing about Maxwell reveals a preoccupation with analysing the effects of his so called 'signature [directorial] style' (Walsh 2004; Pogrebin 2000), which is considered to comprise 'a wilful numbness' (Brantley 2006); 'flat tones' (Pogrebin 2000); a 'laconic-ironic' attitude (Walsh 2004) and art 'which combines pitch-perfect orchestration of the deadening rhythms of contemporary American speech with an acting style that, in its monotone affect, borders on the autistic' (McNulty 2003).

This apparently restrained or constrained performance is what appears to signify most productively for theatre critics who set out to isolate and identify the director's intervention. Wayne Alan Brenner included an overheard snippet of conversation in his review of *Drummer Wanted* for the Austin Chronicle. He wrote '"It's kind of like", one student was heard was heard to remark with much inflection, "really *bad* acting, but *on purpose*"' (Brenner 2003: 1).

Maxwell has written that he is 'careful' not to put any pressure on actors to 'emote'. However, he is at pains to emphasize the fact that he is not discouraging emotional engagement. As part of an interview with Bonnie Marranca in 2002 he stated that, as far as he sees it, it is '[n]ot a question of why the character is on stage—but why *you* are on stage [as actor]' (Marranca 2002, Author's emphasis). Despite the naturalistic framing of the plot-line and characterization, Maxwell's approach to acting borrows from contemporary performance as it appears to be conceived as a real-time task, a task requiring a significant amount of courage. He has stated that much actor-training is focused upon teaching the actor how to suppress or disguise his or her nerves, so Maxwell's question to the actor, to consider *why* they are on stage, appears designed to reawaken a consciousness of the real 'here and now' of the theatrical moment rather than the fictional 'here and now' of the character. Responding to implications of the designation of his non-psychologically motivated performance as 'deadpan' Maxwell has conceded that:

> [. . .] yes, [in the context of theatre] it is perhaps deadpan; and yes, I can see that it can appear without effect, but not in comparison to real-life, only in relation to plays which the viewers have seen in the past; inconsistent not with reality but only in relation to a viewing history. (Quoted in Mauro 2002)

Maxwell is at pains to point out that the incongruity of his performance-style (if it can be termed as such) is that it disrupts the established acting conventions employed in more traditional theatre contexts. An exception to the tendency to focus upon acting can be found in a more extended piece of academic writing by Markus Wessendorf, who, in 'The (Un) Settled Space of Richard Maxwell's *House*' draws a parallel between the way that both actors and characters appear 'not at home in their own bodies' and argues that this amounts to 'an acting style and a character dramaturgy that are equally anti-mimetic' (Wessendorf 2001: 447–449). By analysing both the internal (intra-diegetic) signs deployed within the fictional world of the play and the external (extra-diegetic) signs world of the auditorium, Wessendorf demonstrates that Maxwell's 'signature style' is not as superficial or inane as the majority of critics would allow. Within this piece Wessendorf comments upon the cultural forces at work in the fictional world of the play. By tracing the relationship between directorial work, acting and characterisation I intend to challenge claims made by critics elsewhere that Maxwell's work is a repetition of the 'laconic-ironic downtown school of playmaking' (Walsh 2004: 103) or that he is 'an anti-phony phony for the smart-set cynics' (Feingold 2003). By paying attention to the cultural forces at work in the lives of his characters, I intend to pursue Judith Butler's proposition that a 'monologic masculinist economy [can] operate to effect relations of . . . racial, class and heterosexist subordination' and so understand, for example, a 'laconic' character as behaving in response to his or her own social environment (Butler 1990: 13–14). Furthermore, not only could Maxwell's character development be understood to represent an attempt to foreground the illusory nature of the self-governing Humanist subject, but also that any emotional hesitancy on the part of the actors is an attempt to draw attention to the rarely acknowledged Humanist ideology at the centre of the Strasbergian strain of Method Acting. [1]

The performance-oriented approach to 'acting' is shaped through a particular discourse, which has long been sceptical about psychologically motivated acting and psychologically rounded characters. Following Willem Dafoe's interview with Philip Auslander in 1984, a Performance Studies approach to 'acting' appeared to imply that the best function for acting, within deconstructive theatre, was for it to be made visible as a task-based activity. Critical vocabularies were appropriated from other disciplines in order to describe on-stage activity as 'non-acting or 'acting'; 'matrixed' or 'non-matrixed' (Kirby 2002). Foreman has resisted providing psychological motivation for his performers by requesting that their movements are disassociated from their speech. Swettenham describes this as a 'mechanical approach' whereby Foreman 'ask[s his actors] to execute specific physical movements as they say any given line, without necessarily giving them any motivation for those actions' (Swettenham 2008: 69). The performers' preoccupation with attempts to multi-task, according to Foreman, help prevent them from becoming relaxed, or feeling at ease on stage. He writes:

> Performers normally want two things. One is to be loved, and the other is to find a way to be relaxed onstage. The basic Stanislavsky method, as it has been taught in America, trains an actor to find a way to be relaxed during a performance, even within a highly emotional scene. (Foreman 1992: 41)

Method Acting[2] in particular, has been revealed by Performance Studies to be 'logocentric' (Auslander 1999) and shown to rely upon the Humanist understanding of the autonomous self-governing subject (Hornby 1992). Given the resistance to acting in the performance field, it appears incongruous to find a practitioner such as Maxwell who engages with the rhetoric of Method-acting, whilst employing other, more performance-art influenced means to defamiliarise traditional theatre conventions. The enunciation of the function of acting within Maxwell's work invites a reading framed by a Performance Studies epistemology, however, his rationale for resisting traditional theatre practice appears nostalgic for the very concepts deconstructive practice seeks to resist.

In his introduction to *Acting (Re) Considered* Phillip Zarrilli suggests that:

> [E]very time an actor performs, he or she implicitly enacts a 'theory' of acting—a set of assumptions about the conventions and style which guide his or her performance, the structure of actions which he or she performs, the shape that these actions take (as character, role, or sequence of actions as in some performance art), and the relationship to the audience. Informing these assumptions are culture-specific assumptions about the body-mind relationship, the nature of the 'self', the emotions/feelings, and performance context. (Zarilli 2002: 3)

Maxwell's work offers a fascinating proposition for Performance Studies scholars because the 'theory' of acting being presented appears at odds with the 'theory' of staging. The approach to acting marks a clear break with naturalistic method-driven practice as actors occasionally appear to stand at one remove from their characters. Additionally, the language used by the director to justify or explain the work (as 'realism', for example) initially is grounded in the dominant principles of the discipline under scrutiny (Marranca 2002). However, the unusual performance techniques employed extend beyond a deconstructive reluctance to reveal the self through performance. The static demeanour of the actors and their refusal to observe naturalistic rules of proxemics, (which would, for example, have lovers and siblings standing close to one other) works to emphasize the notion that some aspect of performance and acting is being re-figured or challenged. Actors occasionally appear slow to pick up on cues, they employ an erratic register, so that one minute they speak at normal volume, the next they raise their voices to shout without any apparent shift in mood or attitude. Although the dialogue runs smoothly for the most part, actors also appear to make eccentric choices about which words they will emphasize, thereby appearing to alter the author's intended meaning. In this chapter I argue that Maxwell and company are staging an intervention into traditional modes of performance and actor training as a way of instigating dialogue about subject formation, identity and language as they are performed both onstage and off. In particular, I read for signs of an anti-Humanist attitude.

This anti-Humanist analysis of Maxwell's approach to acting and characterisation is informed by a Foucauldian understanding of the term. Foucault declared 'the death of man' at the end of *The Order of Things*, by which he is commonly held to have announced the demise of the Enlightenment belief that mankind was governed by 'reason'. The Humanist conception of the human subject is dependent upon the idea that each individual has the facility to make autonomous decisions in isolation from external social or cultural forces; that the individual is self-governing and able to act upon his or her own free will. Alongside Foucault, the *Annales* school of French historians was also influential in galvanising an anti-Humanist theory of historical development, positing that 'the impersonal forces of geography and demography governed the destiny of mankind'; and '[a]nti-humanism's main proposition was that the autonomy of the individual subject was an illusion'. In addition, the *Annales* scholars argued that, 'the Humanist tradition had been wrong to assign the central roles of human affairs to the conscious mind and free will' (Windschuttle 1998: 5). More contemporary meditations upon Foucault's theories of subject formation and power provide further relevant materialist frameworks for considering culture and cultural practice as sites of subject formation. Vicki Kirby usefully outlines the pertinence of Judith Butler's work by asserting that

[. . .] Central to Butler's argument is a conviction that culture is capable of producing ontological (ways of being) and epistemological (ways of knowing) frames of reference which are so powerful that they congeal into the apparent invariance and irreducibility of material reality. Indeed, for Butler, we are subjected to/through the weight of these material truths and live them as defining parameters of identity. (Kirby 2006: 24)

For Butler the illusion of autonomy is developed in and through language, a facet of cultural production that she considers to be, 'a discursive configuration that orders information into normative patterns and practices of intelligibility and legitimacy' (Kirby 2006: 24). 'Ways of knowing' and 'ways of being' certainly appear to be forcefully reiterated by Maxwell's characters who regularly map out idiosyncratic value systems and world-views. These belief-indicators are reinforced by using local or particularised speech patterns, and the parameters of each character's sense of ambition extend alongside a willingness to revise, or look beyond the local. Despite the ostensible limitations visible within each world-view, the characters live under the illusion that they are self-governing and that they are able to make autonomous decisions. The plays often reveal their opportunities to be restricted by economic responsibilities to their families; geographical location; physical impairment or economic class. The conflict between the illusion of freewill and the restrictions of characters' day to day lives builds dramatic tension in many of Maxwell's plays, and the rehearsal and realisation of this conflict is articulated through the argot by which they are constrained.

In addition to the dramatisation of circumstance, Maxwell's work also provides an opportunity to explore the effects of 'racial, class and heterosexist subordination' upon actual bodies. He regularly works with a mixed company of professional and untrained actors, a practice which enables the audience to witness not only how an undisciplined body realises a dramatic role, but how this body fails to repress signs of cultural subordination as it struggles to cope with the task in hand. Maxwell has spoken of the way that Method training provides actors with strategies for subsuming what is commonly referred to as 'stage-fright', and states that he considers any performer willing to dispense with these strategies as 'brave' (Pogrebin 2000). By analysing the work of both trained and non-trained actors in Maxwell's productions, I hope to foreground a twofold critique of the Humanist subject. In addition to the representation of straitened social circumstance I will analyse the vexing circumstance of performance itself and consider how signs of nerves or exertion reveal bodies responding physiologically to their immediate cultural environment. Maxwell's work acts as a critique of the Humanist values of Method-training by demonstrating how it requires actors to ignore the reality of their immediate socio-cultural environment in order to imagine themselves into an absent, fictional reality. According to David Krasner, the Method actor's licence to retrieve an emotional response represents an act of 'free will', a defining feature of the Humanist subject. By interrogating references to ideas of autonomy, self-determinism and free will within Maxwell's plays and the discourse of Method-acting I will demonstrate that narrative and casting fruitfully combine to provide a critique of the illusion of Humanist autonomy.

Maxwell's anecdotes about his experience of Method-acting classes draw attention to the assumption that an actor, as part of his or her creative response, will internalise the fictional character's given circumstances in order to find an emotional response to the text. [3] In a direct attempt to resist this imperative, Maxwell has taken the decision to intervene and test the outcome of experiments in which he attempts to 'relieve' his actors of this 'pressure' or the 'burden' to engineer an emotional response [4]. Rather than ask his actors to retreat into an imaginary version of their character's inner psychology, he asks them to focus upon the nature of their task on stage, as actors, and to re-evaluate whether they feel an emotional response to be appropriate to the immediate context. The distinction between the two approaches lies in the prioritisation of different levels of 'reality' for the actor. The Method-actor is asked to temporarily imagine the fictional world of the play to represent their primary 'reality' for the duration of the performance, and to ignore the contingencies of the present theatrical environment as far as possible. Maxwell's actors, by contrast, are encouraged to hold the present reality of the performance environment at the forefront of their minds and to consider any decisions about characterisation in the context of the project underway. This approach tends to result in the actor interpreting their character differently from performance to performance as they intuit the different context and atmosphere leant by each new audience and their colleagues' different interpretations within a changing theatre environment. [5]

Maxwell's experience of actor training at Illinois State University appears to exert a considerable influence upon his approach to theatre-making. He set out to resist and explode much of the received wisdom imparted during his training in his work with Cook County Theater Department in Chicago (1992–1997) and regularly makes reference to aspects of his early acting experiences whilst explaining the rationale for his work. [6] For example, in response to the often repeated suggestion that his actors' use a 'deadpan' style of acting, Maxwell refers to terminologies used in 'acting classes':

> I worry that [deadpan] gives the impression that I'm asking actors to 'play a negative' which is a phrase that gets bandied about in acting classes that I actually agree with. I'm careful when I speak to actors that I do not want them to feel any pressure to emote, which is different than saying, 'don't emote' or 'don't feel', 'don't reveal'—and then also focus finally on what they *are* doing, as opposed to not doing. To me, this is what keeps it from being deadpan. [. . .] Seems to me deadpan

is a deliberate denial of emotion and emoting for effect (especially in comic acting)—I need to make a distinction between emoting and emotion. Emotion exists around things, in this case, the stage, whether we affect it or not, for the player and the audience. This has led me to relieve the burden of 'emoting' by the player. Emoting creates another reality separate from the stage reality. By not emoting, the line between character and actor blurs, I think.[7]

Maxwell's articulation of the Method-actor's imperative to retrieve an emotional response as 'the burden of emoting', is fascinating: it appears redolent of the phrase 'the burden of representation' which is customarily attributed to gay actors, or actors of colour when invited to occupy a role which serves as a metonymic representation of their marginalised or oppressed social group. Chronicling his experience of realising black characters, as a black actor, on stage, David Wiles confesses that, despite his training, he felt ill-prepared for the feelings of ambivalence the portrayal of 'black characters' raised for him.[8] He states:

Method asks me to forget the spectators. It simply doesn't offer tools for forging a relationship with them. It suggests instead that my relationship with the audience will be taken care of by immersing myself in the character's life. It will not. (Krasner 2000a: 172)

Both Maxwell and Wiles articulate a sense that their training did not confront the effect the presence of the audience has upon the experience of live performance for the actor, and that the pressure to continue to employ Method-skills within this environment proved 'burden'-some. The failure to acknowledge the immediate performance environment troubles or encumbers the actor with complex emotional responses that are not resolved by retreating into the imaginary world of the character. The desire to avoid pitfalls presented by the internalised 'burdens' of Method-trained actors appears to lie at the heart of Maxwell's direction and his decision to work with actors who have not necessarily been schooled according to the dominant Strasbergian influenced Method-driven technique.

Much has been written over the last twenty years about the fall from favour of Method Acting in North American acting schools and theatre departments. Richard Hornby has written what he describes as 'an unashamed attack on the American acting system' (Hornby 1992: 1) and David Krasner has responded by attempting to retaliate against what he considers to amount to 'method bashing in the academy' (Krasner 2000: 3). Hornby sets out his dissatisfaction with the persistence of Method Acting in his text *The End of Acting* (1992). He cites 'Method' as the dominant mode of actor training in the United States since the 1920s. He conceives of it as a 'mimetic theory' adapted from Stanislavski's early teaching, to suit the needs of a 'highly individualist, capitalist society'

(Hornby 1992: 5). In summing up the basis of 'this Strasbergian ideology' as he describes it, he states that:

> Theatre imitates life, the more closely and directly the better. The good actor therefore repeats on stage what he does in everyday life, drawing on his personal experiences, but, more important, reliving his emotional [. . .] traumas. Strasberg specifically maintained that an actor, through an interesting process called affective memory, should learn to simulate in himself a dozen or so real-life emotions, which he could then call up singly or in combination for all possible acting situations. The actor plays himself, not somebody else; acting is basically a form of emotional release. Actor training is primarily a process of coming to know yourself, and of removing emotional inhibitions. (Hornby 1992: 6)

Hornby sees Strasberg's teachings as contributing to a solipsistic approach to acting, in which the emphasis relies upon the actor attaining a certain degree of self-knowledge. He argues that this approach has the resultant effect of marginalizing other performance skills, such as vocal projection, movement vocabularies and contextual knowledge of the plays, and that these skills are understood to be peripheral aspects of an acting 'style' rather than fundamental components of a rounded education. Furthermore, Hornby writes of the 'pernicious influence' he sees the '"realism/style" dichotomy as having had upon [North] American acting'. He writes, 'It is obviously based in Cartesian dualism. [According to Strasberg's approach] Realism is supposed to be internal, personal, real, and emotional; style is external, conventional, artificial and cold' (Hornby 1992: 214).

David Krasner's edited collection; *Method Acting Reconsidered* goes some way towards addressing Hornby's criticisms. Louise M. Stinespring, for example, challenges Hornby's assertion that Method teaching has not responded to the challenges offered by poststructuralism by contributing a Derridean reading of Meisner's repetition exercise. She works to show how this inflection of Method teaching invites the actor to respond to the contingency of the theatrical present (Stinespring in Krasner 2000: 97–109). In addition, Krasner also takes the time to respond directly to Hornby and Dennis C. Beck by discussing the appropriation of Stanislavski's methods for both Humanist and poststructuralist purposes on either side of the Iron Curtain (Beck in Krasner 2000: 261–282). However, in contrast to Stinespring and Beck, Krasner himself appears reluctant to question the hegemonic status of the Humanist conception of selfhood and its centrality to his vision of Method-acting. He writes:

> Notions of character and actor and how they are related depend on certain philosophical conceptions of free will and determinism. In Method acting, actors are recognized as being guided by their own intentions; in contrast, non-Method acting frequently views actors *as*

subjects to the imposition of external events. (Krasner 2000: 17, Author's emphasis)

Krasner suggests that without the individual creative input from the actor, characterization is invariably dull and repetitive and will not support the audience's suspension of disbelief. He argues that when actors are not invited to develop roles according to Method training, they are ultimately reduced to the status of puppets. Indeed, for him:

> Determinists subordinate any seeming higher, transcendent reality to the status of illusion. Actor's inquiry into things spiritual is futile, once they accept their own material presence, they are given over to what David Mamet calls 'the actual courage of the actor', a courage that when coupled with the lines of the playwright [creates] the illusion of character'. Actors cease to graft their individuality onto the role and accept their position as *ubermarrionettes.* (Krasner 2000: 20)

Krasner and Hornby's exchange, if it can be described as such, provides a way of understanding the concept of the 'burden of emoting' which Maxwell suggests that the method-trained actor internalizes. The notion of non-Method actors being 'subjects to the imposition of external events' is redolent of Maxwell's desire to see actors think about 'what they *are* doing' in so far as he expects the external events taking place in the auditorium to have some bearing on how they choose to interpret their role in that particular instance. Maxwell capitalises upon the aspects of 'determinist' approaches to acting which Krasner derides. He asks actors to put spiritual considerations aside in order to 'accept their own material presence' and also to accept, to some extent, their position as *ubermarrionettes.* Ironically, the resultant effect often enhances, rather than detracts from the convincing realisation of character as the fictional figures are often themselves shown to be *ubermarionettes* of larger cultural forces. This feature of the work broadens the potential for identifying theories of subject formation within the world of the play, and demonstrates how Maxwell's casting policies draw attention to the influence of cultural forces within the world at large. In very reductive terms, Maxwell's practice can be seen to be drawing attention to the way in which people are profoundly affected by their environment.

Krasner's invocation of 'free will' provides an alternative way of thinking about the cultural materialist approach to subject formation in Maxwell's work. Maxwell's characters have been identified by Markus Wessendorf as, 'losers in a society that reveres self-exposure' (Wessendorf 2001: 455). Indeed, many of Maxwell's characters are blue-collar workers, defined primarily by their chosen occupation and living in the suburbs of a large city. They find it difficult to articulate or disclose their true feelings, and take refuge in popular cultural references and inane anecdotes. Maxwell alludes to the constraints that location, class, race, ethnicity, gender place upon self-realisation by creating a sense that both the spatial and aspirational mobility of these characters is somehow inhibited, as if, in a similar way to non-Method actors, they are, 'subject[s] to the imposition of external events'. In *Boxing 2000* two characters bemoan the closure of a local baseball field; *House* sees the Mother participating in a local community civic group, to little real effect, and the Father reminisces about a now defunct 'Concert Hall/Sports Facility' (Maxwell 2004b). The withdrawal of municipal facilities, to make way for commercial outlets is a reoccurring theme in Maxwell's plays. His characters appear socially aware and well informed of the changes, but are also, despite joining community activist groups, shown to be powerless to prevent the relentless co-option of public land. In addition, Maxwell's untrained actors demonstrate that they are 'subject to the imposition' of the professional theatre environment by failing to disguise the signs of exertion as they struggle to remember their lines and to master stage-fright. The failure of the actor to exert his or her 'free will' in becoming, as Krasner would have it, 'ultimate creators' of psychologically motivated characters provides a fruitful excess of signification in Maxwell's work, which can be interpreted both as part of the characterization and a comment upon the project of representation itself. Maxwell's narratives show free will to be something of an illusion in the contemporary Western world, so it appears fitting that Krasner's celebration of method acting suggests that an actor robbed of the opportunity to create an internalised emotional response to a character is an actor denuded of his or her free will.

Pete Simpson's portrayal of Frank in *Drummer Wanted* provides a compelling example of how the actor's distance from the inner psychology of the character can signify fruitfully in both 'real' and 'fictional' worlds to animate the issue of autonomy and free will.[9] Simpson's character is temporarily 'subject to the imposition of external events' as he is forced to be cared for by his mother after a motorbike accident. The two characters, Frank and 'Mom', are shown to enjoy a fraught relationship in which they express their desire not to be left alone and concomitantly, their sense of despair that they will never be left alone or achieve independence. In terms of the depiction of Frank's sense of agency in the fictional world of the play, his aspirations revolve around his desire to make a studio recording of his music, and yet he appears impeded by a sense of immaturity. His mother exclaims that 'You haven't finished growing up yet. A man can't go through life like this! Where are you going? You're not going anywhere!!' (Maxwell 2001: 28) Frank is given the type of language customarily associated with adolescent male characters, he repeatedly shouts at his mother to 'Shut the fuck up!' and makes lewd inappropriate references to past sexual encounters. At the outset of the play Frank expresses his hatred of accident victims who pursue compensation claims. Because he was hit by his friend 'Rey', he initially states that he does not intend to sue. However, as the play progresses his attitude alters and he puts increasing pressure on his mother to talk to her lawyer-friend about pursuing a claim. Towards the close of the play the pair find out that Frank has been offered $150,000, a sum which, Frank reveals in his closing speech, will enable him to realise his aspiration to make a recording. It appears significant, in relation to my reading for signs of agency and self-determination, that Frank's sense of self-realisation is buoyed by his financial reward. It transpires that he took no active part in progressing the claim, a feature of the narrative which further undermines the role he is given in determining his own future. It is possible to argue that in this piece Frank's sense that he is 'breaking a vicious circle' is illusory.[10]

In terms of Simpson's portrayal of character, several facets of his character's inability to 'move on' are realised physically. During the 2002 and 2003 productions in both Paris and London, despite, or perhaps because of, the splint he wore to keep his (fictionally broken) left leg straight, Simpson's rare and deliberate movements around the stage were marked by a clumsy heaviness. He retained a stiffness about his torso, keeping his shoulders hunched and his arms hanging by his sides. He occasionally shook his head to as if to remove stray locks of hair from his eyes. For the duration of the performance his eyes raked back and forth over the audience and when, during the performance I witnessed at The Barbican in London, late-comers were admitted, he deliberately turned his head to watch their entry and subsequent location of seats. He spoke rapidly and alternated between different modulations of speaking or

Figure 2.1   Ellen LeCompte and Pete Simpson play mother and son in *Drummer Wanted*. (Photo: Michael Schmelling.)

shouting within the same sentence, despite the fact that his lines provided no apparent motivation for these sudden shifts. Simpson maintained the same physical demeanour during his songs, apart from jerking with a kind of unconscious convulsion as he strained to meet the higher notes. The tension visible in his stance, his fixed glare at the audience, and his shifts in modulation signify as a deliberate contrast to the relaxed and consistent behaviour expected of a Method trained actor. However, the awkwardness of his posture also signified to capture, apparently by accident, a certain adolescent discomfort at self-expression and emotional revelation, as represented by 90s portrayals of teenage boys by Keanu Reeves and Beavis and Butthead.[11] The self-consciousness of Simpson's performance is in keeping with his character's self-conscious refusal to amend his expletive-ridden language in order to speak in more respectful terms to his mother. Both actor and character appear somehow constrained, or troubled, by the task in hand, which is to animate, or communicate through the demeanour of a rather boorish, ungracious, inarticulate young man. The only moments of the character's liberation from his linguistic torpor occur as he performs a karaoke version of a soft rock ballad which ironically works to express his fear of being alone and his search for love. Although it is not clear whether he intends these expressions of love for his mother, the vocabulary and sentiment of the songs provide a stark contrast to the macho language he uses elsewhere in the play. Just as Simpson, as an actor, gives the impression of being constrained by his self-conscious performance style, so his character appears trapped within a certain mode of behaviour, as if incapable of exercising the free will to temper his words in order to improve his relationship with his mother. His only moments of grace occur when he borrows the demeanour of the rock-star and someone else's language in order to sing a song. Simpson's characterisation brings to mind the poststructuralist and anti-Humanist approach to language which contends that human subjects are created in and through language. The various opportunities Frank's attitude and demeanour compromise demonstrate that language here is 'a discursive configuration that orders information into normative patterns and practices of intelligibility and legitimacy' (Kirby 2006: 24). Simpson's body language, reminiscent of a forced and performed arrogance, amplifies his performed linguistic arrogance. His awkward stance signifies as both 'bad acting' and as insightful characterisation. Maxwell has confessed to writing from the perspective that 'we're all limited in some things' (Ellis 2005) and indeed, by encouraging Simpson to find a mode of performance in which he appears constrained, he facilitates a synchronicity between the perceived execution of the acting task and the perceived limitations of the character. Simpson does not bring his character to life by imagining himself as the character, but rather enables the audience to glimpse a broader sense of unease as he is asked to suppress the training which enables him to appear relaxed and at ease on stage.

For non-professional or untrained actors this strategy is clearly not as beneficial. Maxwell regularly works with a range of different types of performers. He draws from a pool of long term collaborators (Gary Wilmes, Jim Fletcher, Brian Mendes, Sibyl Kempson); and also invites participation from: amateur actors recruited through adverts in *Backstage* and local libraries (McNulty 2003); actors who may not be classically trained but who are regulars in the downtown New York acting scene; graduates from acting school and musicians or playwrights who choose to turn their hand to acting for a short period of time. Maxwell has stated that the process of introducing new collaborators to his work, 'helps keep *me* new' because he is, 'learning about them and from them, and they are responding to the situation in a new way' (Gorman 2007: 238). He has also stated that, 'the combination of trained and non trained people creates some interesting and unexpected effects' (Pogrebin 2000).

Maxwell's desire to embrace the 'unexpected effects' emphasises his desire to explore the contingencies of the present theatrical moment, to encourage spontaneous and unrehearsed moments to interrupt an otherwise routine performance. He also makes the distinction between 'performers' and 'people' stating that, 'he wants his characters to sound like real people, not actors trying to sound like real people'. During the audition process he states that, 'There's not a specific quality that I'm going for, for me, it's a process of removing the things that are encouraging the person to be a performer as opposed to a person' (Pogrebin 2000). During the course of an interview conducted in 2006 Maxwell and Mendes returned to the notion of karaoke as a performance form, in an attempt to articulate what they found to be a genre of performance that was 'alive' and resisted being soured by performance 'contrivance'. Mendes stated that he enjoyed the fact that the performers in this context 'had no front' and suggested, 'that is why karaoke is so beautiful, because it negates preconception in a way. You see individuals for who they are in a performance environment' (Maxwell and Mendes 2006: 350).

The attempt to de-naturalise performance 'contrivance' and the 'front' that trained actors possess is central to Maxwell's work. In the past he has used exercises borrowed from Lecoq's neutral mask technique to help actors 'flatten their characters' and 'focus on the task and resist the impulse to define a character emotionally' (Wehle 2001: 5). This interpretation of mask work, when combined with the problem of theatrical 'contrivance' and a performance 'front' suggests that in both 'real' life and life on stage, Maxwell considers people to rely upon a kind of behavioural mask to intercede between their 'real' selves and their 'performed' selves.

Theorists documenting the rise of 'radical amateurism' within contemporary experimental performance have variously commented upon its ability to problematise the notion of performance as a capitalist enterprise (Cochrane 2001, Kear 2005); its potential to interrogate the traditional value judgements determining the amateur and the professional (Bailes

2005) and perhaps most relevant to a discussion of Maxwell's work, the refusal of 'alterity' (Alvarez 2006).[12]. Alvarez has written in detail about the pertinence of Maxwell's work to 'a neo-romantic attempt to radically rethink and transcend Western acting conventions in order to encounter . . . a more immediate, direct contact with an authentic being-in-the-world'. For her, this results in Maxwell's 'cancelling the appearance of virtuosity and replacing it with the perceived authenticity of the awkward, un-trained amateur' (Alvarez 2006: 234). Drawing upon Michael Sidnell's work on Coleridge and his concepts 'ipseity' and 'alterity', which, in performative terms can crudely be defined as 'becoming oneself' and 'becoming another', Alvarez argues that radical amateurism's potential lies in 'displaying the mechanics of performance'.[13] She argues that:

> The amateur's inability, in this sense, to achieve a state of alterity, that is, virtuosity or mastery in a convincing and therefore undetectable embodiment and fusing of performer with role or task, inadvertently displays the mechanics of performance; the strings, so to speak, are visible, fracturing the illusion. (Alvarez 2006: 239)

For Alvarez, because the amateur actor is unable to convincingly take on the role of anyone other than themselves, the audience are privy to an apparently unmediated glimpse of a 'real' person, a staging of an apparently 'authentic' human life. It is possible to extrapolate then, the notion that it is actor training, and most usually Method-training, which enables the actor to appear indistinguishable from role and to achieve this state of alterity. For trained actors Method-acting skills provide a set of behavioural 'masks' behind which to hide. Alvarez discusses *Henry IV (Part One)*, one of the productions which featured a number of untrained or amateur actors. She commented upon how the audience response appeared split between those sympathetic to the 'romantic-nostalgic allure of the amateur performer' and those who were, deeply offended by what they saw to be an inept and disrespectful staging of the Bard (McNulty 2003, Feingold 2003). Alvarez frames Maxwell's approach as a positive innovation, and demonstrates how the 'discursive configuration' of traditional theatre values comes to bear upon the work:

> Metaphorically, the amateur grappling with the formal constraints of theatrical artifice becomes a dramatization of the struggle between authenticity, individual identity, and the social forces, codes and conventions that impose standards of what is deemed to be competent performance. (Alvarez 2006: 249)

As intimated above, Alvarez's positive reading of the amateur participation in *Henry IV (Part One)* is one of very few positive responses to make it into print. The general antipathy of a great deal of audience members was echoed in newspaper reviews and even resulted in the London run of the show in the main house at The Barbican Centre being cancelled. Louise Jeffreys, one of the Artistic Directors responsible for the decision focused upon the proliferation of amateur actors whilst expressing her misgivings about the show when she stated 'The thing about non-professionals doing Shakespeare is it just taps into everything you hate about amateur productions, whereas with his other work it has a fragile, touching feel' (Ellis 2005).

Jeffreys' observation raises an interesting question about the application of a directorial approach which has to date, concerned itself with foregrounding realist theatrical contrivances, to a non-realist text. Although, as Alvarez has pointed out, the inclusion of the amateur works to defamiliarise the cultural institution of theatre, it is possible to consider that this piece did not receive the customarily positive reception because Maxwell's particular use of non-professionals works most productively to critique Method-acting rather than classical acting.

Maxwell's 2006 project, *The End of Reality* represented an opportunity for him to continue his interest in interrogating both the use-value and problems associated with acting resources derived from Method.[14] Casting a mix of established and non-established performers, Maxwell continued to explore the possibility of showing 'real people' on stage by giving two of the least experienced actors lengthy monologues. Maxwell wrote the majority of the script for *The End of Reality* (2006) having already met and cast the six participants. As a result, the characterisation for '1' is, to some extent influenced by Maxwell's knowledge of Bradshaw's manner and speech patterns. Maxwell has revealed that he initially wanted this character to use 'Hip-Hop' vernacular when he spoke, but was relieved when he finally completed the casting as Tom's real-life and on-stage demeanour rendered this type of vernacular inappropriate (Gorman 2007: 245). As mentioned previously, one striking aspect of *The End of Reality* is the length and complexity of the speeches given to non-established actors such as Hidalgo[15] and Bradshaw. In contrast to the long-term Maxwell collaborators, the less experienced actors were allocated lengthy monologues at several intervals in the play. The play alludes to issues of race and ethnicity, with Bradshaw, Delinois and Hidalgo being African-American and Hispanic. Bradshaw's character is the chief security guard in charge of an unspecified 'lobby citadel' in New York (Company publicity 2006). His monologues reveal a nostalgia for his 'old neighbourhood', a longing for a time when people did not equate 'success' with 'selling out'. Although he appears to gain solace from Christian beliefs and work, the script contains a number of suggestions that he is lonely and frustrated and others perceive him to be a 'failure'. Tom's Goddaughter Marcia ('5'), confesses to Brian that, '[h]e watches *Seinfeld* every weeknight. Dotes on his cat. Needs distractions like his email and his phone. But no one is mailing him. And no one is calling him. It's sad'

Figure 2.2 Jim Fletcher as King Henry IV. (Photo: Michael Schmelling.)

(Maxwell 2006: 19). Furthermore, after Marcia has released their assailant, Tom reveals that he feels the 'law enforcement community is laughin' at me', that they think, 'what kind of operation is that, can't—can't we detain people ?', (Maxwell 2006: 33).[16] As Frank's language in *Drummer Wanted* is made up of idiosyncratic imagery (in his case macho-adolescent slang), so Tom's is punctuated by quotations from *The New Testament* and references the importance of 'family' and 'community'. He repeatedly talks about the importance of origins, of remembering 'where you came from and how you got to where you are now'. He also intimates the difficulty of taking the 'right track', suggesting that abductee, Jake, avoided 'selling out' by joining the criminal fraternity. According to Tom, Jake came 'on board initially . . . but fell off' (Maxwell 2006: 5). Later in the play Jake returns to taunt Tom with his new associate, at one point he addresses him directly as 'sell out', apparently confirming Tom's previous apprehension (Maxwell 2006: 43).

In *Drummer Wanted* and *The End of Reality* Maxwell outlines both the benefits and limitations of Frank and Tom's rhetoric: their deep-seated beliefs lend succour to a certain extent, and the characters' repeated attempts to find reassurance lends a sense of vulnerability. Towards the close of *The End of Reality* Tom delivers a speech in which he attempts to come to terms with the loss of the 'old neighbourhood'. After having taken this new reality on board he confesses to experiencing a sense of 'agony' and instability:

> I feel untethered now, I can't feel my feet beneath me. This is a new sensation. Floating, my equilibrium gone, I have lost control of my life. How can I claim to have control over my life if I haven't any sense of myself, of my former self and new self has not been defined. (Maxwell 2006: 44)

Figure 2.3   Thomas Bradshaw, Alex Delinois, Sibyl Kempson and Jim Fletcher fight in *The End of Reality*. (Photo: Michael Schmelling.)

By allowing space for his characters to give voice to a particular world-view and to articulate the world according to a particular vernacular, Maxwell builds characters with integrity. He dramatises the way in which their chosen mode of communication, 'orders information into normative patterns and practices of intelligibility and legitimacy'(Kirby 2006: 24). These characters come undone when they are forced to confront their lack of agency and question the 'intelligible' or 'legitimate' status of their value system. In the extra-diegetic world of the play, the amateur actor's struggle with formal acting dramatises 'the struggle between authenticity, individual identity, and social forces'; in the intra-diegetic fictional world characters similarly struggle to understand how their futures are shaped by social forces rather than a self-motivated destiny. Bradshaw's character realises that he must change and rather than see himself as 'saved', instead actively ask God for salvation and pursue a new way of conceiving the world. Simpson's character must accept his lapse in integrity by accepting the insurance pay-out. The rhetoric of both Frank and Tom's language initially relied upon a sense of self-sufficiency only to give way to the realisation that in order to move forward they must turn their backs on received value systems and embrace a less certain future.

The End of Reality provides fertile territory to investigate how an untrained actor realises the role of what Wessendorf might refer to as 'a loser'. In this play the mix of established and non-established actors is equally balanced between cast members. Thomas Bradshaw presents an interesting case study. Although Bradshaw has studied acting in the past, he does not claim to be a 'trained actor'. [17] His entry in *The End of Reality* programme does feature one other acting credit (Young Jean Lee's *Pullman* 2005), however, he primarily identifies as a playwright.[18] In terms of the animation of character, Bradshaw's performance differs from Simpson's in a number of ways. Whereas Simpson's sense of vulnerability appeared to emanate from the withdrawal of a set of skills that would enable him to play to his strengths and fall back upon a comfortable, relaxed mode of performance, Bradshaw appears exposed by not appearing to have recourse to a set of performance skills that would allow him to relax on stage. During the performances I attended in New York and London, his rather hunched stance appeared innate rather than learned and during his longer speeches Bradshaw often spoke too quickly, so that the sense of the complex language was difficult to follow. His physical bearing also appeared a little incongruous, as he would take up and fiddle with props or sway very slightly as he spoke. Bradshaw also appeared slightly ill at ease when directly addressing the audience. In contrast to the economy of Mendes' and Fletcher's movements, these barely perceptible gestures created a resonance of vulnerability. Towards the end of the piece he deliberately turned his body outwards to face the front of the stage, and began to address the audience. In contrast to Simpson's confrontational and unrelenting glare, Bradshaw's surveillance of the audience appeared comparatively timid and forced, as if he found the situation uncomfortable and was deliberately recalling an instruction to move into this position, rather than feeling that the moment of direct address could be spontaneous. Although these actions were most likely to be spontaneous and accidental, they did signify productively to contribute to the realisation of the fictional character. In addition they also demystified certain accepted conventions of acting by drawing attention to that which is customarily suppressed.

By encouraging Simpson to adopt an alternative non-Method driven approach to acting and by allowing Bradshaw's idiosyncratic tics to remain visible, Maxwell is encouraging his actors, along the same lines as his characters, to lose a layer of skin.[19] By creating plays which reveal the labour (or 'work' in Oswald's terms) involved in maintaining a coherent sense of identity Maxwell demonstrates not only the illusory nature of the stable, autonomous Humanist subject, but also culture's ability to produce 'ontological frames of reference' which affect physiological transformation and so create a tangible and 'material reality' (Kirby 2006: 24). The signs of exertion manifest the difficulty of the task, and so call into question the normality of any successfully performed sense of composure. For both characters and actors, the demeanour of self-assurance is shown to be an acquired skill which is taught and practiced, rather than inherent.

In the past Maxwell has confessed to being 'rather fond of "bad acting"' (Wehle 2001) and states he is drawn to the untrained actor because:

> [. . . .] a lot of what training does is allow you to cope with the fear of performing, to deal with that extraordinary thing, to go up in front of people and perform their tasks. I think a lot of the time training allows you to deny the anxiety, the fear. And I would prefer to see people afraid and brave'. (Quoted in Pogrebin 2000)

Although the untrained actors in Maxwell's work are not participating in 'amateur theatre proper' and are apparently part of a 'new form of directed amateurism' the signs of their nerves are harvested in order to draw attention to the effects of environment upon the human subject (Kear 2006: 37). Although the untrained actors exercise 'free-will' in electing to participate, their apparent liberty to participate in a 'foreign' practice or to explore new creative territories is constrained by the signs of their body's unpreparedness. They do not fit easily into this environment because their sense of vulnerability becomes evident as their body responds to the pressures of the new situation. The trained actor, by comparison is equipped to deal with the pressures of changing environments, and granted licence to express him or herself creatively on stage. He or she is equipped with the skills to exercise what Krasner calls 'free-will'. By asking trained actors not to rely upon these skills and by inviting untrained actors to risk exposing their vulnerability Maxwell draws attention to the invisible role that training and education play in equipping the human subject for life. The sense of unease manifested by the untrained actors employed by The New York City Players accretes and amplifies the suggestion that a subject cannot transcend the limitations presented by his or her own environment without external assistance. Directorial and dramaturgical strategy combine to demonstrate 'free-will' and autonomy to be, if not illusory, to be the preserve of a privileged few. Ironically, Krasner argues that the Method-actor needs to transcend the 'here and now' in order to give the performance 'definition', whereas Maxwell would appear to be pushing for the opposite stance—to achieve definition by returning to the fact of the here and now.

3   Passionate Indifference
Cook County Theater Department

On Thursday 12 January 2006 I found myself in a New York bar near
The Kitchen, having just witnessed the opening night of the New York
City Player's *The End of Reality*. Later that evening, in conversation
with Brian Mendes, cast member, and long-term Maxwell collaborator, I
learned of Cook County Theater Department's role in shaping key relationships between playwright-director Richard Maxwell and significant colleagues. As part of our conversation Mendes related an anecdote regarding
a Chicago newspaper critic who, in an attempt to equate the company's
emotionally minimalist acting style with such unbridled enthusiasm for
experimentation, had entitled a Cook County profile, "Passionate Indifference. Unable to recall the name of the critic, or whether the description
came from a company member, or from the critic himself, Mendes shouted
over to Maxwell, asking, 'who came up with the term "passionate indifference" in relation to Cook County?' without hesitation Maxwell replied, 'I
did.' Mendes raised his eyes heavenwards and responded with a wry smile,
as if this some element of this exchange typified their relationship.[1] This
determination of Cook County's work struck me as significant because this
juxtaposition of 'passion' and 'indifference' seems an apt description for
Maxwell's more recent work. This informal exchange prompted me to look
into the work of Cook County Theater Department in order to explore a
possible aesthetic lineage from Maxwell's work with The New York City
Players (NYCP) to Cook County Theater Department (CCTD).

CCTD's name comes up in numerous interviews and after-show discussions, as if Maxwell's ideas have some kind of origin or genesis in these
early experiments. Maxwell co-founded Cook County Theater Department in 1991 with three friends he had met either through his fellowship at Steppenwolf or from college in Illinois.[2] Of the founding members,
Maxwell had won an acting fellowship, Mendes worked as assistant to
the actors, including, during his tenure, Albert Finney; Kate Gleason was
working as Steppenwolf House Manager and Gary Wilmes had been to
high school and college with Maxwell and had moved to Chicago to participate in the burgeoning stand-up comedy scene.[3] The impetus to form
the theatre company emanated from their disappointment in discovering

Steppenwolf's reversion to safe, subscription-friendly material when, as students of theatre, they had come to Chicago hoping to work in a radical, risky and vital performance environment.[4] Maxwell has explained, 'I don't want to badmouth Steppenwolf, but when we were working with them what they were producing was not like it was when they were in the Church basement at Highland Park.'[5] At the time of Mendes and Maxwell's internships Steppenwolf had been working towards a production of Mary Chase's 1950 play *Harvey*, a play about, as Mendes put it, 'a giant white rabbit'. The early company members had each learned about Steppenwolf's 'organic . . . spiritually indigenous work' as part of their college syllabus and had come to associate the company with a raw, emotionally heightened acting style rather than the more family- friendly fare they experienced (Vonnegut 2000: 68). Their disappointment and drive to forge new discoveries at the cutting edge of theatrical experimentation led them to form Cook County Theater Department and embark upon their first project, a deconstruction of Rogers and Hammerstein's *Oklahoma!* (1943) entitled *Swing Your Lady* (1992).

Although Maxwell has stated that when he left Chicago in 1994 and moved to New York, it was part of a 'deliberate decision to break with Cook County' he repeatedly acknowledges the importance of his experience with the company in shaping ideas about his various approaches to acting and performance.[6] Part of Maxwell's desire to break with CCTD came from his frustration with the need for each creative decision to achieve unanimous approval. He has described this collaborative approach as 'beyond democratic' because the ethos of the company prescribed unanimous, rather than majority agreement upon each and every creative and practical issue (Marranca 2002). It would appear, on the one hand, that the 'break' with CCTD is a significant and deliberate feature of any record of Maxwell's career. However, for me; the real extent of the 'break' is thrown into question by a number of issues. Firstly, the notion of constructing Maxwell's departure in terms of a kind of rupture fits a little too neatly with a traditional Western positivist version of history, which seeks to 'begin with differentiation between the *present* and the *past*', secondly this version of events runs the risk of eclipsing the significant work of the company itself and finally, it threatens to disguise or occlude the ongoing nature of his working relationship with several members of the company (De Certeau 1988: 2). For example, before the demise of the company at the end of 1997 (but after his departure for New York), Maxwell had asked CCTD to perform in a production of his play, *Burlesque*, (1995) in New York and Chicago; and CCTD mounted their own, independent production of *Flight Courier Service* which appeared in Chicago having been directed by Wilmes in December 1997.[7] Furthermore, many ex-CCTD members have been cast in performances of Maxwell's post-CCTD plays or have continued to work as designers or musicians. Most notably, Wilmes has appeared in *Billings* (1997) *House* (1998); *Boxing 2000* (2000); Mendes in *Joe* (2002); *End of*

Reality (2006); Gleason in the original version of *Flight Courier Service* (1997) and *Burger King* (1997) Each of the four founder members, plus Vicki Walden, a long-term CCTD member, appeared in *Henry IV (Part One)* (2003). Additionally, In 2008 Lara Furniss designed the set for *People Without History*. Ultimately, I am hesitant to construct Maxwell's departure from CCTD as a definitive rupture or break as I consider it runs the risk of marginalising the importance and integrity of an approach to artistic collaboration forged in and through early experiences of working as a devising company. Although Maxwell is undoubtedly the single author and director of his work, my understanding, from having witnessed rehearsals, and having spoken to collaborators, is that his methodology borrows as much from a devised approach to theatre making as it does from an autocratic model which is customarily associated with, what Derrida has termed, the 'theological' role of the traditional director or playwright.[8] I do not intend to imply that Maxwell's approach is a devised one, but I do wish to explore the notion, which customarily gets overlooked when considering the oeuvre of a single playwright and director, that collaboration, from both new and long-term participants, is a key feature of his work. In addition, input from ex-CCTD members and the experience of having worked with CCTD is instrumental in influencing some of Maxwell's recent dramaturgical concerns. The focus of this chapter, therefore, will be to revisit the work of CCTD with a view to analysing the extent to which Maxwell's current practice manifests both a continuation of ideas developed with the company and a marked departure from this work.

I am aware that in retaining the logic of the 'break' or 'continuation' that I am engaging with, rather than resisting, what De Certeau might term a 'positivist' approach to historical research, however a self-reflexive historiographical methodology will foreground the ideological imperatives offered by this approach. I am also aware that the questions I have asked of reviewers, performers and even the videos of the performances after Maxwell had left the company have been tempered by a desire to map out a relationship between the past and present and to look for traces of rupture and continuity between the work of Cook County Theater Department and the New York City Players. Indeed, in setting out to search for signs of break and rupture I may be shaping a version of events which is purely fictional, such is the paradox of historical research. Historiographical theory by writers such as Thomas Postlewait and Bruce McConachie have made visible the ideological values imposed by historians pertaining to set an agenda of priority in identifying exclusive noteworthy events and topics. By embarking upon this historiographical project I intend to challenge the dominance of a certain version of the US theatre canon which tends to exclude small scale experimental theatre operating outside of New York and make visible the contribution of members of CCTD to Maxwell's current oeuvre.

Given the proliferation of academic writing about the difficulty, if not impossibility of documenting history in the contemporary climate of self-reflexivity, it is tempting to conclude that this chapter will inevitably be flawed, partial and incomplete. To give due consideration to each and every hidden ideological imperative governing this approach to historical research would necessitate a chapter (at the very least) dedicated entirely to a recapitulation of the aporias and pitfalls of historiographical methodology. Any historiographical project should acknowledge work by Derrida and De Certeau who warn against the illusory, yet seductive, potential of the archive. In *Archive Fever: A Freudian Impression* Derrida describes 'archive fever' as a type of 'homesickness, [a] desire to return to origin', suggesting that a symbolic truth-potential is conferred upon objects or facsimiles identified as 'archival' or 'original' and that the compulsion to consult this material is tempered by a physiological sense of nostalgia as much as a rational desire to uncover 'the truth' (Derrida 1996: 71). Similarly, De Certeau warns that historiography might 'have us believe' that a '"beginning" situated in a former time might explain the present [. . .] historians begin from present determinations. Current events are their real beginnings' (De Certeau 1988: 11).

Exercising ideological vigilance, in addition to foregrounding the problem of 'rupture' and 'continuity', necessitates an acknowledgment of 'current events' determining my starting point and a commitment to remaining sceptical about the 'truth-value' of the fragments of archive amassed to date. Joseph Donohue provides a treatise upon the problems of amassing 'evidence and documenting' in any historiographical project, warning that a 'plenitude' of material cannot speak for itself, but instead must be supported by 'lucid, conclusive argument'. In setting out a scheme of ethical 'obligations' Donohue suggests that:

> [u]ltimately, then, questions of scholarly evidence and documentation come down to what I perceive to be the author's fourfold obligation to be faithful to the subject, true to sources, fair and frank with readers and deferential to tradition. Fidelity to the subject requires, of course, a sustained scepticism much as the opposite of blind trust. Just as truthfulness to sources calls for an accuracy of treatment and a respect for the circumstances of origin much different from breezy confidence. (Donohue 1989: 194)

As with much historiographical theory, Donohue ultimately emphasises the agency of the historian/historiographer in shaping and constructing a version of events rather than reporting on past events with supposed ideological transparency. Perhaps one of the most useful ways of justifying, or conceptualising this investigation is to borrow Michal Kobialka's logic and to articulate it as an 'enunciation' or 'version' of history which is akin to a 'performative act', which will 'always be fragmentary' (Kobialka 2002: 6–8).

In amassing an 'archive' of resources I have drawn upon the generosity of ex-CCTD members who have granted me access to video documentation, photographs and copies of performance programmes and agendas; I have interviewed several company members, in person and via email, and have consulted online archives for *The Chicago Reader* and the *Chicago Tribune*. Video material has been drawn from private collections of rehearsals, run-throughs, and on one occasion, the documentation of a lengthy discussion between company members.

Interviews with ex CCTD members have been extraordinarily fruitful, I have conversed in detail with three of the founder members (Maxwell, Mendes and Wilmes). Inevitably each interviewee recalled events in a different light, and attributed different levels of priority to the various aspects of the work. Subsequently, each 'partial' recollection will go on to have some bearing upon my reading of 'continuity' or 'rupture'.

With the growing popularity of online archives I have been able to access reviews from several Chicago newspapers dating back to the early 1990s. I have amassed reviews from a range of journalists, however the majority of lengthy reviews have been written by Justin Hayford, a theatre reviewer employed by the *Chicago Reader* who demonstrated considerable enthusiasm for the work, and a fierce loyalty to the company. He states that he adopted a deliberate approach to the company's work, testifying that

> [t]he mainstream press almost never bothered to review [CCTD's] work [. . .] I took it upon myself to follow their work closely and to write about it as much as I could, not only because I found it engaging but because it was clear that precious few critics had any interest in or tolerance for their aesthetic.[9]

Much of the material available from non-company members is available as a result of Hayford's personal championing of avant-garde theatre work in 1990s Chicago. Although it is difficult, as an outsider, (and in particular as a non US resident) to determine the editorial policy of *The Chicago Tribune* and *The Chicago Reader*, Hayford appears to suggest that these were more independent newspapers and implies that their political allegiances did not perhaps fit as neatly with the Republican cultural heritage forged under Reagan and Bush (Senior) during the 1980s and early 1990s as more mainstream publications.[10]

Cook County Theater Department was inaugurated in 1991, at which time founder members plus Chris Sullivan, Erica Heilman, David Pavkovic and Tony Sacre began to work towards their first production entitled *Swing Your Lady*. The piece was based upon Rogers and Hammerstein's 1943 musical, *Oklahoma!* the company retained the dialogue of the original production, but wrote new melodies and lyrics to replace existing songs. The company spent nine months rehearsing the production and raising funds from local supporters and benefit nights before mounting it at their dedicated venue, The Loft in 1992. The company went on, with various different members in attendance, to mount ten further productions at the same venue. Their repertoire included *Fable* (1993); *Nothing and Advertising* (1993); *Clowns Plus Wrestlers* (1994); *Minutes and Seconds* (1994); *Burlesque* (1995); *Elimination* (1995); *Tosca* (1996); *Home* (1997); *Summerstock: Wizard of Oz* (1997) and *Flight Courier Service* (1997).

The Loft was situated at 2255 South Michigan (described in reviews as 'off-Loop' or Chicago's 'south Loop') a hybrid living/performance/rehearsal space that Wilmes and Maxwell had converted out of their expansive rented accommodation, which had once been home to a car showroom. According to Hayford, '[t]hese days that neighbourhood has been aggressively developed with a million 'luxury condos' all over the place. But back then it was pretty much a wasteland. Kitty corner from their space was a boarded-up Burger King and an abandoned Amoco station. It was a bit of an adventure to go to their theater.'[11] Documentary records of the living quarters reveal that The Loft consisted of a two-tiered open-plan living/performance space. Footage of the space reveals a leisure-space giving way to an expanse of linoleum- covered rehearsal space without walls or partitions to formally delineate the areas; piles of discarded props and set items were stacked in corners and domestic cereal bowls and coffee cups sat alongside tools and large items of set which were under construction. Furthermore, the identity of the Loft as a 'domestic' space is reiterated in several of the videos of run-throughs and rehearsals as Baby, Maxwell and Gleason's pet cat stalks in and out of shot. It is clear that the venue was highly unusual in its function as both a private homely space and a theatre venue attracting paying audiences. Furniss has stated that, '2255 S. Michigan was not a place of work but a home, and CCTD was not a job but our life. We lived together, some of us had relationships, and we all passionately believed in what we were doing.'[12]

Hayford identifies the work of Cook County, along with that of contemporaries, Doorika, as being part of what he saw to be 'a brief second-wave of performance-art based theater in Chicago'.[13] Many of Hayford's readings of CCTD's experimentation as a form of Fluxus performance develops out of this positioning, and indeed the semiotically indeterminate nature of many of the images and scenarios presented by the company share Fluxus' celebration of the quotidian and subversion of artist as impresario (Jenkins 1993).[14] In terms of a wider theatrical culture, Cook County were part of a vital theatre scene, producing work which ran alongside that being produced by Steppenwolf Theater Company, Remains Theater, Goat Island and Sock Monkeys.[15] Stephanie Shaw recalls that:

> CCTD helped haul Chicago out of the tail end years of kitchen sink realism. The city had made a name for itself (mainly through Steppenwolf but also through less fame fated theaters like Remains and Body Politic) by presenting very visceral, straight forward dramas of the scratch and sniff variety. You didn't see a lot of original work of the devised performance variety, although things occasionally got wild at

the Organic, but by the time CCTD came along, the Organic was on the wane. The only other (widely known) theater in town doing this sort of thing was the Neo-Futurarium with *Too Much Light Makes the Baby Go Blind.* [16]

From the early 1960s and beyond Chicago benefited from the wider distribution of theatre funding from the Ford Foundation and the federal government's National Endowment for the Arts (NEA) as these resources contributed to the creation of a vital theatre infrastructure which supported commercial and non-commercial theatre in Chicago. A survey of resident professional theater companies in Chicago testifies to the active theatre scene continuing today (Bowser 1998). According to Hardison-Londré and Watermeir, '[b]y the mid 1990s Chicago was the second largest theater center in the United States with some one hundred and fifty theaters, a rich mélange of commercial venues non-profit companies, a range of culturally specific theaters, college and university theaters, improvisational comedy and suburban dinner theaters' (Hardison-Londré 1998: 381–382). Despite the increase in federal and state funding programmes around this time, CCTD were largely self funded, soliciting contributions from patrons and receiving occasional state grants. Mendes revealed that, 'we received small grants from the Illinois Arts Council but most of the money we raised ourselves. We used to have these crazy fundraisers and fundraising drives. We had a 'prom' one year—that was very successful.' [17]

In terms of discussing theatrical influences, despite working along similar lines and at a similar time to Goat Island in Chicago, and The Wooster Group in New York, company members attest to being only indirectly aware of their work. Mendes recalled that Lin Hixson, Artistic Director of Goat Island had been to see *Elimination* in 1995, but he could not recall CCTD going to see their work prior to this time.[18] Company members also claim to have been influenced by the work of The Wooster Group, being impressed by the 1993 production of *Brace Up!* and harvesting ideas via David Savran's book, *Breaking The Rules.* The company's main aesthetic project was to question received theatrical wisdom and to resist a narrative-driven, psychologically motivated form of acting. Maxwell has stated that the foundation for some of his recent experiments stem from an aesthetic developed with Cook County whereby '[we would] ask actors to respond to being on stage in front of an audience. We would do what we thought the audience wanted us to do, not what we wanted to do' (Marranca 2002). Mendes also divulged that the company would explore exercises, 'relating to questions about what acting asks of us'.[19]

In order to give a rounded sense of Cook County's aesthetic and to set about determining the extent of Maxwell's break from/development of this work I will analyse a number of examples of work viewed on video and DVD. One of their most interesting pieces is perhaps the first piece, *Swing Your Lady.* Wilmes has revealed that the company would improvise to explore different methods of delivering the lines, experimenting with different voice pitches and modulations. Despite frequent discussion by commentators this piece is rarely discussed in any detail. The performance was not recorded and I have been unable to locate a review, furthermore no samples of the adapted score remain.[20] In addition to the elusive *Swing Your Lady* I will also refer to *Clowns Plus Wrestlers, Burlesque, Nothing and Advertising* and *Minutes and Seconds.*

Consulting *Chicago Reader* critic Justin Hayford I confessed that I had found it surprising how difficult the CCTD video documentation was to read or interpret. I confided that, over the years, the company appeared to have experimented with so many different forms and voices, that it was almost impossible to 'put a handle' on a single creative methodology. Hayford agreed, and as part of his celebration of their spirit of experimentation, suggested that:

> [i]n essence, they were messing around, trying things out, hoping to hit upon new ideas and new forms. I don't think they cared much about continuity of vision. It was really experimental work—not just avant-garde—because they were experimenting with ideas and techniques to see that might come out on stage.[21]

Taking an overview of work produced between 1993 and 1997 it is however possible to identify, if not to 'explain', a number of reoccurring themes, or features of CCTD's work. An interest in 'found' texts and 'found' movement characterised their early work, a feature which could be seen to emanate from minimalist dance and performance forms, or, as Hayford has suggested, the heritage of Fluxus performance art (Hayford 1997a). In addition, the work rarely followed a teleological line of narrative development and instead would draw upon a number of different texts. *Clowns Plus Wrestlers* included material quoted from five such texts: Shakespeare's *Hamlet*; Turk Pipkins' *Be a Clown*; Lou Banach's *The New Breed—Living Iowa Wrestling*; a homonymic version of *Hamlet* by Kenneth Koch and Robert Ainsley's *Bluff your Way in Math*. The cast, crudely divided to designate 'clowns' or 'wrestlers', either recited sections of text simultaneously, creating the effect of a random, indecipherable mass of overlapping voices, or took turns to recite sections from one of the texts whilst standing in an illuminated portion of the stage. *Minutes and Seconds* again resisted linear development and drew upon a multivalent form consisting of a number of different scenes featuring repetitive movement sequences or encounters with everyday objects. The intention appeared to be to mimic the dissociated stream of tangentially related images and conversations commonly associated with dreaming. In terms of textual material, *Minutes and Seconds* featured a conversation between an actor/character referred to as 'Dave' and an actor/character referred to as 'Roberto'.[22] Dave asked Roberto (who was installed in a tall wooden tower to his right) about an ongoing feud he had with his neighbours, and Roberto answered him in Italian. These exchanges took place at repeated interludes inserted between other scenes. At several intervals Dave ran onto the stage and appeared to consult a hand-held watch to time the duration, a possible reference to the temporal preoccupation indicated in the show's title. In terms of the visual composition of the piece, one cast member performed a dance with shoes upon her hands, later replacing the shoes with paint cans. Another entered, upside down, through a high doorway, and skied across the ceiling; another enlarged an image of his face using an overhead projector, which was somehow installed onto a pram frame and covered with a white sheet. The form of these pieces, created towards the middle of CCTD's career, is perhaps most usefully theorised in terms of the desire to engage with an intertextual use of found-texts, as featured in the work of The Wooster Group; the

Figure 3.1   Rebecca Rossen, Roberto Argentina, Chris Sullivan and Vicky Walden in *Minutes and Seconds*. (Photo: Lara Furniss.)

desire to discover a non-rational, dreamlike mode of composition and a celebration of vaudeville, or popular forms of theatre and entertainment.

Whereas *Clowns Plus Wrestlers* relied upon costuming for much of its visual effect, *Minutes and Seconds* made use of slide projection and experimental lighting effects.[23] Lara Furniss, the designer for this piece, had engineered a set which called for coloured lanterns to be shown through a paper backdrop and significantly enlarged images of each cast members' face projected onto the walls of the stage.[24] During both *Clowns* and *Minutes*, cast members would sing their lines using a high-pitched monotone, or invade the centre-stage area, sometimes en masse, occasionally alone or in pairs, to perform a sequence of repetitive actions. The movements, when accelerated, resembled contemporary dance movement, however most of the performers appeared to resist imbuing the movements with a level of finesse or virtuosity that one might customarily associate with the trained dancer's body, and in so doing could be understood to draw their inspiration from postmodern or minimalist dance (Rainer 1996: 293).[25] *Nothing and Advertising* also employed both high-pitched vocal delivery and unison movement sequences but also appeared to have a more easily identifiable 'theme'. In addition to exploring the notion of 'nothingness' the piece also repeatedly engaged with a sales rhetoric, borrowing phrases and slogans from TV advertisements and exhorting consumers to consider what was missing in order to confront the material goods they 'wanted' or 'needed' in their lives. At one point Wilmes and Maxwell engage in a lengthy exchange in which Maxwell (as 'Rich') convinces Wilmes (as 'Gary') that his life is somehow lacking a certain material object, and that he can ascertain this from the way that Wilmes walks. After a lengthy, comparatively sophisticated, speech about 'social needs', which outlines, 'an incomplete understanding of the needs people satisfy and the consumption of goods' Wilmes interrupts Maxwell to ask, 'did you say fuck?' puncturing the rhetorical effect of the more academic tone being employed. *Nothing and Advertising* employed musical accompaniment on piano, throughout, and featured performers who appeared to sing, rather than deliver, their lines. This use of music differed from the more recognisable songs and refrains performed as part of *Burlesque* or *Clowns and Wrestlers* because the performers appeared to be improvising the notes sung, whilst attempting to retain the grammatical sense of each line.

The reliance upon arresting visual effects, dance sequences and garbled, barely-discernible declamation, points to a medium that attempts to undermine the primacy of the written word in performance. The deliberate obfuscation of meaning through text would suggests that the company were calling upon an audience to create meaning by attributing each of the sign-systems deployed with equal significance. By robbing them of the security of meaning through traditional dialogue or verbal exposition, the company were challenging the expectations an audience member might bring to a piece of traditional theatre. The apparent desire to both

Figure 3.2   Roberto Argentina, Gary Wilmes and Vicky Walden in *Minutes and Seconds*. (Photo: Lara Furniss.)

engage with avant-garde experimental techniques and the evocation of popular cultural forms such as clowning, wrestling, slapstick humour and vaudeville stage routines was also designed to puncture any preconceptions an audience might bring about the elitist or highbrow nature of the theatrical medium. Wilmes' question, 'did you say fuck?' after Maxwell's considered 'social needs' speech and the incongruity of watching a leotard-clad performer recite from the introduction to *One Thousand Avant Garde Plays* both point to a desire to render intellectual rhetoric absurd and to frame a more popular, quotidian mode of address as more 'authentic' or 'truthful'. Footage of discussions held during *Swing Your Lady* along with records of company interviews reveal a strong desire to avoid creating material which might be seen to be 'pretentious' or 'too politically correct'. Mendes has provided a useful insight by revealing that company members would warn each other against potential precocity by shouting 'blow it out your ass!' [26]

Burlesque provides an example of a production, which attempts to interrogate the theatrical form whilst insisting that characters communicate through the medium of song or casual vernacular. The piece borrows the cabaret format, using a compère or MC to introduce different acts, and yet each 'act' appears to self-consciously represent a different part of the narrative exposition of Mark and Martha's story. The MC was given lines reporting on the history of the American stage, detailing how 'Off-Broadway' and 'Off-Off-Broadway' theatre came into being. This piece could be understood to be 'metatheatrical' due to its self referential form, and yet this description seems somehow incongruous because the development of a traditionally high-art, experimental drive to deconstruct does not sit comfortably alongside the celebration of low-brow popular cultural forms. [27] This difficulty in describing or naming the process points to one of the most arresting and idiosyncratic features of CCTD's work: the integration of avant-garde theatre practices of the 1990s and popular theatre.

The drive to create a productive tension between textual material and its mode of delivery provides the most obvious instance of continuity between the work of Cook County and the New York City Players. As mentioned previously, Maxwell and Wilmes' scene in *Nothing and Advertising* includes an intellectual analysis of 'social needs', a frame of rhetoric which is not characteristic of Maxwell's solo writing, and yet the dialogue preceding and following on from the more academic speech feature the banal or everyday topics of conversation (they discuss Rich's desire to grow his hair), and guttural grunts of macho assertion and exclamation (such as 'yeah man!' and 'right!') which do feature in several examples of Maxwell's work with New York City Players. The character of Mark in *Burlesque*, could also be seen to be an early incarnation of Father in *House* (1998) as he also employs a quasi-teenage vernacular.[28] Clad in a silver glam-rock jumpsuit, Wilmes delivers his lines in a manner redolent of popular cartoon characters, Beavis and Butthead[29], and performs soft rock ballads to the accompaniment of a hand-held cassette player.

Other features of CCTD's mode of performance can be seen to have had an enduring effect upon Maxwell's writing. The feature of his work which is commented on most frequently by critics and academics is his approach to acting and direction. Critics have described his 'signature style' or 'trademark' performance routine as comprising 'a wilful numbness' (Brantley 2006); 'flat tones' (Pogrebin 2000) and a 'laconic-ironic' attitude (Walsh 2004). In relation to Cook County's performance style, Hayford has interpreted such interventions in terms of actors 'behaving' rather than 'acting'. He offers an illuminating insight into his view of the relative efficacy of the company's approach to physical and verbal performance in the following quotation:

I've always been struck by how little 'acting' and how much 'behaving' goes on in a Cook County production. Performers walk on treadmills, scamper up heating pipes, sing about their cars while executing movement sequences, all without posture or pretence or any actorly concern for motivation. The company's physical language has been rich and evocative in and of itself. But whenever the performers had to speak there were problems. They have long struggled to 'just' deliver stretches of dialogue or recite found texts as matter-of-factly as they might drink a glass of water or change clothes. At best their deadpan delivery created delightful comedy. At worst it made long sections feel passionless and irrelevant. (Hayford 1994)

Maxwell's later approach evidences a honed technique resulting in NYCP performers being able to realise texts in a 'matter of fact' manner and yet avoid forsaking passion. Reviewing *The End of Reality*, Brantley registered his surprise at the efficacy of such a technique. Describing Sibyl Kempson's articulation of character Shannon Kennedy, he wrote, '[the fact] that Ms Kempson speaks as if she were reading a bus schedule perversely makes the fear more credible—a fact of life instead of a moment of self-dramatization' (Brantley 2006). Other critics have described the emotionally restrained quality of some of Maxwell's characters as evoking a fear of self-exposure. Sarah Hemming describes the effect of such revelations as akin to witnessing 'a sense of vulnerability', she suggests that, 'Maxwell's characters seem to have lost a layer of skin' (Hemming 2005).

In Maxwell's post-CCTD work much of his writing and direction coalesce to produce a style of performance which appears to be shadowed, or informed, by failure. As quoted in my previous chapter, Markus Wessendorf has described his characters as 'losers in a society that reveres self-exposure' (Wessendorf 2001: 455) and Brenner reports that he has heard the work described as 'really bad acting . . . on purpose' (Brenner 2003), demonstrating, as discussed elsewhere, that failure both informs the thematic and methodology of the work [30]. This interest in the aesthetics of failure can also be found in Cook County's oeuvre, an aspect of their work developed in pieces such as *Minutes and Seconds, Swing Your Lady* and *Tosca*. In interview Mendes, as director of *Tosca*, told Hayford that:

> [e]very time we pick a show we try to ask 'what would be the greatest challenge?' [and] the question became 'well if you can't do that, what can you do?' And that is really how we approached the whole thing. We went in knowing we couldn't do it, so what would be left after we failed? (Hayford 1996)[31]

In *Tosca* the company set out to stage a version of Puccini's opera using only two performers (Wilmes and Walden), both untrained singers, to perform all twelve characters. In review Bommer wrote that 'Mendes has compressed Puccini's passionate tragic opera into a playful seventy-five minute multi-media deconstruction. [Walden's] singing barely meets the opera's minimal demands. Clearly homage is not the point' (Bommer 1996). Mendes accentuated the difficulty of the performance task by asking just two performers to realise an entire cast. However, whereas Maxwell's interest in failure extends to an interest in procuring a rehearsal aesthetic across set and props, Mendes' interest in failure in *Tosca* appears to have been limited to performance, as the set was reportedly sophisticated and impressive. Hayford described it as an, 'improbably lyrical stairway-within-a-cocoon' (Hayford 1997b). Collaborating with Stephanie Nelson, Furniss had built a large set revolving around a giant staircase and a cocoon ceiling. Painted portraits of each character were projected onto the set 'to introduce the characters and help introduce the concept that Gary was playing *multiple* characters.'[32] Nelson created puppets to act out a 'dumb-show' version of events between scenes. According to Furniss, it was a 'full-on visual feast, and when the curtains opened on opening night, we got a standing ovation (which isn't normally done in Chicago fringe theatre!)[33] Additionally, looking back on his experience of directing the piece, Mendes recalls, 'Gary was amazing' reinforcing the fact that the success of the performance, in his eyes,

Figure 3.3   Gary Wilmes and Vicky Walden in *Tosca*.
(Photo: Lara Furniss.)

should be measured through the performers' commitment to performance, rather than to more traditional evaluations of virtuosity and mastery.

An interest in the sense of vulnerability and humanity that Sarah Hemming suggests can be achieved by presenting non-virtuoso performances, can also be glimpsed in the very first CCTD show, *Swing Your Lady*, particularly in the company's decision to substitute a pre-recorded excerpt of local black Chicago residents for themselves performing the scene in which the male consorts bid for their partner's picnic hampers in *Oklahoma!* Labelled 'non-actors footage', Wilmes provided me with a DVD of edited sections of film in which approximately fifteen African-American male adults and children took turns to read lines from the hamper bidding scene directly to camera. The edited version of the footage appears as a compilation of talking-heads style footage in which Chicago locals gradually increase the amount of money being offered, and deliver asides upon the quality of the food and the increasing stakes. For example, one character complains about having a 'three day bellyache' from Ado Annie's sweet potato pie and another asserts that the rising price is 'too rich for my blood'. Although the quality of the final recording is compromised by the noise of heavy traffic in the background, once the sections have been edited into order the footage provides a highly effective and amusing realisation of the bidding section of the scene. Many of the 'non-actors' are hesitant; they look in the wrong direction, or stumble over difficult phrases. However, others invest great enthusiasm in their roles, imbuing the lines with a sense of authenticity, as if these words naturally trip off their tongues and comprise a natural part of their day-to-day speech. I can only conjecture, but I imagine that the natural scansion of many of the lines in the mouths of local African-American Chicago residents must have contrasted starkly with the delivery of the lines by the largely Caucasian cast of CCTD. Maxwell has revealed that the company chose to tackle *Oklahoma!* as it was 'probably the most American show you can think of'. He also claimed to find the dialogue almost archaic and foreign-sounding and has stated that, 'its language felt so strange in [our] mouths' (Oswald 2006: 5) and, '[it has] no resonance today' (Marranca 2002). The insertion of this section of 'non-actors' film footage into CCTD's production worked productively to foreground the absence of non-white faces both in the film version of *Oklhahoma!* and in the stage version of *Swing Your Lady* and to underscore the irony of its being considered, as Maxwell has pointed out, an almost quintessential representation of early American culture. In addition, the non-actors footage is resonant because the sudden presence of a community of voices, for whom the language does not appear archaic or foreign, draws attention to the way that subjects can be identified, and indeed, garner a sense of identity from vernacular phraseology and local patterns of speech. By pursuing his interest in vernacular developed in this early CCTD piece Maxwell has been able to begin to explore issues of class and social mobility in his later work.

Minutes and Seconds featured performances of failure, insofar as actors attempted to perform impossible tasks, such as skiing upside down, washing broken plates and dancing with paint tins in place of shoes. Maxwell does not call upon NYCP performers to enact such specific tasks, but he does call for them to engage with the various pursuits of acting, singing and occasionally stage fighting when they have perhaps only been partially trained in one of these disciplines. Maxwell works with both professional and amateur actors, and as a result, the experience of watching his work often includes witnessing a performer who does not necessarily have sufficient training to be able to meet the high production values expected by the professional stage. In attempting to sing, the actor's voice might break under the strain of meeting a higher note, or his or her body may show signs of exhaustion or clumsiness it attempts to cope with the demands of a prolonged fight sequence. The interest in quotidian 'tasks' appears to have been transformed in Maxwell's later work to an interest in a task-based approach to performance. I would argue, however that the effect remains the same, if not signifies in a more heightened way given that the tasks relate directly to the perceived efficacy of the performance, and the more narrative-driven, minimal appearance of Maxwell's later work means that the audience have a more direct emotional investment in the actor's ability to communicate. In Maxwell's later work, acting and performing become high-risk activities.

Although the scope of this essay does not allow for a detailed analysis, the use of music would also appear to be a crucial part of the work of both companies. *Burlesque* perhaps serves as an interesting example of a transitional piece, as it serves as an example of an early play written by Maxwell, performed by CCTD, but not devised by or with the company. *Burlesque* featured characters entering and exiting a stage area set up as if for short vaudeville turns, so the stage was wide yet shallow and housed a number of microphones on stands. As part of, or in-between the scenes which dramatised the development of main characters Mark and Martha, performers would take up position before the microphone and sing original songs, also written by Maxwell. Mendes sang a song, in character as Subterfuge the Destroyer that called for the audience to look beyond his character and recognise his identity, first and foremost, as an actor. Sporting a gorilla mask and accompanied by acoustic guitar, Mendes sang, 'There's no room for both of us on this stage' before switching to a falsetto to implore, 'feast your eyes on me, I'm doing something, my name is Brian'. In contrast to songs featured in *Clowns Plus Wrestlers* and *Nothing and Advertising*, the songs in *Burlesque* appear to relate to both the diegetic world of the performance and the non-diegetic world of the auditorium. In addition to creating dissonance between the content of what is spoken and how it is delivered, the use of singing in *Burlesque* works to draw attention to the risks associated with the task-based nature of performance. Although this dual aspect of description and re-enaction does not necessarily continue seamlessly into

Maxwell's NYCP work, the presence of songs in his NYCP plays often allows characters to communicate emotions they appear otherwise unable to express and gives the audience the opportunity to witness the performer labour under the strains of a new, potentially over-demanding task.

Significant points of continuity between the work of CCTD and NYCP appear in the tensions created between the content and performance of text; the invocation of the risk of failure in the completion of quotidian and performance tasks and the use of music to create further tension between exposition and genre. Other features of Maxwell's work with NYCP, which appear at a nascent stage in the work of CCTD include an interest in an overall aesthetics of failure, a desire to draw attention to the vulnerability of the performer at work on stage and an interest in theatrical and every-day vernacular. This overview may give the impression that CCTD's work closely resembles Maxwell's work with NYCP; however this is not neces-sarily the case. Video footage of Cook County's work gives an impression of a stage densely populated with figures, props, items of set and multi-media projection. The stage is rarely empty, and the spectator is regularly called upon to distribute attention between two or more events taking place simultaneously on stage. A certain amount of chaos appears to character-ise the work of Cook County, as if the company intend to maximise the potential for moments of semiotic resonance created by chance, by means of an accidental collision of tangentially related signs rather than through a pre-determined script. By contrast, Maxwell's later work tends to have a rather austere approach to staging, with a minimal amount of second-hand furniture and props being employed to furnish the setting. Key items of machinery or set will occasionally feature as in *Joe*, in which a custom-made conveyor-belt was suspended above the performers' heads to lend the effect of a blanket of twinkling stars, or as in *Boxing 2000* in which a min-iature boxing ring was pulled on stage mid-way through the performance.[34] Maxwell's use of innovative staging techniques is most often discussed in relation to *House* in which Jane Cox based her design on a replication of the company's rehearsal studio, even down to the minute detail of the pay-phone and takeaway menus pinned to the wall (Wessendorf 2001: 446). Overall, the visual effect of Maxwell's NYCP work differs greatly from that of CCTD as it does not feature an excess of visual information, or invite the audience to negotiate their way through a proliferation of multi-media stimuli.

Another contrast can be identified again in relation to an economy of signification. Whereas Cook County eschewed psychologically motivated characterisation and a teleological structure, Maxwell's post CCTD work exemplifies a deep investment in the linear narrative form and the devel-opment of three-dimensional characters. The later work demonstrates the simultaneous struggle of both actor and character to articulate their intended message, and so although the material resists a singular, more tra-ditional interpretation, the characters featured in each play are delineated in detail. They are given character names, costumes are tailored to lend an insight into an interior psychology and they are shown to adapt according to changes of circumstance over the course of the play. Many characters are identified in relation to their blue-collar jobs, such as the home removal workers in *Billings* (1996) and the security guards in *The End of Reality*. Characters in CCTD's work, by comparison, were difficult to define, because the performers appeared, to a certain extent, to be performing themselves. Cast members always employed their given names on stage, and dialogue often worked to describe the task they were involved in onstage rather than to lend an insight into an otherwise repressed or hidden identity (Hayford 1994). In addition, CCTD performances appeared to be shaped in terms of a musical, rather than narrative composition. Each performance would be fixed so as to observe a pre-determined order, but the structure would be determined by decisions about the relative tone and pace of each scene, rather than by a desire to pursue a line of narrative development through to a point of closure.

By comparing and analysing the work of both CCTD and NYCP I consider myself to be in a stronger position to asses whether Maxwell's departure from CCTD can, or should, be conceived as a deliberate 'break'. On one hand there appear to be more examples of aesthetic continuity than rupture. Not only does Maxwell repeatedly refer to the work of Cook County when explaining his recent interest in actors 'behaving' rather than 'acting', it is clear that an overall interest in the performative potential of risk and failure can be identified in the work of both companies. Further apparent examples of continuity include an interest in resisting intellectual rhetoric; the drive to create a certain degree of dissonance between the delivery of text, and the content of the text itself, and an interest in popular theatrical and musical forms of entertainment. However, an appraisal of the overall appearance and effect of the two companies would lead me to conclude that the two performance styles are, at least superficially, very different. CCTD prioritised the use of found text; employed deconstructive strategies such as inter-textual juxtaposition; the amalgamation of high-brow and low-brow cultural forms and a chaotic and multivalent approach to semiotic composition. They eschewed linear narrative and traditional approaches to characterisation in favour of presenting their own company members as participants rather than characters in the scenarios being explored on stage. Furthermore, appraisal of CCTD's video footage reveals an investment in visual and image-based vocabularies. This prioritisation of visual images suggests an approach deeply invested in the autonomy of the audience member in negotiating an original pathway through multiple signs and sign systems. By contrast, Maxwell's work is often visually minimal. Scruffy, or second-hand set items and props often lend the setting a utilitarian feel, as if the audience member is about to witness the actors perform a walk-through or rehearsal, rather than a honed performance of the play. Actors remain in role throughout the play and deliver lines in which they attempt, rather clumsily, to express their commitment to loved ones and aspirations for the future. With the exception of *Burlesque*, it would be difficult to confuse a Cook County performance for a later Maxwell performance; the two approaches are compositionally and aesthetically distinct. In conclusion, I would argue that a clear aesthetic break exists between the two bodies of work. However, in terms of a methodological break, I do not consider the distinction to be quite so pronounced. Although Maxwell regularly writes his plays prior to embarking upon the rehearsal process, a number of examples exist of him beginning with a rough draft which is transformed through numerous incarnations before being fixed as a definitive blueprint for performance.[35] In addition, he occasionally matches actors to characters before having completed the play-script and then writes material with a particular actor in mind (Gorman 2007). Another key aspect of methodological continuity lies in his continuing collaboration with former Cook County members. Although he employs colleagues such as Wilmes, Gleason and Mendes as performers, long-term collaborators play a key role in explaining the ethos of task-based performance to untrained actors and new recruits.[36] Mendes has acknowledged that out of the creative arguments characterising early Cook County rehearsals has developed a deep mutual respect and trust which allows Mendes, Wilmes and Maxwell to be open and frank about their perception of the production underway.[37] Therefore, despite the fact that Maxwell, by identifying as director and playwright, would appear to be working as sole author, and to be presiding, in what Derrida would term a 'theological' manner, over all aspects of the production, an appraisal of his continued association with ex-Cook County members serves to undermine this designation.

It is possible, of course, that other ex-company members would not agree with this interpretation, and argue that this reading presents an overly positive representation of collaboration between NYCP and CCTD, however, one of my reasons for wanting to pursue this line of argument revolves around my sense that the dialogues initiated by CCTD about theatre, the commitment to theatre as a vital cultural form; and the experience of struggling to decide how to shape and form an original piece of theatre, urgently inform a crucial part of Maxwell's methodology, and that the nature of his commitment to theatre as an accessible cultural form was shaped by his work with CCTD in the 1990s.

4 'I Got Balls, See?'
A Study of Working-Class Masculinity in the Plays of Richard Maxwell and the New York City Players

Downtown New York playwright, Young Jean Lee has said that she, 'chafe[s] at the thought of writing an "identity" play'. According to Karen Simakawa, Lee deliberately avoids nominating 'identity' as an issue within her plays, and so could be seen to be producing work which demonstrates an intertextual awareness of Stjepan G. Meštrović's 'post-race, post-identitarian, post-postemotional utopia(n)' culture (quoted in Shimakawa 2007: 92). It is conceivable that the proliferation of artists creating identity-performances during the 80s and 90s has sated the palates of the New York theatre crowd and so rendered it an 'ex-nominated issue' (Fiske 1987: 135). Richard Maxwell's response to the issue of playwriting and identity politics is similar to that of Lee, and appears to reinforce this point of view. As quoted above, Maxwell has expressed the idea that 'consciously dealing with racial issues in a play is one thing, but for [the play] to constitute a racial statement is boring' (Gorman 2007: 240). His inclination to describe identity statements in this way is perhaps indicative of the effects that the rhetoric of 'post-identity' politics has had upon liberal Western culture. However, notwithstanding his hesitation, I would argue that issues of identity, whether class-based, racial or gendered, lie very much at the heart of Maxwell's oeuvre. Within this chapter I attend to key examples of his work in order to identify a pattern of themes and stylistic devices and argue for the relevance of reading for signs of an identity discourse. In particular, I will argue that the plays evidence a range of attitudes towards subjectivity, failure, class and gender formation and manifest a drive to engage with the discourse of a contemporary masculinity 'in crisis'.

Throughout the chapter I intend to perform readings with a view to analyzing the construction of masculinity and class. In particular I will pay attention to representations of vulnerability, empathy and verbal dexterity. My analysis will include a reading of play-scripts and the discrete contexts of production. I propose that a productive tension exists in Maxwell's work between the scripted dialogue and his approach to staging, which provides an opportunity to read his construction of masculinity and class as performative, innate *and* socially constructed. I will also demonstrate that, in addition to themes developed within his plays, Maxwell's approach to directing and casting is informed by a drive to encourage the audience to read for signs of gender fallibility (a failure to 'repeat' appropriate gendered behaviour). I propose that communication is shown to be fraught and difficult for all of Maxwell's characters, but that male characters, in particular, are shown to experience some kind of crisis as a result of their inability to communicate appropriately in certain contexts. My exploration of male subjectivity will take on board theories drawn from a range of disciplines, including feminism, masculinity studies, socio-linguistics, theatre-studies and behavioural psychology. I will draw upon work by Michael Mangan, Simon Baron-Cohen and E. Anthony Rotundo in order to argue that Maxwell's plays represent 'the "harm" of gender system(s)'; possible manifestations of autism as an example of gendered empathy disorder and the representation of dramatic declamation as a 'feminine' and consequently problematic form for working class men to perform (Rotundo 1993: 291, Baron-Cohen 2003: 137, Mangan 2003: 18). I will also draw upon Judith Butler's work on gender performativity; Jen Coates' work on male conversation and Bob Vorlicky's notion of the theatre as a gendered space.

Roger Horrocks' articulation of a sense of 'masculinity in crisis' in the mid 90s included the idea that '[t]he masculine gender has all kinds of benefits, but it also acts as a mask, a disguise, and what in psychotherapy is called a "false self"'. In contrast to representational discourses relating to issues of race and gender visibility, the main thrust of his argument relates to the pressure men undergo to conform to the normative male role model and the resultant deadening, constricting effects this has upon their sense of ambition and opportunity. He writes:

> Many men are haunted by feelings of emptiness, impotence and rage. They feel abused, unrecognized by modern society. While manhood offers compensations and prizes, it can also bring with it emotional autism, emptiness and despair. (Horrocks 1994: 1)

I consider that Horrocks' determination needs to be extended to include issues of race and class, as the educational opportunities made available to most white middle-class men can be seen to provide them with access to therapeutic discourses of the self, which in turn help temper feelings of impotence. A study of British working class men conducted by Louise Archer, Simon Pratt and David Phillips demonstrates that focus group participants placed a greater value in identifying with manual, rather than verbal skills, and considered participation in Higher Education and non-manual trades as 'feminine' and threatening to a strong, working-class identity (Archer, Pratt and Phillips 2001: 443). Similarly, Donald Warren's analysis of the lower middle class Middle American male demonstrates that, '[h]is 'ideal self' is a physically strong, hardworking, dependable person. Social aggressiveness-ness and verbal ability are seen exclusively as feminine attributes' (Warren 1998: 341). The issues of empathy and verbal dexterity will be key to my analysis of both character and performance style in Maxwell's plays.

Socio-linguist, Jen Coates has observed that stories relayed in casual male conversation regularly, 'reproduce the dominant values of masculinity—emotional restraint, ambition, achievement and competitiveness'. In her analysis of a broad range of conversational narratives she also observed that, 'some of the stories reveal men struggling to reconcile competing discourses of masculinity' (Coates 2003: 65). Most interestingly, she introduces the phrase 'to mask up', a term coined 'by male prisoners to describe the conscious adoption each day of a defensive emotional wall that provides a barrier between the man's real feelings and the outward façade he presents to the inmate group' (Coates 2003:77). Coates' work brings to light the importance of context in shaping patterns of male language and behaviour. In interview Maxwell has indicated his interest in behavioural neutrality and masks, consequently the notion of adopting an 'outward façade' can be seen to be pertinent to an analysis of male characterisation within his work (Gorman 2007: 236). Maxwell appears to be exploring the opportunities afforded by an adoption of 'neutrality' as a survival tactic for the heteronormative male. The risky act of emotional disclosure is dramatised both within the narratives of his plays and by means of experimental staging techniques, in the contingency of the theatrical present.

It is the staging of Maxwell's self-directed plays which perhaps works most effectively to undermine any illusory potential the plays may suggest. The physical and vocal work of the actors, the pacing and staging all appear to be motivated, first and foremost, by a utilitarian drive to 'put on a show', or to 'tell a story', rather than to encourage audience members to suspend their disbelief or invest in any psychological identification with the characters. At times the performances are suggestive of the work an actor might undertake during rehearsal, they perform as if executing a 'walk through' or physical 'scoring' of the play. In addition the actors often *indicate* an emotion or attitude rather than invest their lines with the sense of spontaneous emotional sincerity that has become a convention of contemporary realist theatre. During each performance actors regularly direct sections of dialogue towards the audience, rather than to the relevant colleague on stage. They also identify and watch individual audience members, for example, if they draw attention to themselves by entering the auditorium late, or if they cough or laugh ostentatiously. The sense of 'rehearsal' rather than 'performance' is further reinforced by the constant illumination of the house-lights, which remain up for the duration of most of Maxwell's performances. They also serve as a meta-theatrical indication of self-reflexivity, as if the director and cast wish to actively signal their awareness that they are mounting a performance. It is this drive to keep drawing attention back to the representational nature of theatre-making that will inform my reading of certain aspects of Maxwell's work as 'performative'. Judith Butler's work on the performativity of gender has resulted in the term being suggestive of 'a dramatic and contingent construction of meaning', a definition which I consider to be highly relevant to Maxwell's approach to staging (Butler 1990: 139). Her reference to a 'contingent construction of meaning' provides a means of analysing the specific social and material situation influencing, or determining a certain behavioural utterance. Butler writes that, '[t]he possibilities of gender transformation are to be found . . . in the arbitrary relation between [the stylized repetition of acts], in the possibility of a failure to repeat, a de-formity, or a parodic repetition that exposes the phantasmic effect of abiding identity as a politically tenuous construction' (Butler 1990: 141). By striving to keep aspects of each actor's 'real' personality visible and by asking the actors to '*do* rather than *show*' Maxwell demonstrates that the construction of both meaning and identity is socially and temporally contingent. He also draws attention to the limitations of traditional masculine working class behaviour by contrasting these traits with those of actors trained in the expressive medium of theatrical declamation. Because many of the performance tasks push the actors to the limits of their capability, they frequently run the risk of failing to 'repeat', or communicate to the expected standard, and so expose their shortcomings before the collected audience. In Butler's terms, the actors, in showing, or performing, signs of awkwardness, fail to repeat acts that would signal both the normalcy of their presence on stage, and the normalcy of the mannerisms attributed to their class and gender. I want to borrow Butler's approach in order to argue that the amateur actors' signs of strain provides an audience with the opportunity to witness a subject in process or formation. The actor's compulsion to succeed and the marks of strain emanating from the untrained body could be recognised as signs of a subject 'coming into being' (Butler 1990: 8). Although Butler refutes the notion of a foundationalist subject, an objection that makes nonsense of any attempt to read for signs of a coherent or 'innate' masculinity, she does provide a useful thesis on how 'contemporary juridical structures engender, naturalize and immobilize' the (would-be) subject's sense of agency (Butler 1990:8). Butler will be useful to my reading of Maxwell's work to a certain extent, however, for the purposes of my argument, I will reserve the right to retain the term 'subject' and recognise certain aspects of masculinity as fixed. In my view, rather than representing subjects in process, the male characters and male actors in Maxwell's plays are encultured in a manner more in keeping with de Beauvoir's theory that one 'becomes' ones gender, 'under a cultural compulsion' (de Beauvoir 1973: 301). I want to argue that it is in the realisation of the script that a performative repetition of gender and class is made visible, but also that despite the apparent engagement with a hegemonic masculinity, there are signs of a critical relationship to gender acquisition within the play texts themselves.

The complex and subtle interrelationship between extra- and intra diegetic systems of signification calls for a distinction to be made between the different types of actor employed to perform in Maxwell's work. In simplistic terms, the performers may be categorised in terms of 'amateur' and 'professional', some performers having undertaken professional actor training programmes, or having worked in American theatre companies for a number of years, others coming to acting for the first time.[1] Many of the actors cast in Maxwell's production of *Henry IV Part 1*, for example, were first-time performers and recruited by means of 'Help Wanted' posters in libraries and colleges (Alvarez 2006: 247). The complexity of the issue of actor training emerged during an after-show discussion for *The End of Reality*: Sibyl Kempson and Tom Bradshaw both expressed different ideas about to describe their status as 'professional actors' in relation to the level of training they had experienced, Kempson claimed not to consider herself to be a 'trained actor', even though she has appeared in numerous down-town New York productions and Bradshaw spoke readily of his 'training' despite being an established New York playwright, rather than actor.[2]

Although critics such as Robin Pogrebin have observed that Maxwell's performances are 'deliberately artless' and 'amateurish' and that 'the actors who play these roles don't seem to be acting', a distinction also needs to be made between long-term collaborators who have honed performances which appear to be deliberately 'amateurish' in relation to received models of mainstream performance and more recent cast members whose performances may be marked 'accidentally' by signs of the amateur (Pogrebin 2000). In the case of the less experienced performers, I would argue that their performances accidentally signify in this way because their lack of training prevents them from disguising the physiological signs of nervous strain upon the body and the idiosyncrasies of their style of enunciation does not necessarily match the confident fluency of an actor accustomed to performing on stage before a live theatre audience. However, although these slippages may be accidental on the part of the actors, I consider these signs of strain to be productively garnered by Maxwell in performance. Alexis Soloski's review of *Joe* offers a useful insight into the different effects the two approaches to amateurism might have. This piece employed five different actors to play the eponymous character at different stages of his life. Of the cast, only Mendes possesses an established repertoire of acting roles. Soloski observed that:

> Of the five human actors portraying *Joe* [. . .] Brian Mendes manages the material best. The rest acquit themselves well enough but occasionally appear to strain against the style, aching to act the speeches rather than letting them unfurl. But Mendes finds depths in the flatness. Without deviating much from a monotone, he conveys the emotions that

might be present were the character a real person speaking these lines and not an actor portraying them. (Soloski 2002)

Soloski does not repeat my distinction between amateur and professional, but she does mark the difference between what I have identified as the two approaches at work here by registering the effect of one as 'strained' and one as 'deep'. Although Mendes employs a 'monotone' register, a potential mark of the amateur, his performance is credited for achieving a sense of authenticity. By contrast, the 'amateur' performers enable the audience to glimpse a sense of strain as they struggle to adhere to the discipline of still-ness and monotone required by the director. Maxwell's approach to cast-ing and direction is highly nuanced as he creates an awkward situation for both types of performer. He calls for experienced performers to draw back from the fluent, confident approach internalised by method-trained actors and for the inexperienced to observe strict rules of proxemics and kinesics, which guard against any spontaneous or instinctual desire to move towards, or touch, a fellow actor. For me, these scenarios signify productively both within the world of the play and in the 'here and now' of the auditorium to draw attention to the strain a male or female subject may experience when engaging in social performance. It exists as a gendered performative utterance because it recreates and foregrounds the context of societal pres-sure in the present moment. For Maxwell's male characters, the staging of awkwardness extends beyond the diegetic world of each play, and into the present world of the auditorium. I consider that this 'live' enactment of the actor's risk and the potential of failure constitutes a felicitous coincidence with the 'expression' of gender attributes as found within the fiction of the plays. For Butler, 'gender attributes [are] the various ways in which a body shows or produces its cultural signification' and if gender attributes can be *shown to be* performative then 'there would be no true or false, real or distorted acts of gender, and the postulation of a true gender identity would be revealed as a regulatory fiction.' A performative act is one which 'effec-tively constitute[s] the identity' and gender is shaped through the repetition of performative acts 'through sustained social performances' (Butler 1990: 141). The lack of verbal inflection used by many of Maxwell's performers, and the static, almost tense, demeanor they maintain for much of each performance works both to express the idea of an anxious, working class male body uncomfortable with the declamatory context of 'performance', and to demonstrate a tension between a successful and flawed 'social per-formance'. I consider that that the potential to glimpse the performative moment of gender formation is made possible through the contingency of the 'live' event, and particularly through the presence of an audience to wit-ness the risks involved in public exposure and performance. Furthermore, the response to the tasks being demanded of the actors is marked by gender because, as Vorlicky has suggested, the context of theatrical presentation has been marked as 'feminine'. As a result, an effortless presentation of self-realisation on stage would result in the performer being successful within a feminine domain. Vorlicky argues that when male performers theatricalise an autobiographical self, 'their voices and bodies occupy or share the space that hitherto had been marked [. . .] "for women only"' (Vorlicky 1999: 204). Similarly, Mangan observes the gendering of self-expression and articulation associated with the declamatory nature of the dramatic arts. He suggests that theatre and acting have traditionally been associated with the feminine, 'side of the ideological divide [being characterised by] illusion, display, emotion [and] the body' (Mangan 2003: 18). As a result, the staging of awkwardness, on the part of the male performers, whether honed through rehearsal or leant an air of authenticity by attempting to execute a difficult task, enables an audience to glimpse what might be at stake in any social performance where the subject finds his or herself compelled to 'perform' out of their familiar social context. In Maxwell's performances, the failure to perform appropriately is shown to be contingent and specific to the middle class context of theatre. The pull of competing discourses produces an irony—where the actors 'fail' to achieve a honed, seamless sublimation of self behind character, they actually 'succeed' in reaffirming the kind of traditional masculine identity chartered by gender theorists. It would appear that there are a number of different levels of failure in play in Maxwell's work. In terms of the context of the theatre, the marks of amateurism constitute 'failed' examples of social performance, however in terms of the context of a traditional, working class male environment; the failure to articulate or declaim accurately represents a successful inhabitation of the masculine gender role.

Michael S. Kimmel's 1987 publication *Changing Men* introduced the then emerging field of 'men's studies' and emphasised its grounding in feminism and women's studies. Citing the emergence of an interdisciplinary approach, Kimmel argued for a move 'beyond' the hegemonic 'sex-role' model which 'specified the ways in which biological males and biological females became socialized as men and women in a particular culture'. He stated that:

> [. . .] this sex-role paradigm posits a historically invariant model, a kind of static sex-role container into which all biological males and females are forced to fit. This process of fitting into preexisting roles is called 'socialization'. As such, the paradigm ignores the extent to which our conceptions of masculinity and femininity—the content of the male or female sex role—is relational; that is, the product of gender relations that are historically and socially conditioned. (Kimmel 1987: 12)

In 1983 Joseph H. Pleck also queried the 'MSRI' (male sex role identity) paradigm, which he stated had dominated academic social sciences since the 1930s. His definition claimed that:

An easy and usually accurate way of telling whether a particular argument derives from the MSRI paradigm is simply to note whether it has one or more of the following characteristics: 1) it uses terms like *insecure* or *inadequate*; 2) it emphasizes the potentially psychologically harmful consequences of a man's relationship with his mother; and 3) it views homosexuality as the worst misfortune that can befall a man. (Pleck 1983: 7)

Pleck detailed the assumptions behind the MSRI paradigm, outlining how the psychologically-driven model invested in the belief in an 'innate psychological need to develop sex role identity'. It identified the problem of 'hypermasculinity (exaggerated masculinity, often with negative social consequences)' as an indication of 'insecurity with sex role' and attributed men's negative attitude towards women as a symptom of incomplete sex role acquisition. It also attributed 'historical changes in the character of work and the organization of the family' to the heightened difficulty for men in maintaining sex role identities' (Pleck 1983: 5). I consider that hypermasculinity, the objectification of women and problematic parental relationships, all features associated with this paradigm, reoccur as themes across a number of Maxwell's plays, and although these theories may appear crude and reductive in light of more recent work on gender performativity, Pleck and Kimmel's work represents a useful model for measuring his representations of masculinity against a recognizable social model.

Kimmel and Pleck provide a useful resource to help substantiate what is conventionally recognized as typical masculine behaviour. However, they also provide a motivation to look for social enculturation beyond that of gender and suggest that different masculinities come into play in different contexts. Butler also points to the 'racial, class and heterosexist' forms of subordination that come into play as a subject comes into being (Butler 1990: 15). In Maxwell's performances, the uneasy co-presence of the success of the inarticulate working class male and the failure of the amateur actor demonstrates how an otherwise heteronormative male body can be shown to be deviant when taken out of its conventional context. Although it is difficult to measure Maxwell's critical engagement with conventional masculine gender roles it is clear that he has something to say about emotional revelation, class and verbal eloquence. As I have mentioned above, many of his characters appear inarticulate and socially awkward, prompting one critic to describe them as 'border[ing] on the autistic' (McNulty 2003). Although theories of social determinism have dominated gender studies since the 1980s there are signs of a desire to return to, or acknowledge, the relevance of biology. Working in the field of gender psychology, Baron-Cohen argues for a reconsideration of biological essentialist theories of innate gender difference. Charting the changes in attitude towards social materialist and essentialist theories, he writes:

In earlier decades the very idea of psychological sex differences would have triggered a public outcry. The 1960s and 1970s saw an ideology that dismissed psychological sex differences as either mythical, or if real, non-essential—that is, not a reflection of any deep differences between the sexes *per se*, but a reflection of different cultural forces acting on the sexes. But the accumulation of evidence from independent laboratories over many decades persuades me that there are essential differences that need to be addressed. The old idea that these might be wholly cultural in origin is nowadays too simplistic. (Baron-Cohen 2003: 10)

Maxwell does not appear to be aligning himself readily with any one recognizable theory of gender, hence the need to draw upon a number of different theories here. Baron-Cohen's theory of autism provides a useful way of considering the behavioural traits of some of his characters. Furthermore, although Maxwell's characters do reinforce traditional masculine stereotypes they are regularly presented as failures, or in conflict, suggesting a desire on the part of the playwright to problematise rather than reinforce hegemonic gender identities. In one of his more recent pieces, *Ode to the Man Who Kneels* (2007) Maxwell recreates the hypermasculine archetype of the cowboy, but shows him to be the victim of 'heartbreak' and provides his contemporaries with a number of confessional speeches. Similarly in *The End of Reality*, (2006) the traditonally hyper-masculine environment of security services is compromised by the emotional disclosures of two key characters. Maxwell's approach to gender appears to shift in these pieces, giving characters the opportunity to articulate their discomfiture. The difference is most visible in relation to emotional disclosure and vulnerability. The earlier plays present dysfunctional male characters who do not necessarily appear aware of being constrained by their behaviour whereas the later plays present characters more ready to verbalise insecurities and attempt to describe an emotional landscape.

Maxwell's exploration of social performance and identity includes a pattern of repeated themes relating not only to gender but also to the world of work, the domestic sphere, fighting, sports, family relationships, love and death. Although many female characters populate his texts and pieces such as *Showy Lady Slipper* (1999) features a predominantly female ensemble, the majority of plays call for a largely male cast. The sensibilities of the male characters are customarily revealed through dialogue, although the fight-sequences in *Boxing 2000* and *The End of Reality* also betray attempts to capture the awkwardness of real/performed stage combat. Many of the characters can be seen to have been given lines that point to an attempt to assert their difference from women in order to attain 'hypermasculinity'. Pleck suggests that a negative attitude towards women provides one such marker, and in *Caveman* (1999) and *Billings* (1996) Maxwell has included characters that objectify and speak in derisive terms about women. #3 Mover, for example, confesses that he likes pornography; pointing to a pornographic magazine he is given the lines: '[m]y ex old lady hates it. But I don't care. She looks like she came out of one of those. I like a woman with a nice, high, tight ass' (Maxwell 2004b: 16). Similarly, in *Caveman*, a married character who may be talking within earshot of his wife, asks a colleague, 'Did you see that girl? [. . .] That one with the ass. [. . .] I want to fuck that girl'(Maxwell 2004b: 181). The character of Frank in *Drummer Wanted* shows a similar reluctance to temper his macho pursuit of casual sex by bringing a series of girlfriends back to his mother's house, and the character of Brian in *The End of Reality* appraises a woman by saying 'Baby! I like that! How much?'[3] Interestingly, whilst marking their 'success' in occupying the traditional masculine sex role, these characters go on to be designated as repulsive and primitive by their male and female colleagues. In *Billings*, #1 Mover likens #3 Mover to an 'ape' or a 'caveman' and in *Caveman*, character 'C' is shown in an unsympathetic light as he is unconcerned about his wife's desire to trace their missing son (Maxwell 2004b: 13). A more developed heterosexual relationship is mapped out between characters Fred and Marissa in *Boxing 2000*, although Fred uses similarly objectifying language to describe an ex-girlfriend: '[s]he has a nice body. Big tits, big ass. You know? More than a handful?' Although he repeats his desire to see Marissa, and intends to ask her to marry him, a visit to her house includes the repeated stage direction 'he grabs her', which in performance was realised as a clumsy lunge towards her breasts, indicating that his visit was primarily motivated by the desire to have sex (Maxwell 2004b: 251–256). Although this type of behaviour is not necessarily criticised by all the characters, the sexualized description of female characters occurs across a number of Maxwell's plays and appears to contribute to a sense of the male characters' dislocation from the opposite sex. Other expressions of hypermasculinity include the careful demarcation of the conversational topics the male characters discuss. In addition to the subject of attractive women, topics include hobbies such as motorbike riding, music, body building and drinking. Male characters often appraise each other's bodies, but any homoerotic suggestion is sublimated beneath factual discussions about the use of steroids or workout regimes. For example, in *Caveman* characters A and C discuss anabolic steroids at length, and in *The End of Reality*, Brian confesses that 'I could never be ripped like this guy' indicating his admiration for Jake's physique.

The difficulty of retaining a coherent male sex role identity is often elliptically referred to by characters who might be designated 'effeminate' or emerge through confused confessions by characters speaking in monologue. In *Boxing 2000*, two brothers, Fred and Joe are shown to share a certain level of intimacy as they discuss the problem of a present for their father, but Jo-Jo eventually accuses Fred of being 'so sensitive' and teases him for wanting to go to visit Marissa's house. He shouts, 'Marissa!! I love you !' to which

Figure 4.1   Brian Mendes in *The End of Reality*. (Photo: Michael Schmelling.)

Fred responds, 'Awww. Shut up.' His brother also tells him to 'Quit acting like a woman' (Maxwell 2004b: 212). The salesman character in *Showcase* also demonstrates signs of insecurity and sensitivity, although his monologue employs a cyclical, almost contradictory structure that suggests a clumsy attempt to justify and come to terms with an intimated homosexual experience. In addition to the self-love suggested by the salesman's affection for 'his shadow' (a figure which is literally brought to life in performance via a stocking-masked and clad figure) he dwells upon a recent meeting with an old friend Victor, a friend who had 'books about bisexuality on his shelf' and of whom he asks, 'were we friends or lovers?' He muses over the strange dynamic of an evening meeting with Victor and his boyfriend and describes Victor's attempts to 'grab' him in the men's lavatories. In a similar manner to Jo-Jo's attempts to reign-in Fred's sensitivity, the salesman chastises himself for his insight into a complex emotional landscape. He observes, 'I felt it. Feelings. I SEE it. People come apart [. . .] How come I now feel everyone's pain. I never used to. Damage. Psychic damage.'[4]

The theme of hidden or difficult 'feelings' runs throughout Maxwell's work, a great many male characters either directly attest to 'not understanding' when asked about their feelings or are shown to be incapable of asking crucial, emotive questions of their loved ones. Marissa asks Fred about his imminent fight in *Boxing 2000* by saying, '[h]ow does that feel?' to which he replies, 'How does that feel? How does what feel? [. . .] I don't know! I don't know what you're talking about half the time'. When

Marissa tries to push him by saying 'You can't tell me what you feel like?' Fred responds with sexual innuendo, 'I feel like coming inside' (Maxwell 2004b: 216–217). In *House* (1998) the character of 'Wife' asks her son, 'How come you never tell me your emotions? You're very careful showing your emotions to people. Remember that time at Frico's?' The son's response is marked by a blank entry next to his name in the script. When he finally responds to his mother he responds instead to the mention of a fast food venue in her anecdote and tells her, 'I like tacos' (Maxwell 2004b: 121). Emotional disclosure for male characters, in a number of Maxwell's plays, is restricted to simplistic statements about what they do or do not 'like'. As mentioned above, #3 Mover in *Billings* announces, 'I like pornography'; and the son's example of 'lik[ing] tacos' replicates the many similar statements made by his father, such as 'I like the sound of the cars going by my window' and 'I like Black Sabbath' (Maxwell 2004b: 121–122). In *The End of Reality* Brian responds to Marcia's attempts to analyse his horoscope by saying 'No, I don't like that . . . ' when asked 'why?' his response, like that of the Son in *House* is indicated in the play script by a blank line.⁵ In contrast to female characters such as Lori in *Showy Lady Slipper* and Wife in *Caveman*, who demonstrate a tendency towards self-analysis, the male characters are shown to be extremely reluctant to reflect upon the impact their behaviour might have, or to disclose anything about their emotional wellbeing.

In *Ode to the Man Who Kneels*, Maxwell introduces characters who acknowledge their emotions, but who do not necessarily benefit from becoming self-aware. The play opens with a lengthy monologue from the eponymous character who reveals:

> I'm an actor. Everything I experience in my life, everything I feel, is saying this. You know ? It adds a layer to my life that I wish weren't never there. A voice in my head that says you don't count for shit, because you, what you're experiencing, you're thinking, you're counting . . . It's not a real way to live. And you get used to it. But I feel. That's plain, In any case. I FEEL.⁶

There does not appear to be any therapeutic closure to be had from their confession and these characters continue to suffer *despite* emotional revelation. Furthermore, the act of disclosure is marked as one of difficulty rather than liberation. The General Store proprietor, also referred to as 'The Dashing Man' and 'Pablo', expresses gratitude that his lover can 'read minds':

> . . . I sing for her and her alone. The woman here reads your mind. That woman is the woman you saw in the window. Every man who lives or even passes through is ready to give everything, his life in order to have her! You see? Imagine- she can read your mind. What a relief that is.⁷

In addition to demonstrating a reluctance to share their feelings, many male characters also manifest difficulty with empathetic communication. The exchanges between exclusively male characters are often clipped and monosyllabic, or their conversational gambits tend towards an obsessive attention to detail and a lack of regard for any two-way dynamic. For example, an exchange between A and C in *Caveman* takes the following form:

> C: Were you on the floor today?
> A: Yeah.
> C: Okay. Lot of people didn't show up, no?
> A: Huh?
> C: Don't you think?
> A: Why?
> C: 'Cause it's Friday?
> A: I don't know. Yeah (Maxwell 2004b: 181).

Despite being well disposed to one another, the structure of the conversation is constructed so as to appear strained. A does not respond to C's questions in the customarily affirmative manner to be expected of trusted colleagues. The characters of both Man and Woman in *Billings* also serve as a good example of characters who are ostensibly enjoying a conversation, but who are actually not interested in providing space or time for their companion to respond. During the opening section of *Billings*, despite being on stage with four other characters, Man delivers a monologue for an extended period:

> I like Billings all right. But I think I got a better thing in Minneapolis. . . . It's pretty good. Yeah. It's a good job.I do all right. We should do all right. It's hard work though. I don't know if you've ever done this kind of thing before but it's pretty hard to do. I work a lot . . . (Maxwell 2004b: 9)

He goes into great detail about his past, giving dates of when he moved to Billings and details of the names of old friends and old places of work. Although he addresses the movers, the pauses inserted into his speech do not appear to encourage dialogue. His speech appears one of self-justification, as if this character needs to reassure himself that he has made the right decision to move from Billings to Minneapolis. The character of Frank in *Drummer Wanted* also stands as an interesting example of one who refuses to adapt the tone or content of his speech according to companion. He retains the vernacular of a vulgar teenager whilst in the company of his mother, repeatedly swearing, telling her to 'shut up' and referring to 'muff diving' amongst other macho pursuits. Whilst his mother attempts to talk to him about a financial settlement for his accident he embarks upon tangential monologues. For example, when asked if he would like to talk to her lawyer friend, Frank replies:

> Psssh. I hate the lawyers. Lawyers don't feel pain. . . . I remember this Perto Rican guy. He knew how to deal with pain. I never knew some-one to deal with pain—Whenever I get pain I think about—He—HQ told us we're working with these guys but these guys sucked. [. . .] One thought he had it, had it down cold. Really fucken cool. He knew pain. But he was quiet. I had lotta respect for that. That's how you deal with pain . . . I was gonna tell you something. [8]

Mom's response to Frank's mode of speech is one of resignation, although towards the end of the play her resignation gives way to frustration. She reveals that 'I've gotten really good at not feeling anything' and after Frank calls her a 'bitch', she loses her temper, slaps him and asks '[w]hat is wrong with you? Every time I try to talk to you you pull away. [. . .] You haven't finished growing up yet.' Sickened by her son's greedy pleasure at the out-come of his accident settlement she asks him to leave, mirroring his coarse, inappropriate language by saying, 'Get out fucker'. [9] The adoption of crude vernacular by Frank's mother highlights its incongruity in a mother-son relationship and serves to emphasise the harmful impact such aggressive language might have. The refusal, or inability, of these male characters to adapt their language to social context stands as a further expression of failed social performance in Maxwell's work. Rather than form emotional ties through verbal exchange, these characters alienate those closest to them and reinforce their own emotional and existential isolation.

Further male-identified problems with communication occur when male characters are shown to be incapable of asking significant questions of their loved ones; questions that may have life-changing consequences. In *Boxing 2000*, Fred is unable to verbally ask Marissa to marry him. The exchange is structured as follows:

> Fred: [. . .] I've got something for you. . . .
> Marissa: What is it?
> Fred: Open it . . . It's a ring.
> Marissa: Where'd you get this, Sols?
> Fred: Next to Sol's.
> Marissa: Oh.
> Fred: Do you like it?
> Marissa: I like it. It's sweet.
> Fred: Well . . . Are you gonna answer me?
> Marissa: What's the question?
> Fred: Well, you know what I mean.
> Marissa: You can't ask?
> Fred: Yeah, I can . . .

Marissa: Do you have a plan?
Fred: Plan? What you talkin' about?
Marissa: What is it. Tell me what the plan is.
Fred: . . . Get married.
Marissa: That's not a plan, Federico.
Fred: Why not? (Maxwell 2004b: 223)

There appears to be a significant correlation between Fred's lack of a future 'plan' and his ability to formulate the words to actually ask Marissa to marry him. He fails to secure the desired outcome because he fails to directly pose the symbolic question. Similarly, in *Drummer Wanted*, Frank fails to prove that he has 'got balls' by repeatedly refusing to talk to his mother's lawyer 'friend' who is attempting to secure a financial settlement for his motorcycle accident. At the outset of the play Frank had denied being interested in a settlement as he had been hit by his friend Rey. He stated that, 'No, I'm not like that. I don't care about that. I hate people like that. It's Rey. He's my friend. What am I supposed to do? I just want this whole thing over with.' However, by the end of the play, after having left all negotiations to his mother, he relishes the prospect of receiving a $150,000 settlement, saying that, 'I got balls, see? You saw 'em. I don't apologize for the money. I get the money. I get the money. The money is MINE.' [10] Although Frank might be seen to attain some degree of social success by leaving home at the end of the play, the disintegration of his relationship with his mother, and his failure to credit responsibility for the settlement to his mother, points to an ongoing sense of failure: his behaviour remains deluded and adolescent.

If the earlier examples of sexual objectification and pursuit of male hobbies can be understood in terms of the MSRI paradigm provided by Pleck, then the communicative traits of many of Maxwell's male characters can also be read in terms of Baron-Cohen's theory of 'the extreme male brain'. Although he asserts that his theory does not insist that *all* men manifest these behavioural characteristics, he does argue that '*more* males than females have a brain of type S [a systematic, 'male brain'] and *more* females than males have brain of type E [an empathetic, 'female brain']' (Baron-Cohen 2003: 8). When considering an extreme version of the male brain, Baron-Cohen points to a pattern of communication difficulties which have been charted as symptoms of Asperger's syndrome, a high-functioning type of autism. He describes autism as:

[a]n empathy disorder: those with autism have major difficulties in 'mindreading' or putting themselves into someone else's shoes, imagining the world through someone else's eyes and responding appropriately to someone else's feelings [. . .] They believe in saying what they think, seeing no point in sugaring the pill or spin-doctoring (Baron-Cohen 2003: 137)

By recording character traits of those with autism, Baron-Cohen observes a pattern of behaviour whereby people (mostly men):

> [t]alk only to obtain something they need, or to share factual information. They may reply to a question with the relevant facts only, and they may not ask a question in return because they do not naturally consider what others are thinking. These are people who are unable to see the point of social chit-chat. (Baron-Cohen 2003: 133)

Baron-Cohen's exploration considers a number of high-functioning autistic people, who are highly successful in some areas of their professional life, but who fail to perform appropriately in social situations. Although this may appear to be an extreme version of male behaviour, many of his observations do appear to correspond to the construction of character within Maxwell's plays. Several of Maxwell's characters demonstrate a desire to analyse their emotions, but the language they use is often elliptical and metaphorical, and does not offer much solace. Maxwell appears to be pointing to the potentially 'harmful' features of a gendered system, and in picking up on the relationship between male behaviour and autism he could be articulating his sense that traditional masculine role models are out of kilter with more therapeutically-aware times.

As I mentioned previously, several of Maxwell's later plays demonstrate a shift in attitude towards emotional disclosure. In *The End of Reality* (*EOR*) and *Ode to the Man Who Kneels* (*Ode*), male and female characters are given long monologues detailing a complex emotional landscape. The characters also maintain a more abrupt, or brusque mode of interpersonal exchange, akin to the 'autistic' behaviour described by Baron-Cohen, but when alone or with trusted friends, they reveal the secrets of their otherwise hidden thoughts. These monologues are often confessional in nature and describe crushed aspirations, wounded feelings and broken hearts. For example, the character of Brian, In *EOR* manifests signs of hypermasculinity in his willingness to fight intruders and his crude appraisal of women, but he also appears to burst into tears when Jake is abducted and he confesses his love of Marcia to Tom after her departure. His speech attests to a fear of being 'broken' or 'destroyed' by his grief:

> Fuck!! You don't know. Just that it's true. This will break me. I—I know this for a fact. It will break me. It will destroy me. That's a cold hard fact. I can feel it. I know it. And there's nothing you can do about it. . . . I'm tired of being in control. I'll let fate be in control.[11]

Interestingly, Brian's emotional outburst corresponds with the articulation of a desire to give up 'control', suggesting that his previous containment, or 'control' over his emotions contributed towards an overarching sense of control over his life as a whole.

EOR's Tom also proves an interesting object of study, appearing to eschew hypermasculine argot in favour of a more modest, devout language. Although he participates fully in the fight sequences, he also confesses to a number of insecurities: he fears he will be ridiculed by his colleagues in the police force when Marcia releases their intruder; he confesses to having inappropriate sexual feelings for his Goddaughter and repeatedly mourns the loss of respect in his 'neighbourhood'. Tom repeatedly recites from *The Bible* and voices regret at the breakdown of interpersonal relationships. The presence of the female security guards and a devout male Head of Security tempers the otherwise hypermasculine activities at the centre of the play. Tom confesses to Brian:

> I know we're in the future now. I can feel it. I'm not stupid. But I can't help clinging to the past. I miss the old neighborhood . . . And I thought the only thing left in this neighbourhood untouched are the churches. Well I was wrong. They tore down that Holy Cross to make way for a hi-rise. Can you imagine ? A Church. A home for believers.[12]

Tom's tentative faith and willingness to verbalise and share insecurities with a male friend represents a shift in characterization for Maxwell away

Figure 4.2 Jim Fletcher and Greg Mehrten in *Ode to the Man Who Kneels*. (Photo: Michael Schmelling.)

from an apparently ironic representation of gauche, inarticulate males to include more obviously complex and contradictory characters.

Ode is set in the mythical Wild West and revolves around the arrival of a cowboy to a town named Grid. The play is punctuated by a number of songs, the last of which includes the lines:

> Look how the frozen cowboy stands
> Sings the songs in his head
> Look how the frozen cowboy stands watching the sunset
> . . .
> Keep the melody in your head son
> Keep it just in your head[13]

As in *EOR*, *Ode* features a number of male and female characters who discuss their emotions, in dialogue and monologue. The character of The Dashing Man serenades his lover, confesses that he is desperately in love with her and reveals that he is impotent. The Kneeling Man reveals himself to be 'an actor' and discloses a kind of schizoid existence in which 'you're not in the real world. You're recording. You're storing it up for a moment when you can use this for later'. He also states that he gives himself 'three days' to get over his heartbreak, but towards the end of his monologue reveals that a year later he is, 'still stuck on day two'. Indeed, the issue of emotional disclosure and vulnerability appears to be at the centre of this play, which suggests that the admonishment to 'sing the songs in your head' and 'keep it just in your head' relate to advice on how to preserve male dignity. The central cowboy figure, also named 'The Standing Man' and 'Daniel', exerts his influence over the other characters by assassinating the male characters and taking sexual ownership of the females. In contrast to other characters in the play, The Standing Man is brutal and maintains a hypermasculine demeanour, however even he is given a number of revelatory disclosures, which undermine the customary illusion of a self-sufficient and emotionally reticent cowboy. His lines include some unusually poetic descriptions. After having told The Kneeling Man that he 'looks stoopid', he goes on to describe a strange landscape: '[w]hile under the earth there is a labyrinth of cave passages where albino fishes swim with no eyes in a sea beneath the sea of dirt.'[14] During a later scene, in the General Store, The Standing Man reveals, '[t]he Dashing Man wipes tears from the face of the Standing Man' and he asks the proprietor to organize a band of warriors with 'broken hearts':

> I only take men with broken hearts. Makes 'em brave, I reckon. You just don't care whether you live or whether you die. The broken hearts makes the pain tolerable. These are men for me and I'm for them, Pablo. Do you know? [15]

Although The Standing Man's actions are brutal and greedy, his language betrays an emotional vulnerability out of keeping with traditional representations of the cowboy.

A number of sections of *Ode* indicate that the characters take on the role of a kind of narrator; lines of dialogue are interspersed with lines describing the characters and their thoughts. For example, The Standing Man describes himself as follows:

> The Standing Man is convinced that he is not a killer. ("He cannot lie. He simply cannot. If he was to lie, he would become undone. So he simply does not") That he never killed. The half-life and the sickness. A constant half-life. The Standing Man wants to be close to you. He does.[16]

These lines attribute an incongruent sense of moral integrity and a contradictory depth of emotion to an otherwise amoral character. However, there is a repeated disparity throughout the play between what the characters say and what they do. They repeatedly assert their loyalty, but then behave in a contradictory manner, appearing to realign loyalty with little conscience. If the survival of the cowboy, an established hypermasculine male archetype, depends upon his 'keeping it just in his head' then it is possible to read this play as being about the male experience of emotional sublimation. Elsewhere, in plays such as *House* and *People Without History* Maxwell writes with an intertexual awareness of the dramatic canon and in *Ode* he could be recognized to be paying homage to Sam Shepard's cowboy figures. Shepard invokes cowboys and the frontier of the Wild West in plays such as *Cowboy Mouth*, *The Tooth of Crime*, *Mad Dog Blues*, *Cowboys#2* and *True West*. Florence Falk, describing 'men without women' in Shepard's plays, suggests that the popular understanding of the frontier is that it is: 'the domain of the male Homo Erectus, whose bulging muscles and veins streaked with violence bespeak daring and conceal any trace of vulnerability' (Falk 1981: 91). Falk argues that the image of the cowboy represents a 'lost machismo' and 'glorifies the male: costumes him in unfeeling masculinity' (Falk 1981: 90). Shepard's cowboys are in keeping with the archetypical brutish male, however Falk argues that the characters are 'developed with unflinching irony' and created in order to draw attention to the performed nature of gender. She writes:

> To succeed, Shepard's males play at being *Men*, his females at being *Women*; that is, both sexes act out not necessarily what men and women *are* but how they imagine men and women *behave*. (Falk 1981: 95)

Like Shepard, Maxwell appropriates the archetype of the cowboy, but does not rely upon an ironic reading to draw attention to dysfunctional survival tactics. By giving the cowboy, and his male counterparts dialogue that acknowledges emotional difficulty, Maxwell breaks with the tradition of representing the cowboy as 'emptied of intellectual curiosity' (Falk 1981: 92) and shows him to be more emotionally intelligent and profound. Maxwell's earlier characters such as Frank from *Drummer Wanted* and the eponymous *Joe* hint elliptically at some kind of emotional malaise, however his later characters are given lines which explicitly describe emotional turmoil. As with Brian and Tom in *EOR*, these later characters offer a representation of a contradictory masculinity. Ironically, despite their new found ability to share their emotions, the characters in his later pieces do not achieve a new level of emotional wisdom, or find a way of transcending their wordly anxiety. By verbalizing their grief they demonstrate another, previously hidden facet of their character, but unlike most contemporary Hollywood narratives, are not rewarded for this self-realisation (White 1992: 146). They remain the same and continue to behave in the same way ostensibly after the close of the play. It is significant that the later characters verbally reveal their emotions, as the practice of sublimation, the exhortion to 'just keep it in your head' appears to have been central to their ability to maintain their position as a heteronormative male. The later characters bear the outer signs of hypermasculinity, and they are still participating in this culture, yet they are also given lines which enable them to verbalise a sense of disquiet about their emotional solitude. This work continues to represent the 'harm' of masculinity and yet does not solely rely upon irony to destabilize traditional gender roles.

Although Baron-Cohen has theorized masculine communicative and empathy deficits in terms of an extreme, borderline-autistic male brain, a number of other theorists have pointed to issues relating to verbal and social articulation as a recurrent problem of, and for, contemporary male subjects. Coates observes that narratives appearing in female speech provide opportunities for self-disclosure, 'men's first person narratives focus more on achievement and triumph . . . and are not designed to reveal feelings or to lead into talk where feelings can be compared and discussed (Coates 2003: 73). In addition to Horrocks' argument that the contemporary 'crisis' of masculinity is characterised by a kind of 'emotional autism' Rotundo argues that twentieth-century consumer-driven culture has robbed both men and women of 'even the rudiments of a language to discuss community and connection' (Rotundo 1993: 284). Such observations about the restricted potential for self-expression for the contemporary male appear somewhat incongruous in the context of the documentation of Western culture's growing interest in 'therapeutic culture'. Documenting cultural shifts during the Regan years, Robert M. Collins describes the emergence of a 'self-referential quality of American life in the 1980s' and a shift away from the traditional 'New England self' towards the 'California self'. According to Collins the 'California self' rejects traditional Protestant values in order to develop a solipsistic theory of self-interest. He writes, 'the California self, by contrast, is the self "taken to the max", a self that chooses, feels pleasure and pain, dictates action and even has things like esteem, efficacy and confidence' (Collins 2007: 153). This apparent tension between, on the one hand, a culture that is embracing self-analysis and taking a therapeutic interest in articulating emotional needs and a more working class male culture that finds its vocabulary diminished, perhaps provides an insight into the pertinence of much of Maxwell's work. The values promoted by his characters often appear deliberately outmoded, and certainly out of kilter with the therapeutic shift towards self-disclosure. Even the disclosure of personal information in pieces such as *EOR* and *Ode* does not bolster the characters' sense of themselves as functional, humanist subjects. For me, this tension is heightened through the realisation of character by the amateur and professional actors employed by Maxwell. The stillness and emotional reticence of many performances contrasts with the ubiquitous method-acting approach to performance deployed in the majority of main-stream Western theatres. In addition, the incorporation of performance tasks such as singing or fighting, creates a risky scenario in the 'here and now' of the theatrical event in which the actor engages with the discourse of gender and class performativity. In discussing the opportunities afforded to men by the 'toughness/tenderness' discourse, Rotundo observes that, 'we are disabled in choosing the wise risk from the unwise, and tend to value risk as its own form of good. In this manner, we are all hurt by the cultural configuration of manhood.' (Rotundo 1993: 291). When working class men are called upon to delimit the behavioural codes at their dis-posal, because they are both on stage and in character in Maxwell's work, the specific nature of the performative risk is made visible. The traditional masculine codes of behaviour recorded by Pleck and Kimmel and the gen-dering of verbal proficiency, as described by Vorlicky, Coates and Man-gan, point to the complex proposition faced by male working class subjects when attempting to disclose intimate information to their peers. Maxwell's characters demonstrate repeated signs of ineptitude or failure in relation to emotional revelation and empathy and so achieve success in observing tra-ditional gender and class role behaviour whilst failing to build sustainable relationships. The character traits are repeated across a number of plays and are shown to correspond to a pre-existing notion of gendered behaviour. In addition to exploring identity by means of invoking culturally specific codes and attitudes, Maxwell also encourages the actor's unease to signify as an instance of performative repetition of gender and class. By retaining metatheatrical references to the process of putting on a performance, Max-well situates his actors within a context which, as Mangan and Vorlicky have pointed out, is customarily gendered as 'feminine'. As a result the real and/or performed unease of the actors signifies as the emotional restraint expected of traditional working class American males, when situated in a context of emotional disclosure. This aspect of his work can be considered 'performative' because unease represents a failure to repeat either the tra-ditional attributes of the professional actor, or the traditional attributes of the working class American male, and as a result shows identity formation to be 'phantasmatic' and a 'politically tenuous construction' (Butler 1990: 141). The staging of awkwardness and social ineptitude points to the particular 'harm' that hegemonic male role identities inflict upon male subjects who find the contemporary 'Californian', or therapeutic discourse unpalatable. Maxwell's work may not constitute a definitive 'statement' about identity, a welcome feature given Butler's warning that, '[g]ender ought not be construed as a stable identity or locus of agency which various acts follow' (Butler 1990: 140) but rather encourages an exploration of the social performance of identity in specific racial, class and gendered contexts.

5 Concert Hall Slash Sports Facility

The Anthropological Space of Richard Maxwell's Theatre

Searching *You Tube* for clips of Maxwell's recent productions, I chanced upon a composite of stills from an Oslo-based company, Verk Produksjon-er's 2005 production of The New York City Player's *House*. A three-minute montage animates a collection of production photographs organised sequentially to provide a reminder of the exposition of the play. Although the sequence of staged conversation, fighting and murder is recognisable from the 2001 production of Maxwell's own play, and despite the fact that Maxwell's approach is not always consistent, several elements of this production gave me pause for thought because they went against my understanding of a Maxwellian 'logic'. Initially I found it difficult to identify precisely what it was I found to be at odds with my understanding of his methodology but something about a subtle but discernible level of *finish* marked my perception of this production as being different from Maxwell's own. Although the information about the overall production is minimal, and my perception correspondingly flawed, the composite did provide a prompt to re-evaluate my existing ideas about Maxwell's use of space.

The key to addressing this conundrum lay in my sense of something being awry with the Norwegian production's apparently hermeneutic self-sufficiency, I turned to semiological texts that have sought to define minute and precise elements of the mise en scène. I turned to Gay McAuley's *Space in Performance: Making Meaning in the Theatre,* which provided me, in turn, with an overview of Anne Ubersfeld's 1970s socio-political 'taxonomy of stage space'; and Una Chaudhuri's *Staging Place: The Geography of Modern Drama*, which worked to explore the possibility that a seemingly closed or self-referential realist fiction might contain in itself, a 'hermeneutic principle' pointing to naturalism as 'ideological crisis'.

McAuley conducts an analysis of a number of theatre semioticians, comparing, in particular, the ways in which they try to refine distinctions between the different permutations of 'real' space and 'fictional' space; on-stage space and off-stage space; imagined and actual space. Firstly she introduces Ubersfeld's distinction between 'stage space' and 'scenic place' suggesting that:

The stage space is a straightforward notion, the stage itself glossed as 'the playing area', but the 'scenic place', as she conceives it, is more complex. It is both the fictional place where the action is occurring (the Forest of Arden, Nero's palace in Rome etc.) and 'the toplogical . . . transposition of the major features of the social space experienced by a particular group within a given society' (McAuley 1999: 18)

Secondly, McAuley foregrounds tensions arising from attempts to adequately describe the difference between props and set which *represent the fictional world of the play*; props and set which indexically *refer to an outside world* (for example, windows, doors, photographs) and *geographical indicators described verbally by characters*. Taking issue with Hanna Scolnicov's evocation of theatrical space 'within' and theatrical space 'without', McAuley points out that:

The "within" and "without" categories distinguish between what she calls "perceived space" and "conceived space". I would suggest, however, that, while the offstage can perhaps be claimed as conceived space, the onstage is always both perceived and conceived, stage space and scenic place in Ubersfeld's terms. (McAuley 1999: 21)

McAuley's work in setting a 'taxonomy of spatial function' represents an invaluable tool in helping to understand what might be at stake in a number of Maxwell's plays. This attention to detail is particularly useful as Maxwell's work appears to follow an eclectic logic by borrowing from contrasting theatre disciplines. On one hand, by employing linear narrative structures and psychologically developed characters Maxwell observes the traditions of realist theatre; on the other, by developing a utilitarian mode of performance and introducing sudden, and unexplained, leaps in time, he acknowledges recent strategies developed by experimental practitioners such as Richard Foreman and The Wooster Group. The elision of one set of theatre conventions with another creates a productive tension through which both the language developed to describe theatre and the process of performance itself is made strange.

I will attend to what McAuley would describe as both 'performance' and 'textual' signs by analysing the staging of a number of productions alongside sociological and topographic references to fictional worlds made by Maxwell's characters. At the outset of the chapter I will identify what I have termed a 'rehearsal aesthetic' within Maxwell's work and consider the issues arising from Maxwell's decision to draw attention to the signs of labour and preparation customarily suppressed in realist theatre. I want to argue that Maxwell actively discourages 'denegation', a practice which Ubersfeld describes as encouraging the audience to momentarily 'forget' that the scene unfolding before them 'has no consequences outside the confines of the stage space' (McAuley 1999: 40) and that his position therefore resists an immanentist view of art, which would hold that the work of art is an 'autonomous, rounded and organic whole that seeks to unify and universalize experience and transcend the temporal dimension' (Sayre 1989: 57). Elsewhere in the chapter I explore Una Chaudhuri's proposition that 'the erasure of spatial particularity, one of the hallmarks of postmodernism, is represented in drama through the figure of America' (Chaudhuri 1995: 4). This section of the chapter identifies locations, buildings and communities described within plays such as *Billings* (1996), *Showcase* (2003), *The End of Reality* (2006) and *Good Samaritans* (2004a) and argues that they are usefully read in relation to Marc Augé's theory of the 'non-place'. The nominated locations are customarily associated with 'dead-ends'—a spatial metaphor employed to describe constraint of opportunity or social mobility, which invites a reading of 'non-places' through the lens of the myth of the American Dream. The final section of the chapter builds upon the myth of the American Dream as it is spatially realised in the symbolic landscape of the American West and represented in plays such as *The Frame* (2006), *Ode to the Man who Kneels* (2007) and *Cowboys and Indians* (1998).[1]

In formulating Maxwell's use of space, I want to argue that several of the places constructed within the dramatic space of his plays, are redolent of Marc Augé's theory of 'non-places' (1995) because, like the 'concert hall slash sports facility'[2] of my title, (in being a transient or multi-purpose location), they are apparently without 'character' (Augé 1995:82); they are akin to 'the airports and railway stations, hotel chains, leisure parks and large retail outlets', spaces that for Augé, 'cannot be defined as relational or historical, or concerned with identity' (Augé 1995: 77). Conversely, I also feel inclined to describe Maxwell's use of theatrical space as what Augé would term an 'anthropological place' because he acknowledges the theatre building as a place where people come together to think about identity and community. In Augé's terms, this would imply a place in which the social is 'engendered' and in which 'journeys have to be made' (Augé 1995:81). I want to argue that Maxwell frames each performance as a discrete event and purposefully acknowledges the coming together of actor and audience by making visible the marks of preparation, labour and rehearsal that would normally be suppressed in a conventional realist production. These marks are made visible through, what I want to characterise as a 'rehearsal' aesthetic and his tendency to use received techniques of *Verfremdungseffekt* to remind the audience that they have come to see a play. Ubersfeld describes theatre's function in terms of a 'bring[ing] together of actors and spectators' and marks it as a socio-political phenomenon which provides an opportunity to analyse hegemonic social process. Her analysis of theatre space argues that the relationship between actor and spectator depends . . . on both the physical form of the auditorium and the [dominant] form of social organization' (McAuley 1999: 18).[3] If Ubersfeld's reading of the theatrical event can be deemed relevant here, then it would point to the theatre as a place of historicity, a site which shapes social relations and would subsequently represent, in Augé's terms, an 'anthropological place'. Maxwell works to keep these ideas in the forefront of the audience's imagination.[4]

Markus Wessendorf has described Maxwell's work as 'oscillating between the two modes of contemporary theatre' and 'the theatre avant-garde that originated in the 1960s' (Wessendorf 2001: 455); an observation that goes some way to explaining his idiosyncratic approach to theatrical space. It is Maxwell's 'proclivity for narrative structure, social milieu and quotidian dialogue' which marks his engagement with contemporary American theatre, and his 'staging and acting techniques that owe more to performance art' (Wessendorf 2001: 455). In addition to these disciplinary or generic influences, Maxwell's approach to space could also be explained in terms of a postmodern approach to scenography. For Robert Cheesemond this includes an 'insituist impulse to frame the theatrical with reality and reality with the theatrical' (Eynat-Confino and Šarmová 2000: 159). Maxwell invokes both the theatrical real and the offstage real by animating a fictional world that deliberately acknowledges and addresses its audience.

To return to the 'troublesome' Verk Produksjoner photographs—they reveal a playing area of approximately 60 metres by 30 metres; the back wall and floor are draped with an expanse of white paper pulled from a wide roll mounted in the grid. Stage right stands a bare tree (apparently real) and a coil of orange chaser lights. Stage left stands a tall pile of boxes—the boxes are all the same size, and are stacked about 2 metres high, so that the top of the pile is aligned with the top of the paper roll. Upstage, a lone box has been extracted from the pile and placed upstage right. The actors are clad in casual contemporary clothing; and, as in Maxwell's production[5] a young boy, approximately ten years of age, plays the role of 'son'. In terms of the discordant features, I would identify three main elements which appear out of place. Firstly, several shots show the son in some kind of dressing-up costume, in place of, or in addition to his original 'son' costume. In one shot he wears a death-head mask—a hood pulled over his head with a plastic skeleton face at the front. In this shot he appears to be wielding some kind of weapon; in another he poses in a dragon costume—he leans forward on one leg and poses for the camera whilst holding a toy bow and arrow. Secondly, during a fight sequence between the two male adults, the pile of boxes is demolished and a tear created in the paper wall. Finally, a number of images show various actors standing on the lone (upstage right) box as they sing their song. Heads are thrown back in exertion and they appear to be delivering their song towards the back wall of the auditorium. The set struck me as being exceptionally clean and well preserved. Although the boxes showed signs of having been repaired with parcel-tape and the costumes looked appropriately worn-in, there was something about the level of 'finish' apparent in these images which made the actors appear 'styled' or 'attended-to' by a team of diligent stage managers. What had struck me was a sense that the additional costumes and the symbolic use of set was somehow 'excessive' when matched against Maxwell's production of his own play. The deliberate 'costuming' of the child; the deliberate act of choosing to represent domestic 'order' and 'disorder' through the actors interaction with their minimal environment (a tear in the back wall, a pile of boxes knocked over) seemed to have enabled me to identify the understated within Maxwell's production.

These differences, although subtle and barely discernible given the format, prompted me to attempt to identify and qualify Maxwell's approach to space. Albeit with minimal visual evidence, I felt that I could somehow ascertain that the Verk Produksjoner's version differed most dramatically because it appeared to offer a closed hermeneutic fictional world within which to locate this domestic drama. In intuiting this production as 'closed' I am invoking a structuralist reading or tendency which is perhaps best described in poststructuralist terms. In *Structuralist Poetics: Structuralism, Linguistics and the Study of Literature*, Jonathan Culler outlines the arguments raised against structuralism, outlining what Derrida considers to be the main problem in attempting to define structures and units within a structuralist analysis:

> This closure, it would be argued, testifies to the presence of an ideology. . . . To make any postulated effect the fixed point of one's analysis cannot but seem a dogmatic and prescriptive move which reflects a desire for absolute truths and transcendent meanings. (Culler 1975: 244)

Leaving the problematics of my own search for 'absolute truths' and 'transcendent meanings' to one side for the moment, Culler's description of the study of structuralist poetics reveals that hermeneutic 'closure' is associated with a singular, immanentist ideology. In this instance, the production appears to have been created according to an ideology of realist contemporary theatre which maintains a clear distinction between signs belonging to what McAuley identifies as 'theatre space' and 'audience space'. Maxwell's productions, by contrast refer to a more eclectic range of ideologies, which work to problematise received understandings of a delimited theatre space.

Ironically, given that I have designated it 'closed', this production apparently followed a theatrical logic which permitted props and information from off-stage to be introduced to support the unfolding of the play. This logic relies upon viewing conventions that can incorporate foreign objects, not necessarily named within the script, into the world of the play. Whereas in more experimental or postdramatic theatre, off-stage is often framed as belonging to the non-fictional world of the auditorium, for the purposes of this production audiences are invited to conceive of off-stage as an extension of the world of the play. For example, the mask, dragon costume, child's weapons and musical accompaniment were all introduced from 'off-stage' and yet they do not appear to puncture the hermeneutic self-sufficiency of the fictional world as they serve to diegetically bolster and maintain the fictional illusion. This contradiction, (when items from outside of the scenic place can be brought onstage without hermeneutic disruption) points to a space of 'denegation'. For Ubersfeld, denegation is:

> . . . the psychic operation that permits the spectator to see the physical reality of what is happening onstage, to accept it as reality while knowing (or forgetting for brief instants) that this reality has no consequences outside the confines of the stage space. (Ubersfeld 1996: 23)

This inducement to 'forget' is clearly a key convention supporting theatrical realism. Ubersfeld interestingly describes it as a 'psychic operation'. It is a learned reading convention which encourages and allows the spectator to accommodate contradictory aspects of the diegetic and extra-diegetic world, which might otherwise puncture the self-sufficiency of the hermeneutic world, and draw too much attention to the constructed nature of the fiction. This term is highly pertinent to Maxwell's work because, to date, he has largely adopted the form of realism. His plays are written according to realist conventions and the direction of the plays also maintains continuity of character and location. However, I want to argue that Maxwell introduces features that disrupt established reading conventions. In several pieces certain events that signify, for me, as 'careless' or 'clumsy'[6] disrupt realist conventions and draw attention to the nature of the theatrical activity underway. Maxwell's 'rehearsal' aesthetic is related to what has been termed an 'amateur' aesthetic elsewhere (Alvarez 2006, Bailes 2005) however I see this conception being played out more persuasively when related to scenic place and theatrical space. It is this co-option of a rehearsal aesthetic that acts as a reminder of the performance as a labour-intensive 'event' which has been prepared specifically for a group of spectators, more conventionally known, of course as, an audience. Although the quasi- realist form of *House* may initially appear to promote denegation and invite the audience to 'forget' and accept what they see as 'real', Maxwell's actual production was designed to appear unfinished and so potentially encourages an audience to address latent expectations set in place by realist viewing conventions; to consider the labour expended in preparing for this event and imagine how a framing of rehearsal as labour might raise questions about the theatre as a paradigm of social organisation (McAuley 1999: 19–20).

I have identified my sense of the 'out of place' of the Oslo production of *House*, by describing its level of *polish,* or *finish.* By contrast, in his own production of *House*, Maxwell appears to have procured a deliberately 'unfinished' look to his set. In consultation with designer Jane Cox, Maxwell decided, for the back wall of the set (as 'scenic place' this should have been a domestic interior), to replicate the wall of the rehearsal room the company had been using in New York.[7] Markus Wessendorf observed that the wall was 'around 7 feet high with a payphone and a Chinese take-out menu attached to it' (Wessendorf 2001: 446). In contrast to the unblemished white of the paper backing the Oslo set, this wall was grubby and suggested a functional, transitory space, rather than a maintained playing area. Analysing Maxwell's use of space in *House*, Wessendorf has described this 'home' as in keeping with Chaudhuri's 'problem' of the 'geopathological' home characterising much Modern drama. He also describes the fictional place (the scenic place) as 'alienating' and 'undecided', adjectives which potentially figure it as one of Augé's anonymous non-places. However, when read in terms of dramatic space, a hermeneutic identifier which allows for both textual and performance signs to cohere, I consider it to deliberately invoke 'rehearsal' as a process of preparation for meeting the audience. This wall is perhaps the most explicit reference to the rehearsal space in Maxwell's work. More subtle references include incongruous items of furniture being used or appropriated as they might during rehearsal rather than during a 'final' performance. I am thinking in particular of the dining chairs used to stand-in for the car during Mom and Frank's journey to the karaoke bar in *Drummer Wanted* and the dining tables in *Good Samaritans* which provide a bed upon which Rose and Kevin make love. In both shows, up until the point of re-appropriation the chairs and tables have been used in accordance with their function, and have been selected so as to be in keeping with the domestic interior being represented. However, in the two instances described the actor/characters subvert the conventional use-value of the items of furniture and instead use them to represent something else: another, very different item of furniture and a motor vehicle. This type of re-appropriation suggests a sudden shift in direction, as if an element of child's play or improvisation has insinuated itself into the chosen form. In terms of theatrical coherence, although accustomed to reading a montage of theatrical texts, these two moments signified, for me, as incredibly naïve and manifested a gauche disregard for realist conventions. Had the production introduced, prior to this moment, a convention of improvising with the furniture, then this would have helped explain the moment of subversion, but a sudden, singular breach of convention signified for me as surprising, clumsy and 'amateur'. Observing the terms of 'denegation' this was such a blatant breach of convention that I, as a spectator, could no longer 'forget for a brief instant' that this was just 'part of the play'; I found it impossible to accommodate it as part of viable on-stage activity and subsequently, this action did appear to have, in Ubserfeld's terms 'consequences outside the confines of the stage space' (Ubersfeld in McAuley 1999: 40). These instances of re-appropriation as deliberate 'signs' of rehearsal, are incorporated to cite the *process* of rehearsal and make visible the labour behind theatrical illusion.

I will introduce more items of incongruous furniture in relation to *The End of Reality*, a production of one of Maxwell's plays developed in 2006.

The following anecdote lends an insight into my sense that the 'unfinished' has become important to Maxwell's aesthetic. At the end of one *End of Reality* rehearsal in January 2006, I watched Scott Sherratt, stage manager, attempting to mend one of the tables being used as the security desk in the 'lobby citadel' (as it was described in the promotional material).[8] He mentioned that he was waiting for some new hinges to arrive to reinforce the tables so that they would be able to bear the weight of the actors as they fell against or rolled over them during the fight sequences. I remember asking him in surprise, 'you mean you are going to use *these* tables?' I was shocked to discover that these tables were not stand-ins, they weren't just 'making-do' until the 'proper' tables arrived. At first glance, the tables resembled trestle tables used for pasting wallpaper: in actual fact they were fold-out tables with iron legs and a fairly thick wooden surface. Maxwell had chosen three such tables to represent the security desk featured in this show. Perhaps it was partly a result of the promotional citation of the play as being located in a 'lobby citadel', but I was expecting something much more finished, something resembling receptionist Amanda's desk in the television programme *Ugly Betty*, some kind of lofty polished 'work-station' finished with a matte, stain-free veneer.[9] Logically, it would follow that if a fictional office building was important enough to employ a team of fictional security guards, then it would warrant investing in an impressive front desk. In addition to the make-shift tables, I was also surprised when Maxwell decided to retain a scruffy strip of tape, originally laid down to give the actors some sense of how to move about the space in the final set. Although the white floor was refreshed after each performance, the gaffer tape, placed there during rehearsal, remained in place. It was this aspect of his work which, in hindsight, I realised, must be about Maxwell's actively encouraging a set which bore visible traces of the rehearsal room. In contrast to the dining chairs and utilitarian tables in *Drummer Wanted* and *Good Samaritans*, the *End of Reality* tables had never been in-keeping with their fictional environment. Nor were they in keeping with the design for the rest of the set which included smart back-lit side panels, a projection screen and numerous floor and back panels painted a brilliant white. By failing to apply the same production values to all aspects of the set and by subverting the expectations relating to where makeshift objects 'belong' Maxwell causes slippage between different sign-systems. As McAuley observes, customarily rehearsal spaces (and by extension, stand-in props) used during rehearsal are 'never seen by the public as the rehearsals are very much part of the hidden domain of theatre production' (McAuley 1999: 70). McAuley, usefully points out that despite being hidden from view, the specific nature of rehearsal spaces can influence creative decisions made during the production process:

> The rehearsal space is never a neutral container and, however black and empty it may seem to the observer, it is likely to imprint aspects of its own reality on both the fictional world that is being created and

even on the physical reality of the set that will ultimately replace the mock-up so carefully indicated within its confines by means of gaffer tape on the floor and bits and pieces of furniture. (McAuley 1999: 74)

A final example of an apparently misplaced prop or object lies in the robot which whirrs onstage at the end of *Joe* (2002). This robot appeared home-made, with recognisable bits of domestic gadgetry soldered together. The robot, clad in the same red top as the other Joes entered on what resembled caterpillar tracks from a child's toy tank and a camcorder stood in place of its eye. It resembled a more fragile and makeshift version of the robot Johnny 5 from the film *Short Circuit* (1986).[10] Given that *Joe* had also featured an impressive 'star-curtain' machine, which rotated to create the effect of twinkling stars above the heads of each embodied Joe the sudden intervention of gauche machinery seemed mystifying. I found it difficult to make the mental transition and accept this machine as 'deliberately flawed' or 'amateur'.

Thanks to a conversation I had with Mendes about *Joe*, I came to realise that the company are discouraged from thinking about a production as 'fixed' or 'finished' once it has opened. Mendes contradicted my assumption that the 'first night' of a production necessarily represented some kind of goal or point of completion. He stated that company members are encouraged to interpret their roles anew each night and to respond to the change in venue, change in audience, and change in atmosphere. This attitude marks a refusal to engage with a teleological epistemology of theatre-making which distinguishes between the rehearsal process prior to the show and the finished production once it has opened. The teleological model could be regarded to be in keeping with an immanentist approach to art, an approach which regards the art object as 'an autonomous, rounded and organic whole that seeks to unify and universalize experience and transcend the temporal dimension'. According to Sayre, anti-immanentist art: 'refuses to stop confronting [the viewer], distancing, isolating him (Sayre 1989: 58). As Wessendorf suggests, this aspect of Maxwell's work bears traces of the influence of avant-garde practitioners such as The Wooster Group and Richard Foreman.[11] Of The Wooster Group's work, Bonnie Marranca has argued that, 'what is actually being staged . . . is the life of the rehearsal room' (Marranca 2003: 11). In relation to Foreman, Arnold Aronson argues that '[t]here is a determinedly homemade quality' to his work, even when he is working with a substantial production budget:

. . . props gleaned from secondhand shops; set pieces and especially the scenic painting purposely subvert the slick, polished look of commercial theater in which even dirt and decay is carefully, even beautifully, designed. . . . Part of this can be traced back to Foreman's Brechtian roots and Brecht's desire to "show that you are showing" (Aronson 2005: 162)

Artists such as The Wooster Group and Foreman have become associated with a deconstructive approach to theatre, whereby hidden ideological imperatives within traditional realist theatre are fore-grounded and marked as value-laden and hegemonic. Much of this work has revolved around disturbing the coherence and self-sufficiency of the spatial distinctions described by McAuley. She comments that traditionally the 'audience space' and 'practitioner space' are 'quite rigidly demarcated and conceptualized in terms of front and back ("front of house" and "backstage")' (McAuley 1999: 25). Although these artists do not necessarily physically integrate with the audience they do draw attention to the traditional 'ownership' of spaces by employing direct-address and eschew an ideology of denegation by framing the overarching aim of their work as being to mount a production. According to Aronson, for Foreman this amounts to 'an almost aggressive frontality. . . . in an age in which the thrust stage is ubiquitous and environmental performance not uncommon, Foreman's productions engage the audience head-on in a dialectic between stage and auditorium' (Aronson 2005: 162). If the immanent art object is one which is free of ideology and 'out of history' (Sayre 1989: 6) then Maxwell's work, by referring to the material circumstances of production and immediate socio-political concerns, can be deemed to deliberately eschew this status.

In order to position Maxwell as against the immanence of the art-object, I want to mark Maxwell's 'rehearsal' aesthetic as a deliberate means of drawing attention to the contingency of the theatrical event; the social organisation of theatre-going and the 'denegative' viewing conventions which suppress signs of labour in preparing for performance. The casual use of furniture stands as just one example of many other theatrical elements he employs to denaturalise the conventional mechanisms of realist theatrical illusion. Other techniques would include his decision to keep the house lights up throughout the production; his encouraging the actors to speak as if using direct-address even whilst engaged in dialogue with another character; his encouragement of the actors to make eye-contact with members of the audience (most notably, late-comers in *Drummer Wanted*). I want to argue that although Maxwell largely engages with realism, his interruption of denegative reading conventions draws the audience's attention away from the fictional world and toward the immediate circumstances of their coming together to watch a play. This approach resists hermeneutic self-sufficiency and the accusation of immanence by drawing attention to the temporal dimension of the production and extending an invitation to consider the different experiences of space for different social groups. In Ubersfeld's terms, it invites audience members to meditate upon the 'consequences' of this production in the outside world. This invitation is extended both through the experiences of space occupied by situating blue-collar workers within the scenic place of his plays and by making visible the traces of rehearsal in the dramatic space of the theatre.

Following an exploration of Maxwell's refusal of the psychic process of 'denegation' I intend to pursue spatial issues arising from fictional as well as textual elements of his work. Augé's examples of non-places are recognisable within many of Maxwell's (fictional) scenic places. There is also much to be said about Maxwell's contribution to ongoing debates about the representation of America and its being employed to represent 'placelessness' by commentators such as Cheesemond, Baudrillard and Chaudhuri (Baudrillard 1986, Chaudhuri 1995: 4, Eynat-Confino and Sarmová 2000: 159). Although Augé's theory of 'non-places' is highly relevant to many of Maxwell's settings, the dialogue and relationships developed between his characters also resists many of the negative implications of this term. The apparently heterogeneous object of America invoked by Baudrillard and Chaudhuri is complicated by the sense of a collective investment in community represented in Maxwell's oeuvre. Charting the development of 'geopathology' and Modern drama, Chaudhuri claims that:

> At midcentury, a new discourse enters the dialogue and changes the established terms of the drama's engagement with place, displacing as well the dramatic structures that had served the geopathic model. The new discourse centers upon the figure of America, explicating it, first as a betrayal of place, and then finding in it a muted celebration of placelessness. (Chaudhuri 1995: 15)

Although Chaudhuri focuses upon 'the figure of (a represented) America' rather than an actual invocation of the 'real' America, the values attributed to America as a metonym for the dissolution of culture are freighted with negativity. Her chapter 'America and the Limits of Homecoming' analyses examples of work by Sam Shepard, Harold Pinter, Caryl Churchill and George C.Wolfe, in order to demonstrate how the concept of 'home' becomes impossible when there has been a 'dissolution of [a] homogenous idea of culture' (Chaudhuri 1995: 91). Acknowledging the negative associations in Pinter's *The Homecoming*, she writes, 'America . . . is an abstraction, almost a nonplace. The associations that the characters supply for it conform largely to the stereotype that has existed in Britain since midcentury of America as a technologically advanced but culturally sterile zone of material comfort' (Chaudhuri 1995: 113). The 'stereotype' of America as culturally limited has been similarly perpetuated in Baudrillard's *America*, a philosophical, but largely uncritical response to his experience of travelling across the United States. Attempting to work through his compulsion to theorise this experience, he claims that there is:

> No charm, no seduction in all this. Seduction is elsewhere, in Italy, in certain landscapes that have become paintings, as culturalized and refined in their design as the cities and museums that housed them.

Circumscribed, traced-out, highly seductive spaces where meaning, at these heights of luxury, has finally become adornment. It is exactly the reverse here: there is no seduction, but there is an absolute fascination—the fascination of the very disappearance of all aesthetic and critical forms of life in the irradiation of an objectless neutrality. Immanent and solar. The fascination of the desert: immobility without desire. Of Los Angeles: insane circulation without desire. The end of aesthetics. (Baudrillard 1988: 124)

At times, Maxwell's characters do appear deliberately 'unrefined', however the sense of gregarious humanity within his work celebrates an alternative value-system: that of human affection and personal investment. Baudrillard has asked, '[w]hy do people live in New York? There is no relationship between them. Except for an inner electricity which results from the simple fact of their being crowded together' (Baudrillard 1988: 15). Maxwell can be understood to respond to this question with affection for his fellow Americans. Whether his characters are located in the city or in the suburbs, Maxwell regularly demonstrates profound relationships between characters and the investment they have in the moral and capital wealth of their local community. His characters are often shown to be unable to effect change, but this does not mean to say that they are unwilling or without motivation. For example, the character of 'Wife' in *House* joins a civic group to discuss the building of a new fast-food restaurant on a local road; similarly Fred and Jo-Jo mourn the 'de-struction' of a baseball field in *Boxing 2000* (Maxwell 2004b: 113, 207). Baudrillard's evocation of America is one of superior (if 'fascinated' detachment) and Chaudhuri has charted its adoption as a metaphor for transglobal capitalism and cultural sterility. Maxwell's representation of America breaks with this tradition of distanced description and evokes a sense of this country through a series of often complex and contradictory characters. These characters are customarily blue-collar workers or manual labourers with a modest education. Along a similar trajectory to Forced Entertainment, Maxwell does not write plays about influential, socially mobile decision-makers, but instead creates theatre about lower class, socially constrained characters affected by corporate and legislative decisions.[12]

In Maxwell's work the concept of a heterogeneous America becomes impossible as different voices; both from the city and the suburb compete to communicate their thoughts, and occasionally, feelings about their lives. Augé does not specifically refer to America when describing the phenomenon of supermodernity; however the landscape of 'airports and railway stations, hotel chains, leisure parks, large retail outlets' does resemble America as a pioneer of trans-continental travel and Western global enterprise. His vision of supermodern 'excess' is not reduced to that of the 'non-place', instead he articulates this vision as a way of encouraging us to 'relearn to think about space' . . . 'without treating it as the uncrossable horizon' (Augé

1995: 36, 40). Augé's 'non-places' are characterised by an 'overabundance of events, spatial overabundance and the individualization of reference' whereas his 'anthropological place' is inhabited by a subject who, 'does not make history; he lives in it' (Augé 1995: 55). In parallel to the work of Augé, Maxwell both evokes the repercussions of supermodernity and those seeking to resist the erosion of meaningful cultural exchange.

A number of Maxwell's plays reference the aforementioned, 'airports . . . railway stations, hotel chains, leisure parks,' and 'large retail outlets', the types of location cited by Augé as 'non-places'. Samuel Collins has identified Augé's theory of 'non-place' as 'describ[ing] a situation in which these [people] have been dispersed and . . . act fundamentally alone without any particular reference to their common history or similar experience, each occupying a discrete seat in the airplane or lane on the highway' (Collins 1996: 5–8). The characters inhabiting such locations in Maxwell's plays are shown to be isolated and without direction, and could be considered victims of 'supermodernity' (Augé 1995: 30). Augé argues that, 'non-places mediate a whole mass of relations, with the self and with others, which are only indirectly connected with their purposes. As anthropological places create the organically social, so non-places create solitary contractuality' (Augé 1995: 94). *Flight Courier Service* (1997) sees a hapless young man fall into life as an international drug mule. His air stewardess describes the 'crappy little room' in Times Square that she 'barely sees for 3 days a week' when she is home, as her time at home is spent sleeping.' She also complains that 'this job takes up all my life on a plane to someplace in Asia where I end up being 80 per cent of the time. Living out of a suitcase. I mean, no offense . . . but I hate Malaysia' (Maxwell 2004b: 39). *Billings* (1996) is set partly on an Amtrak train and features a couple and their removal team transporting their furniture from Billings to Minneapolis. They move from one apparently identical city to another hoping for difference, only to move into a house half the size of the one they left, immobilised by the offloaded furniture which has been carelessly crammed into their new, under-size home. The character indicated as 'Man' projects his imagined impression of Minneapolis: 'I try to think about what it looks like there. I try to picture it in my mind . . . It's hard. I see lots of tall buildings. I wonder if that's right. I see lots of streets. I see lots of lights. I wonder if that's right' (Maxwell 2004b: 10).

Burger King is set, as one might expect in a hamburger restaurant, and managed by an unusually positive and philanthropic manager who encourages his staff to 'think about the food we make in regards to the community . . . The consumer—in the larger sense nourished by us. By you and by me. Our food going out, entering the community' (Maxwell 2004b: 58). In amongst lines of dialogue typifying trivial jargon and casual slang are exchanges that reveal a surprising depth of feeling. Chubby Bef, a character from *Burger King*, voices her concern about worker's rights and creates a list of demands for her manager. Her list prompts Sherry to respond:

Where is there a place where someone can't always do our jobs for lower pay? Name one. They start at $5.15. You don't want to work for that? That's okay. We'll pay $4.75. And they will. And people will work for it. Mexicans or whatever. (Maxwell 2004b: 63)

This speech brings the under represented experience of the 'working poor' and US immigrants to light. In their discussion of American Frontier Culture John A. Agnew and Joanne P. Sharp point to the widening gap between rich and poor in the mid 1970s as a contributing factor towards America's sense of itself as a 'victory culture'. They observe that:

The American Dream of equal opportunity and progress for all faces significant challenge when the model can no longer function to generate increased incomes for more than a minority of the population. (Agnew and Sharp 2002: 95)

Maxwell does indeed situate his plays in the type of 'non-places' Augé imagines, however his characters are not typical of the customers or user-groups whose identities, Augé suggests, are temporarily erased; rather Maxwell's characters are the workers supporting the service industry. The comparison of Augé and Maxwell's work reveals the bourgeois bias in Augé's own work, which limits its reference to the people populating 'non-places' as 'customers, passengers, users, listeners'—people who have disposable income available to use these facilities rather than the people who turn to them in order to sell their labour and subsequently generate income (Augé 1995: 111). Augé's theory of non-place is certainly useful to read alongside Maxwell's depiction of fictional locations, as it provides a pertinent way of describing these settings as 'supermodern' and frames his characters as victims of 'supermodernity'; however my sense is that Augé's text retains traces of the cultural superiority found in Baudrillard and creates an uneasy distinction between the kind of meaningful cultural exchange he considers might take place in European market-places and the depersonalising experience of transit hubs and service facilities. He dwells upon the depersonalising experience of using the service or transport facilities without attending to the experience of the workers providing the service. Maxwell, by contrast, regularly takes the experience of the workers as his central theme and creates scenarios which reveal characters attempting to hold on to a notion of America as a 'victory culture' whilst acknowledging the hand that fate has dealt them in providing the service industry as a means of employment.

Showcase (2003) contains a similarly sympathetic portrayal of a character's ambivalence about his job. It takes the form of a site-specific piece, located and set in a hotel room. A salesman talks to his shadow (a figure 'literalised' by an actor completely clad in black) describing an emotional and spiritual malaise brought on, in part, by the illness he is experiencing.

He appears isolated and trapped in his hotel room, describing how 'dry' he finds the air and his penchant for turning out his lights in order to observe the people in other rooms:

> All alone in the dark, all I want is to be alone and watch other people in THEIR room. I'm the guy who turns out the lights to watch the other rooms. If you turn out the light here you create a one-way mirror. People can't see you but you can see them. When I close the door, I know I am alone.[13]

His temporary inability to leave the room leaves him robbed of purpose and identity; he prides himself on his expertise in manipulating people and brokering deals, but makes it clear that,

> We're not going to make deals in the hotel room. They're made out in the city. Out in the open. On grass. On concrete. Out on the streets, in other buildings back rooms and churches. They happen of their own accord. They go by feeling and intuition.[14]

The salesman's description of where deals are brokered and his meditation on his solitude in the hotel room correspond with Augé's description of 'solitary contractuality' and 'organically social' spaces. The outdoor locations ('anthropological places') are credited with bolstering the salesman's agency in helping close the deals. By contrast, the hotel room has the capacity to diminish his sense of agency, reducing him to a voyeur, invisible behind his window. Although the salesman is accompanied in the small hotel room by an audience, whom he directly addresses towards the start of the piece, and his shadow, who is literalised through the body of another actor wearing a black body stocking from head to foot, his monologue betrays an extreme sense of solitude. He alternately confesses to confusion and insecurity about his relationship with a friend/lover, Victor, and his increased sensitivity to other people's pain, 'How come I now feel everyone's pain. I never used to'.[15] Ironically, his view of his relationship with his friends and other colleagues and strangers he comes into contact with appears to be remote. He describes encounters dispassionately, and cuts short his conversational gambit with the audience, disclosing that, 'Well, I'd like to ask where y'all from but I get tired of all the stories. Nobody's really from anywhere anyway anymore'.[16]

Good Samaritans provides a further example of a male character experiencing a kind of involuntary confinement. Kevin, a middle-aged addict has been referred to a rehabilitation centre by a judge. In Maxwell's 2004 production a highly realistic set portrayed a stark, classroom-like setting furnished with utilitarian furniture and industrial cleaning equipment. The text has Kevin describe the centre as 'clean', in contrast to the warehouse he is enlisted to work at. He describes the

Figure 5.1   Jim Fletcher in *Showcase*. (Photo: Unknown.)

view from his small dormitory window as being paradoxically that of 'churches and liquor stores'. Rosemary, the centre head describes her work in pragmatic terms, announcing to Kevin that, 'I don't want you here. You don't want to be here. That's what we have in common'.[17] Relating the highpoints of his gambling career to Rosemary, Kevin recounts the places he has visited:

> We went up and down on boats. 12 miles out NO ONE can touch. I remember Iceland and Asia. Monaco and Park Place. Everywhere I'd go, I'd be like "Look. That's me. I'm crawlin' up the food chain"'.[18]

Rosemary punctures his enthusiasm by reminding him, '[A]nd now you're here', to which he responds, 'And now you're here, too'. Their exchange figures the rehab clinic as a place of low aspiration, a place for people running low on luck, whether attending as a 'client' or social worker. The idea of it being surrounded by 'churches and liquor stores' lends it some poignancy, the buildings represent starkly contrasting pastimes available to the local community. As in the case of the Salesman in *Showcase*, the rehab clinic represents a location of temporarily enforced enclosure for its main character. The action of the play revolves around Kevin's entrances and exits into the clinic as it is being swept, cleaned and organised by Rosemary. Their initially antagonistic relationship mutates into mutual affection and they make love. Rosemary confesses to Kevin that, 'I don't even care who you think you are. If you're a loser, or a coward, or a zero. It makes no difference to me. Because I love you. That's what I do. This is the unalterable universe we come to be and I LOVE you.'[19] Although the rehab clinic could initially be designated a 'non-place', given that it is a space 'formed in relation to certain ends', the value placed on interpersonal support and affection by the character of Rosemary transforms it into an important social place. One of Rosemary's songs has her describe the world as a glass globe, 'spinning like it's spun'. She extorts the audience to 'get off if you don't fit' and not to 'break bones cos' they won't knit'[20] These lyrics provide an insight into a compassionate worldview, which envisions life as a complex and fraught endeavour for even those with the most privileged beginnings. When Kevin returns, after temporarily abandoning Rosemary, he confesses, 'I slipped, baby. . . . I fell off a little bit', referencing her image of the world as a spinning glass globe.[21] As with *Showcase*, there are numerous points of correlation between the location of the play, spatial metaphors embedded within the text and descriptions of the characters' life-stories. Although the rehab clinic could be seen to be a transitory place, where the 'clients' are 'identified (name, occupation, place of birth, address) only on entering or leaving' (Augé 1995: 111) Maxwell animates an otherwise sterile environment by having his characters 'engender the social' and form a meaningful relationship. Furthermore, one of the central characters is shown to have a profound sense of investment in her surroundings, to envision it as a place of healing and nurture. Although the proliferation of non-places such as the rehab clinic could be seen to be symptomatic of the excess and overabundance of supermodernity Maxwell does not construct it as a depersonalising space; on the contrary, it is a place of emotional growth and fulfilment.

The End of Reality mourns explicitly a lost 'anthropological place'. The character of Tom (chief security guard) repeatedly talks about how 'this neighbourhood has changed';[22] how even churches are being demolished to make way for 'hi-rises' and how 'success means a kind of selling out, of being bed-fellows with the same elements that we know will destroy the neighbourhood'.[23] Tom's reference to selling-out represents the most explicit reference to a perceived relationship between personal aspiration and environment in Maxwell's work. The play is located in the foyer of a large office block, described, as mentioned previously, in the promotional material as a 'lobby citadel'. Despite his status as Head of Security, Tom is shown to feel insecure. He acknowledges that, 'a lot of people think because they got a badge like this, (. . .) they can go around like a police officer arresting people'. The status of his job is diminished in relation to that of a police officer. Furthermore, at the outset of the play Tom discusses the possibility of his appearing as an extra in a film with Brian. He says. 'I think that would be so great. Just so there's some record that I was here. You know? Can you hook me up with that? I was thinking of getting some headshots'.[24] Again, the perceived glamour of the film industry provides a stark point of contrast with Tom's job as a security guard. Later in the play he voices his concern that his police colleagues will ridicule him for not being able to restrain the intruder: 'the law enforcement community is laughin at me? . . . can't we detain people?'[25] He also feels the need to remind Brian that he is in charge: 'Why is it I always have this question in my head when I talk to you? . . . Who's in charge. Do you think you're in charge?'[26] The arrival of Tom's God-daughter provides further insight into his diminished sense of self-worth. She draws a picture of his home life:

> He misses the old people. He watches Seinfeld every weeknight. Dotes on his cat. Needs distractions like his email and his phone. But no one is mailing him. And no one is calling him. . . . He took me to Letterman. And he came back an audience hero. He's like, "I was in the audience!" . . . You have to realize. He is living that half-aware, medicated or otherwise drugged out existence . . . [27]

Tom's immediate environment, that of his place of work, appears to have contributed to a diminished sense of self-esteem. This impression is reinforced during the play as a member of his team is abducted and he is repeatedly provoked by a criminal gang. His sense of feeling 'untethered' and off-balance is also undermined by his sense of change in his local neighbourhood. In addition to the bulldozing of churches he perceives a diminished sense of community and a reluctance to aim high aspirationally. In a speech that 'goes out to the angels of the old neighborhood' he claims that:

> We are afraid of success and that fear takes on very real proportions, being as close as we are to—rubbing elbows with the famous and important. Success means a kind of selling out. Of being bed-fellows with the same elements that we know will destroy the neighborhood. . . . We remember times when there was a real community here. A community that manifested out of a kind of necessity of survival. . . . In the old neighborhood, you have to pay homage, show respect, show your face now and then, show that you haven't forgotten, where you came from and how you got to where you are now.[28]

Tom's perception of change identifies a shift in values, he points to a different way of 'tallying' values in his family. His anecdote about the local church being destroyed to create space for a high rise building acts as a further allegory for a shift in values away from moral and spiritual concerns to a capitalist drive for profit. Throughout the play there is a close relationship between Tom's diminished self-esteem and the changes to the landscape of the city. As with the salesman in *Showcase* and the character of Donald in *Burger King* Tom has a sense of deep investment in his work despite the

pervasive sense of emptiness and frustration he experiences. The steadfast-
ness of their collective faith in the redemptive potential of work exemplifies a deeply entrenched faith in what we might refer to as 'the American
Dream', 'an ideology which stresses that anyone can be successful given
hard work, luck and unintrusive government' (Agnew and Sharp 1989: 83).
These characters experience a sense that their value systems are out of kilter
with a changing cultural landscape, but they are reluctant to confront the
idea that their faith in equal opportunity may be unfounded.

As previously mentioned, a number of social commentators have
observed a diminishing sense of 'triumph' for America since the end of the
twentieth century (Agnew and Smith 2002: viii) arising from the apparent
need for the population to begin to 'renegotiate' a sense of national identity (Agnew and Sharp 2002: 97). Tom Engelhardt partly attributes this
blow to America's self-image to the defeat in Vietnam and the end of the
Cold War, which left the United States with no singular, readily identifiable
enemy (Engelhardt 1995). Similarly, according to Agnew and Sharp 'the
end of victory culture' has come about:

> . . . because the United States has become less distinctive in terms of its
> self-defined virtues—individual liberty, wealth and democratic institu-
> tions—and more distinctive in respect of its historic vices—impover-
> ishment, violence and crass vulgarity. (2002: 84)

Other commentators identify a troubling of America's identity with Frederick Jackson Turner's proclamation that, 'as of the 1890s the historical
American frontier was settled' (Mogen, Busby and Bryant 1989: 28); so in
order to continue its 'Manifest Destiny', to seek out new frontiers and maintain its national identity America needed to 'invent a new, post-hegemonic
purpose and vision' (Agnew and Smith 2002: x). The end of victory culture
had, according to Agnew and Sharp, 'a profound effect on the national
psyche. . . . The personal identities of many American men were particularly affected' (Agnew and Sharp 2002: 96). Although I do not necessarily
believe that Maxwell intends his characters to deliberately and symboli-
cally represent a national sensibility, this call for a re-imagined sense of
national identity in a 'post-hegemonic' age does provide a pertinent lens
through which to read his work. Many of the male characters discussed so
far hold onto the myth of the American Dream, insofar as it promises that
hard work and a sense of civic pride will reap rewards; however they also
find themselves in social environments and locations which cause them to
doubt the actual potential of their upward mobility.

The imaginary landscape of the Western frontier has been widely
employed in American literature as a metaphor for the American Dream.
Mark Busby, David Mogen and Paul Bryant conjecture that, 'historically,
the frontier mythology has created a symbolic vocabulary that has been
employed to express and interpret the American Dream, to articulate,

examine and criticize American values' (Mogen, Busby and Bryant 1989: 4). Charting the hold the concept has on the imaginations of the American people, they explain that the concept of the frontier:

> . . . begins with a sense of wonder at the infinite possibilities in the expanding world of the Renaissance explorers, for the frontier as the margin of the known opened the possibility of wonders in the unknown. The frontier as the limit of the settled and developed offered the possibility of new land, new resources, seemingly inexhaustible, yet to be gained. (Busby, Mogen and Bryant 1989: 4)

The myth of the American Dream and the opportunities offered by the untamed West reoccur more obviously in three of Maxwell's plays explicitly located on the frontier. *Cowboys and Indians, The Frame,* and *Ode to the Man who Kneels* feature characters who journey, or who live on a Western settlement. As with examples of Maxwell's work discussed above, environment has a significant bearing upon the characters' sense of opportunity. The frontier initially offers the promise of discovery and a new beginning to the Westward-bound but towards the close of each piece the characters have found themselves troubles and difficulties anew.

According to Agnew and Sharp:

> The mindset of limitless possibility was reinforced by the frontier experience of individual social mobility, of the energy of a youthful country in contrast to the social stagnation and economic inequality of "old" Europe. Americans were free to set themselves up in the vast expanse of "empty" land available on the frontier, discounting the presence of natives whose self-evident technological and religious "backwardness" justified the expropriation of their land. All settlers were equal on the frontier, so the myth goes . . . (Agnew and Sharp 2002: 83)

The opportunities offered by the frontier for reinvention and personal growth feature in both *The Frame* and *Cowboys and Indians. Cowboys and Indians* was based loosely on Francis Parkman's book *The Oregon Trail, The Conspiracy of Pontiac* (1849). Parkman himself is realised as an upper-class Harvard graduate who has unrealistic ideas about his own prowess as a leader. His language and attitude reference 'old' European values, speaking in a quasi-Elizabethan prose, 'Damn but my spirits run high!'[29] and belittling his companion, 'Is this an open forum? Captain? I thought I had the floor'.[30] Although his interest is apparently academic, his attitude towards the 'Natives' is one of a tourist and he appears to experience such a violent epiphany in the company of a Native American Chief that he returns to civilisation wheel-chair bound and 'raving'. *Cowboys and Indians'* 'universe of paradox', (as described by critic Peter Marks), sees the characters of Francis and the Indian Chief failing to communicate despite sharing the same language. Incongruously, the Chief speaks a fluent contemporary American argot in contrast to Francis' rather rhetorical style of speech; he also mis-remembers Francis' surname, variously referring to him as, 'Parkham', 'Parkshaw' and 'Parkingson'. An apparently ironic speech has the Chief confess to Francis:

> Speaking for myself, I have loved the whites since the first day I saw them. Yes. They seemed to be the wisest people on earth. I believed they could do anything. Well, I am always glad when any of them come to live in our lodges. . . . You have come far on horseback. It is clear that you like us, or you never should have come so far to find our village . . .[31]

The paradox of his having travelled such a long distance to find the savages 'civilized' is lost on Parkman, who does not appear to take on board the real meaning of the Chief's words. Instead he continues speaking as if the Chief intends to kill him:

> I don't care if you kill me. I'm ready for anything you can give out! If this be my fate, so be it. If this is the place then this is the place. I never thought the place would look like this but how can you know? How can you know?[32]

In this speech, place and destiny are inextricably entwined. Regardless of the absurdity of his encounter with the Chief, Parkman responds as if he has achieved a moment of self-realisation. Parkman's tourist mindset filters out what he deems inappropriate to the surroundings leaving him to dwell on his own version of his encounter with the Chief as the apotheosis of his frontier experience. He returns to civilisation having suffered the 'grief' of madness, destined for an Infirmary and finds Imogene's affections transferred to another. The final speech of the play features him disclosing his intention to write a book about the Indian wars. This vision of the West, albeit a pastiche of the tradition, does bear many of the features of 'the frontier myth' as repeated in the American literary canon. Mark Busby suggests that, ' . . . the wilderness offers the possibility of individual freedom, where individuals can test their sense of self against nature without the demand for social responsibility and the compromise of being part of a community' (Mogan, Busby and Bryant 1989: 96). Parkman, in Maxwell and Strah's play returns to civilisation as if he has tested his 'sense of self', however the main body of the play has shown him struggle to leave the values and social responsibilities of his community behind.

Central characters in *The Frame* also evoke 'old' Europe, being immigrants setting out from 1850s Prussia. Whilst at home, the family had been forced to move from their farm to a more urban area. Mentis, the drunken father of the family, became disillusioned with the parochial community in which they found themselves. The play shows him consumed by desire to make the journey to America, fantasising about the new opportunities this move would afford. However, before he can make the journey he murders the town dentist and is publicly hung for his crime. The remaining family (grandmother, daughter, granddaughter and son) make the journey across the Atlantic and arrive to a reception committee made up of well-meaning philanthropists and already established immigrants. They prepare to join the 'westering' party in search of farmland. Minna tells Munoz Teddy, 'We're poor farmers. We need land to work. That's what we understand. We understand there is land for the takin' out west. We need a lot of land'.[33] However, rather than achieve their dreams, as with the case of Parkman's entourage, the family starts to fragment. The granddaughter (who is thought to have spiritual insight) dies soon after arriving in America, the son remains behind to organise the funeral, and the mother and daughter head out west, accompanied only by a tour-guide. The daughter meets and falls in love with a farmer, Dan, an industrious and devout farmer, leaving the grandmother to return back to their point of arrival alone. The character of the farmer, Dan describes the 'wild' land he has inherited from his father:

> Vast land—took my father's whole life to capture—look, as far as the eye can see (even past those buttes). Feels wide open? Perhaps. But I need it. I need all of it. God gave this to me. Father's land but—I look on it as God's gift, really. And I'll protect it with work til my dying breath.[34]

The closing scene sees the son, Americanized in Brando-esque attire, share his disappointment that he has not become a hero, but is now reduced to stealing and working in a dental machinery factory. The references to dentistry and theft act as a reminder that the son has not achieved any kind of moral or spiritual salvation by travelling to America; by stealing he is no better than his condemned father. America itself, is represented here as a place of opportunity and equality. Willie is scolded for his suspicion of Munoz Teddy's motives towards his sister. He is told to, 'Loosen up. The ladies, when you're—now that you're here. You gotta realize you gotta learn how to treat the ladies. You—here in America. They treat ladies different. You gotta show respect. Show them a nice time'.[35]

The Frame and *Cowboys and Indians* retain many of the values attributed to the mythical West in the tradition of American literature; however the fortunes of their characters depart from convention customarily associated with the frontier paradigm. Characters are shown to remain unenlightened despite their adventures out West. Given that the myth of the American frontier is so deeply entrenched in the national psyche, this could be understood as a critique of the frontier paradigm, and the associated myth of the American Dream. The 'post-hegemonic' vision of America, as perceived by Maxwell appears to be one that argues against the social mobility of American culture and instead reinforces the limitations placed upon the individual by their geographical and social environment.

The frontier landscape featured in *Ode to the Man who Kneels* is dusty, dry and arid. Water, sea, fishes and bathing all reoccur in the fantasies of the characters as they share, confess and sing their aspirations. The settlement in which the characters find themselves is named 'Grid', perhaps an ironic reference to the objective distance of the town-planner's grid. Agnew and Smith point out that, 'space is the abstraction of places into a grid or coordinate system as if the observer is "outside it" or looking down at the world from above (Agnew and Smith 2002: 4). This sense of observers being 'outside' of their settlement reoccurs throughout the play as characters regularly describe the actions they perform in the third person. For example, in the opening lines The Standing Man says, 'Two men are 15 feet apart. The man on the left is standing. The man on the right is kneeling. The standing man is pointing a revolver at the kneeling man. He gives the Kneeling Man a drink from his canteen'.[36]

Maxwell's use of language in this play is highly poetic and densely metaphorical. Dialogue and songs reveal characters adapting to the harsh frontier conditions by fostering an ideology of expediency: they lie, they kill, and switch loyalties in order to survive. The need to 'persevere' and 'endure' are repeated by characters throughout the play. The images of aridity, water

Figure 5.2   Brian Mendes, Anna Kohler, Jim Fletcher and Greg Mehrten in *Ode to the Man Who Kneels*. (Photo: Michael Schmelling.)

and heartbreak are repeated throughout the play, featured both in song and confession. The Waiting Woman describes Grid as a town in decline:

> At one time, Grid was a private paradise mysterious and unknown with gardens and street lamps entered full of possibility. Now, you might find 4 souls in totality. It's all dried up, I'm afraid. This drought that doesn't end.[37]

Further references to drought come from The Dashing Man, who confesses to his lover, The Waiting Woman that, 'I no longer produce fluids from sex acts. Ejaculate with nothing. Nothing is there! O God! It's dry. Curse this drought'.[38] During a nostalgic ballad, the Waiting Woman charts the passage of time and its effect upon her environment:

> And time goes by
> Your sea is dried
> And the Earth cracks apart
>
> The town it falls
> All roofs and walls
> In caves darkest parts
>
> All streams and things
> White fishes bring
> No eyes and they're old
>
> Still further down
> (You're falling down)
> The water gets cold.[39]

In contrast to aridity the characters repeat references, (as in The Waiting Woman's song) to images of water, bathing, sea, fishes and tears. The Standing Man takes the role of narrator at the outset of the piece, revealing that, 'While under the earth there is a labyrinth of cave passages where albino fishes swim with no eyes beneath the sea of dirt';[40] stage directions reveal that 'Tears fall from the face of the Standing man!' and 'The Dashing Man wipes tears from the face of the Standing Man'.[41] In metaphorical terms it would appear that the town is founded on, or has been reduced to 'dirt', whilst 'under the earth' there lies a reservoir or ocean of water. The repeated metaphor of the eyeless and unpigmented fishes hints at a profound darkness, potentially suggesting that the lack of light eradicates the need for eyes, as if the water is sealed off from the light. This inaccessible subterranean water supply haunts the characters in *Ode to the Man who Kneels*, representing an ever-present but unrealisable promise. Similar to the characters of *The Frame* and *Cowboys and Indians* the characters in *Ode to the Man who Kneels* are haunted by the possibility of renewal in the West. Without water opportunities for survival, despite the casts' best promises to 'endure' are limited; they remain in a kind of purgatory of murder, abandonment and heartbreak. As in *The Frame*, and *Cowboys and Indians*, the characters appear to find no joy in their Western habitat. These images of the West deconstruct a tradition which has represented the frontier as, 'the gateway through which one might escape from time into space, from bounds to boundlessness and from the works of God into uncorrupted nature' (Mogen, Busby and Bryant 1989: 5). J. Chris Westgate has suggested that Shepard's invocation of the American West in plays such as *Curse of the Starving Class (1978)*, *Buried Child (1978)* and *True West (1980)* is similarly ambiguous, being 'associated with decay, trauma, loss and regret' (Westgate 2005: 728). He argues that Shepard's plays are much more 'nuanced and paradoxical' than many critics have allowed for, and that whilst his male characters do manifest a nostalgia for the mythic ideal of the nineteenth-century West; Shepard's attitude towards the West does not lend any insight into his own state of being. Maxwell has cited Shepard as an influence on his work and it is perhaps in his plays which offer both a homage and a critique of the Western frontier that this is most visible (Wessendorf 2001: 439).

The interrelationship between environment and opportunity is marked repeatedly in Maxwell's work, particularly in relation to labour and social mobility. His plays feature would-be musicians, social workers, cowboys, soldiers, security guards, provincial characters who attempt to eke a living in a global capitalist society. His characters live with the internalised mind-set of political equality and the apparently 'limitless possibility' consolidated in the popular imagination by the Western frontier and the American Dream (Agnew and Sharp 2002: 83). However, the low-status nature of their jobs subconsciously impinges upon their sense of self-esteem, opportunity and fulfilment. Even when supposedly freed from social responsibility, the cowboys and West-farers find their opportunities for reinvention and self-fulfilment thwarted. According to Mark Busby, as part of 'the frontier paradigm, '[a]n innocent figure (or more likely an ignorant one) undergoes an initiatory experience that grows out of the elements he confronts in the transformed wilderness he faces (Mogen, Busby and Bryant 1989: 98). Maxwell's characters, cowboys and workers alike are not presented with the excitement of an 'initiatory experience'. Given the break with canonical tradition, I want to situate Maxwell's work as resisting established ideas about equality and the freedom of opportunity in contemporary America. Characters buoyed up with a sense of philanthropy and civic pride are shown to suffer extreme anxiety or find their aspirations swallowed up within the larger structures of their corporation. This attention to service-industry occupations and 'blue-collar' employment points to an interest in the now outmoded concept of the 'working class' and a desire to explore the ramifications of under-represented labour. These occupations represent low-status and low-paid jobs in a culture which has experienced, since the 1970s, an increased disparity between rich and poor. Agnew and Sharp refer to the 'working poor' to describe, 'this segment of the population, employed overwhelmingly in the service and retail sectors'. This section of the population, 'experienced rising incomes from 1966 to 1978 but since 1986 experienced both a jump in numbers and a drop in incomes' (Agnew and Sharp 2002: 95). They contend that:

> . . . the setting of wages at the lowest-cost location without attending to the collective consequences for Americans of expanding production overseas without commensurate increases in the earnings capacity for American consumption is seen as a violation of the American promise to its own population. (Agnew and Sharp 2002: 103)

Maxwell's characters appear to have internalised this aspect of the 'American promise' as enshrined in the Constitution and live in faithful expectation that the government have their best interests at heart. However, their lives are shadowed by a sense of unease; of untapped promise and opportunity despite the acceleration and excesses of supermodernity which appear to offer abundant opportunities for adventure and success. They do not voice a sense of this 'violation'; however they are shown to experience a sense of conflict as their own pragmatic sense of what they can achieve falls short of the American Dream's promise of equality and social mobility.

It is significant that, in production, Maxwell strives to retain the marks of labour behind the mounting of each show. His anti-immanentist rehearsal aesthetic challenges assumptions associated with mainstream realist theatre that the fictional world of the play and the 'real' world of the auditorium remain distinct. By refusing to employ the process of 'denegation', which invites audiences to temporarily 'forget' or dismiss extra diegetic information, Maxwell foregrounds the activity of theatre-making and theatre-going as part of social process, as having, as Ubersfeld would have it, 'consequences outside the configuration of the stage space' (Ubersfeld 1996: 23). The slippage between the hermeneutic world of the plays and the auditorium invites a reconceptualisation of the theatre as a place of 'socio-political commentary' (McAuley 1999: 18) and, in Augé's terms, an 'anthropological place'.

6 Conclusion
Inscrutability, Irony and Binary Assignations

My project for this book set out to interrogate a repeated set of concerns identified within the work of Richard Maxwell and the New York City Players. Key themes and ideas emerging for me included: human vulnerability and exposure; the demystification of the illusion of agency and the compulsion and attendant impossibility of performing 'appropriately' in an age of multiplied subject positions. Looking back over the chapters exploring masculinity, the American Dream, non-places and historiography I recognise that my readings have been driven by a certainty that there are many hidden or sublimated meanings to be excavated by detailed interrogation. In my drive to uncover ideologically resistant or anti hegemonic interpretations I have inevitably held back from acknowledging the many different levels at which Maxwell's work can function; that for many, his plays are primarily entertaining because they are funny, or because his songs are uplifting. In terms of form, his plays do tend to observe Todorovian rules of narrative and establish a scene of equilibrium, disruption and a return to equilibrium (Kozloff 1992: 69) and so subsequently can be seen to offer the 'solace of good forms' Lyotard identifies in the realist narrative (Lyotard 1979: 81). In contrast to many of his experimental peers, there is scope here to enjoy Maxwell's work in a comparatively conventional manner; indeed, the pleasurable nature or even the cultural import of the work of NYCP does not necessarily lie in its subversive potential. One might argue that there is sufficient ambiguity about Maxwell's approach that it is impossible to ascertain accurately whether his intention is to be subversive at all.

A number of critics have identified a certain level of irony in his work, and if we take that to mean that there is a disjunction between *what* is explicitly presented, and *how* it is presented, then there does appear to be congruence between irony and what I have been discussing as the intra and extra diegetic signs deployed within Maxwell's productions. For Linda Hutcheon irony is a 'mode of discourse' which enables a receiver or interpreter to discern some kind of presentational attitude *in addition to* the presentation itself. She writes:

[f]rom the point of view of the *interpreter*, irony is an interpretive and intentional move. It is the making or inferring of *meaning* in addition to and different from what is stated, together with an *attitude* toward both the said and the unsaid. The move is usually triggered (and then directed) by conflictual textual or contextual evidence or by markers which are socially agreed upon. However, from the point of view of what I too (with reservations) will call the *ironist*, irony is the intentional transmission of both information and evaluative attitude other than what is explicitly presented. (Hutcheon 1995: 11, original emphasis)

Several of the more sceptical New York theatre critics have described Maxwell's work in terms of an irony they recognise to be characteristic of the downtown theatre scene. As quoted elsewhere, Michael Feingold has described Maxwell as, 'an anti-phony phony for smart-set cynics' (Feingold 2003). Thinking along similar lines, Brian Walsh dismissed audience members who found *Henry IV Part 1* to be ironic (and amusing) as 'avant garde cheerleaders who have no real critical interest in a given show, but rather go out of their way to demonstrate their sophistication by laughing uproariously at any perceived moment of unconventionality' (Walsh 2004: 103). Acknowledging a similarly ironic impulse between Maxwell and Cannon Company's Richard Kimmel, Daniel Mufson has recalled the 'irony and intellectual detachment' in both artists' work:

Each one has acknowledged that a certain level of irony is essential in creating artistic work of integrity today; at the same time, each has expressed frustration with an irony that suffocates emotion or undermines the idea of emotional genuineness or authenticity. (Mufson 2004: 266)

Irony, as a method of communication is considered to activate a mode of reading whereby the interpreter can distinguish between what is stated and what is implied. Readers identify an additional layer of signification which implicitly signals the transmitter's attitude towards what is explicitly stated. This reflexive or meta-critical technique has been discussed as an ideal form for a postmodern age, an age which relativises values traditionally associated with the real (as truthful) and the represented (as fictional or false). Lehmann has identified 'irony' or 'coolness' as a key feature of postdramatic theatre, he writes:

[p]laying with coldness constitutes one of the significant traits of postdramatic theatre. We repeatedly come across a tendency towards 'disinvolvement' and ironic, sarcastic distance. Moral indignation does not take place where it would have been expected; likewise dramatic excitation is lacking, even though reality is depicted in ways that are obviously hard to bear. (Lehmann 2006: 118)

Maxwell himself has stated that, 'for me, it's always more interesting when the sincerity outweighs the irony' (Maxwell and Mendes 2006: 352). He has also distanced himself from an ironic, or parodic mode of presentation:

> [I]rony is parody, which is only interesting to you and is only so interesting. A lot of people think that parody is fine in and of itself. That it's sufficient in terms of a performance, its performative value. But I don't think it is. It's not going to be interesting, for that long anyway, if it stays in the realm of parody. (Maxwell and Mendes 2006: 352)

There is a tension then, between those who align Maxwell's work with the 'cool eclecticism' of a downtown theatre aesthetic (Sellar 2010) and those who identify a drive to provoke genuine emotional engagement. The often-repeated designation of 'deadpan' to describe a 'trademark' acting style reinforces the notion that the majority of critics see a disjuncture between the material presented and Maxwell's attitude to the material. An entry discussing *Ads* in the *New York Times Arts Beat* blog insisted however that sincerity does outweigh parody for AndrewAndrew, 'it's light years from being ironic; the audience actually finds itself identifying with a hologram. It's a true testament to the people involved in this production that a parlour trick on an empty stage could move you to the brink of tears' (ArtsBeat 2010).

Hutcheon argues that irony is not a 'static rhetorical tool to be deployed' but rather 'comes into being in the relations between meanings, but also between people and utterances and sometimes, between intentions and interpretations' (Hutcheon 1995:13). Furthermore, irony has the potential to be *transideological* because it can be provocative when discussing conservative politics and authoritarian when the politics evoked are oppositional or subversive. For Hutcheon, '[t]he transideological politics of irony at once force a distinction between irony that might function constructively to articulate a new oppositional position, and irony that would work in a more negative and negativizing way' (Hutcheon 1995: 16). Citing Ross Chambers, Hutcheon suggests that an oppositional irony would 'target the system' of oppression by 'us[ing] that system, with all the play the system allows, to produce different ends, that is, to change the products of the system, even if changes can only be local and sporadic' (Chambers quoted in Hutcheon 1995: 17). An oppositional irony uses the system without presuming to stand outside of it, whereas a more negative, conservative irony would adopt 'a point of view exterior to the system . . . in a position of power.' Hutcheon's expanded definition of irony provides a useful way of understanding the presence of irony within Maxwell's work. Although it is difficult to establish a uniformity of approach, I imagine that Sellars' 'avant-garde cheerleaders' laughed most uproariously at pieces such as *Showy Lady Slipper, Boxing 2000, Drummer Wanted* and *House,* pieces created between 1998 and 2002. These pieces have the potential to be understood as light-hearted and humorous. The characters speak using the cadence and vernacular of contemporary American speech and discuss seemingly inane subjects such as horse riding; realising dreams; getting a job and music concerts. The stillness of the actors onstage and their marked emotional restraint signal that there is a disjuncture here between the lines being recited and the attitude of presentation. According to Hutcheon, in order to test the progressive or reactionary potential of this ironic attitude we need to firstly identify 'the system' under scrutiny and then read the playwright's relationship to 'the system'. As I have argued throughout the volume, I consider Maxwell to be writing from a post or anti-humanist perspective, so for me, his 'system' is the heteronormative discourse which compels subjects to behave appropriately according to class, gender, ethnicity without considering the harm dominant social forces impose. In order to test his sincerity, Hutcheon would have us measure his relationship to the work. Does he speak from a presumed position of authority, distancing himself from the system, or does he speak with a sense of emotional investment? In these particular examples, where the characters are largely shown to be emotionally expressive through song or combat, it is easy to see a potential to interpret the work as patronising, as if Maxwell has put unschooled actors on stage in order to become objects of ridicule or representing characters limited by intelligence rather than opportunity. However, the repetition of vulnerability as a sign transmitted through the actor's performance and as a sign transmitted through characterisation, for me, overrides any suggestion of stupidity. Furthermore, as I mentioned in the Preface, Maxwell repeatedly demonstrates an interest in the lives of blue-collar workers and, what he describes in *Das Maedchen* as the 'clean, hard-working, middle class' (Maxwell 2010). He is interested in people who invest a great deal of energy and commitment into low-skilled jobs and bestows his characters with details of favourite pastimes; frustrations about the difficulty of family relationships; favourite objects and memories. This detail evidences a genuine sense of affection, rather than a distance or sense of superiority.

As I have suggested, Maxwell's stance is often inscrutable, for those (myself included) who want to claim his work as ideologically progressive, certain aspects of his characters' dialogue, by necessity, *need* to be read as 'ironic'. For example, I interpret the sexist language used by the movers in *Billings* as ironic, and I assume that the playwright has a critical relationship to these values: he is including them as an aspect of characterisation in order to show the character to be sexist. Maxwell has also included what might be considered risqué statements about race and sexuality which, if not understood as 'ironic' could well be considered offensive to an audience familiar with the discourses of multiculturalism and political correctness. In *The End of Reality*, Tom's (scripted as '1') assailants initiate a conversation about race and ethnicity. The characters of Tom and Alex (scripted as

'3' and '4') are played by Thomas Bradshaw and Alex Delinois, both black actors; the character of Jim is played by Jim Fletcher, a white actor. They hold the following exchange:

> 1: Yeah. Where do I know you from?
> 3: Yeah?
> 1: Where are you from?
> 4: don't matter.
> 1: I know this person. I know you. Where do I know you from?
> 3: I know where I come from.
> 1: Africa right?
> 4: Ohhh!!!!
> 1: Isn't that where we all come from?
> 3: What the fuck did you say?
> 1: I said that we all come from Africa anyway.
> 4: Oh!
> 3: Is that right? Hey . . . (walks up to him) I don't come from Africa. Look at me. Do I look like we came from Africa?
> 1: Well . . .
> 3: No no no. Lemme tell you. *I* didn't come from Africa. You got that?
> 4: No, this guy is talking about that scene from True Lies? Did you see that movie? The guy is like gonna die and so he says, you're Sicilian right, and the guy is like yeah, and the other guys like, you know where Sicilians come from? No. And he says Sicilians have kinky hair and dark skin because the moors came over from Africa and fucked your women, and so your grandmother and shit was fucked by niggers, so you Sicilians are all niggers.
> 6: It's not True Lies.
> 4: What?
> 6: True Lies is Arnold Schwartzenegger.
> 3: Yeah, you're right . . . she's right. Hey- (to 1) You can be from Africa. I'm not from Africa . . . You got that?[1]

Experiencing this scene at The Kitchen, New York, both during rehearsal and in performance, I struggled with a sense of unease as I listened to this exchange. My impression was that fellow audience members were also shocked—I perceived barely audible gasps as the character of 3 (Jim) asserted ' *I* don't come from Africa'. For an educated, middle class, liberal audience, this exchange represents a shockingly reductive attitude towards race, and features a white character (and white actor) attempting to humiliate a black character (and black actor) because of his race. My sense is that a liberal audience would also be familiar with arguments about the representation of racism and sexism appearing to condone, or reinforce conservative values, no matter how ironically they are presented. My impression was that Maxwell *must* be being ironic in writing this scene. I wanted to be able to conceive of this scene as ironic because the alternative would negate my investment in this work as subversive, radical and ideologically progressive. I recall that during rehearsal this scene gave the director pause for thought, and it was erased from the play for several days. Sensing the controversial nature of the scene, Scott Sherratt, who was acting as stage manager for this piece, attempted to get a rise out of Maxwell by offering him $50 to reincorporate the scene after it had been cut from the play. It transpired that Maxwell was not necessarily shying away from the risqué nature of the lines, and the scene was reintegrated primarily because it gave the characters a reason to fight towards the end of the scene (Gorman 2007: 240). In interview Maxwell revealed that attitudes to race did inform *The End of Reality*, and he drew upon ideas from an early play *Ute Mnos vs. Crazy Liquors* (1998), which in turn, was based on a transcript of a real trial about a bar fight (the fight took place between bouncers, one of whom was black, and a white customer). Maxwell came across information in the depositions which revealed that the main character's friend had asked 'what's it like being a nigger in a white man's world?' before punching the black bouncer. Maxwell referred back to this instance whilst discussing *End of Reality*, but revealed

> [t]hat's not the reason I wanted to do the play but it reflects, at least in part, a kind of attitude. Where I grew up, you aren't going to find that many black people. I don't know; it wasn't a conscious thing (for *Ute Mnos*) [But] it was in this play. In *End of Reality* it was conscious, I was thinking about it. So maybe it's the first time I'm consciously thinking about race. But it also came up in *Boxing 2000* too, because I was casting lots of Hispanic people, and being deliberate about that and wanting it to have an outer-borough feeling. (Gorman 2007: 240)

Maxwell's critical relationship to racism revealed in interview provides a context with which to retrospectively confirm that I was right about the ironic intention for this scene. However, I think that the ambiguity of his intention is troubling, in that it might, as it did for *The End of Reality*, encourage a conservative reading, which identifies with the negative values of the scene. *Das Maedchen* shows the character of the 'Father' to hold similarly conservative values, which he imagines as a kind of 'honesty'. The recited narrative reveals that:

> The father gets crazy with his honesty. Too much for his own good. This man who has nothing to lose by being honest. Unnerving in his opinions, people call him racist and sexist, homophobic, Jews running Hollywood. Jews take care of each other. It's just what he observes. Does he believe these things or is he trying to get a reaction, see if you're paying attention. It's ugly, but to him, it's how he feels. He's

being honest. He doesn't account for the anger he feels. He sees nothing but hypocrisy in people. He can't stand that. If black people aren't criminals, why aren't any of you friends with them? Show me your black friends! He sits in the room. His ideas about the world; comfortable, not wealthy. (Maxwell 2009: 9)

The character believes that by actively vocalising his prejudices, he is being 'honest', or true to himself. He is stating what he really believes, rather than engineering a more socially acceptable truth. Maxwell's characterisation, in this instance, does construct the Father as reactionary and acknowledges how such ideas might be received in a contemporary Western context. However, in *People Without History*, Maxwell gives several of his soldiers lines of dubious political intent without such a clear nod of reassurance from a narrator. Alice, a peasant healer, has been captured as a prisoner of war by a group of soldiers returning from the Battle of Shrewsbury. During her time as prisoner she has foraged for food to nourish and heal both captors and fellow prisoners. Mendace, one of her captors demonstrates that he is recovering his strength by saying:

Hey! Rhobert. Where is that woman? Robert! Come here. . . . There she is. Hey. You know we're going to rape you don't you? I just said what everybody's thinking about anyway. What's wrong with that? Everybody's thinking—Why haven't we raped her yet? It's only a matter of time. That's what I think. It's not my fault if I just say it. What's wrong with me if I got the guts to say it that way. I'm just the only one who said it that way.
    Pause
It's all there floating in the air, and I brought words to it, to say it that way. (Maxwell 2009: 78)

Mendace's speech, as with dialogue throughout the play, is written using contemporary American phrasing and rhythms of speech despite being set in 1403. Although Mendace's sentiments are those of an unreconstructed male, no doubt typical of a late Middle Ages soldier, the sense of his need to defend his words seems out of kilter with its historical setting, and more derivative of a contemporary culture of self-reflexivity and political correctness. Again, this is a speech about 'honesty', and as with the Father's speech in *Das Maedchen*, a character verbalises ideas he is confident are shared by others, but whose taboo nature discourage the less forthright characters from articulating. This insight into 'honesty' lends a new perspective to the theme of masculinity, openness and articulation. In previous plays we have seen male characters engaging in mundane conversations about work or sport in order to avoid conversations that might involve emotional revelation, suggesting that much of import goes unspoken. Mendace, in *People without History* however verbalises that which would normally remain unspoken. It is possible to conclude that Mendace's defence of his base inclination represents a way of actively foregrounding or criticising the unpalatable, his defence evidences an acknowledgement of the misogyny inherent in his desire. However, for me, I found even the verbalisation of these thoughts distressing. I recognised that this speech served a function to ground the characters with a certain quasi-realist fictional world, but was shocked that these sentiments had been aired at all. Furthermore, I interpreted Mendace's defensiveness as unapologetic, both on the part of the character and the playwright, an interpretation that went against previous expectation and upset my construction of Maxwell's work as ideologically progressive. Subsequently, I became interested in considering why I felt discouraged from reading this speech as 'ironic'. Certainly, a disparity exists between what is articulated and the way it is articulated and it is also possible to define the value 'system' under scrutiny (that of heteronormative patriarchal discourse). So, according to Hutcheon it should be a fairly straightforward task to analyse the author's relationship to the system, asking once again, does he speak from a presumed position of authority, distancing himself from the system, or does he speak with a sense of emotional investment? Although I would draw upon previous experience to conclude that Maxwell's relationship to these words *must* be ironic, I found this instance troubling because it so closely resembled sexist rhetoric and appeared unapologetic in tone. Hutcheon has warned that one of the shortcomings of irony is the risk of reinforcing, rather than deconstructing a certain value set. She writes, '[i]n the ironic discourse, every position undercuts itself, thus leaving the politically engaged writer in a position where her ironic discourse might "just come to deconstruct her own politics" (Moi quoted in Hutcheon 1995: 16). My sense of disquiet leads me to conclude that Maxwell is more brazen than many of his downtown contemporaries; by allowing such an ambiguity to remain he runs the risk of 'deconstructing' or obscuring his own, more enlightened politics. When questioned about his motivation for giving a voice to a non-liberal position Maxwell responded that he had not been conscious of the repetition of the issue of 'honesty' in his more recent work, but on reflection felt that this drive to resist what he saw to be a New York centric liberalism started with *The End of Reality* and was prompted by a desire to suggest that 'we should not be so quick to call these people idiots, that's what we read in the newspapers—in the *New York Times*'.[2]

Reading around *People Without History*, I am reassured to find extra-textual reassurance that Maxwell intends his attitude towards Mendace's misogyny to be critical. In interview with Liz LeCompte, Maxwell reveals that this play is, 'an indictment of male desire':

[Alice is] a woman because I'm dealing with traditional male desire. And *my* desire. I liked imagining a woman who couldn't give the men what they wanted, even though she may be the last woman on earth.

That's why she changed a lot. That's why she's probably gay. (LeCompte 2009: 73)

The ambiguity of Maxwell's position here perhaps reflects a conscious decision to become more inscrutable. In 2004 Brian Walsh suggested that, 'Maxwell's specialty is a persistent deflation of masculinity' (Walsh 2004: 104), however in his later work (*People Without History, Das Maedchen, Ode to the Man Who Kneels*) his intention to 'deflate' is markedly ambiguous. It is possible that this is due to a deliberately renewed relationship to irony, as if Maxwell is driven to obscure any easy understanding of the work as 'ironic' or deconstructive. The representation of women within his work has customarily been sympathetic; with female characters shown to be articulate and motivated (in contrast to the inertia of their husbands or boyfriends), and capable of meaningful friendships and emotional exchange. When wives or girlfriends have swapped allegiance between male partners (as in *House* and *Cavemen*), the humorous potential has been exaggerated by a rapidity which undercut any attempt to judge them as perfidious. The rapidity and thoughtlessness of their exchange of allegiance is so exaggerated that it foregrounds the futility of attempting to believe in them as psychologically-rounded, believable characters. However, in a piece such as *Ode the Man Who Kneels*, the more serious tone of the piece, and the extended exchange between the two female characters results in, what for me is a troubling ambiguity about Maxwell's intention in representing two, almost archetypal characters. As discussed previously, the play is set in a Frontier town named Grid. Residents include 'the Dashing Man', the store proprietor and 'the Waiting Woman' (also known as Mo) who 'talks endlessly about the man who will never arrive'. The eponymous Kneeling Man dies early on in the piece, having been shot by the Standing Man, a vigilante cowboy looking to recruit fellow warriors in town. Mid-way through the piece Juny arrives, coming to take ownership of land she has inherited. Stage directions indicate that 'she is younger than the other girl . . . she talks about animals. And stutters. Stumbles, she has a remarkable gift for not saying anything'.[3] Towards the beginning of the piece the Waiting Woman invites the Dashing Man 'into her bedchambers' and they become a couple. However, the Standing Man shows an interest in her and asks the Dashing Man to pass on his portrait to her. The Dashing Man reiterates his attachment to the Waiting Woman (who, in the intervening minutes has become his wife) telling him, 'I'm pretty relaxed about your flirtation with my wife'. The Standing Man kills the Dashing Man and 'walks into Mo's house'. After a fiery exchange, in which Mo reminds her new suitor that he 'stinks' and is barely worthy of her attention, the couple embrace. Mo has executed a change in amorous allegiance with the rapidity featured in *Caveman* and *House*, but it is not marked by the same humour. In the absence of extra-textual information about his attitude towards the change in allegiance we are left to interpret it either as evidence of the essential perfidy of womankind or as an act of utilitarian necessity.

Elsewhere the Waiting Woman (Mo) is constructed as an ideal wife or partner. She is venerated for her empathy; the Dashing Man proclaims that:

> I sing for her and her alone. The woman here reads your mind. That woman is the woman you saw in the window. Every man who lives or even passes through is ready to give everything, his life in order to have her! You see? Imagine—she can read your mind. What a relief that is.[4]

The attraction Mo holds for 'every man who lives' constructs her as an unworldly ideal, as if she is the representation of an ideal femininity rather than a character in her own right. Her attraction takes on seemingly mythical proportions as male characters are willing to kill in order to be with her. The poetic, sombre tone of this play does nothing, in my mind, to enable us to find signs of an ironic incursion into the rhetoric of the fiction. The figure of the Waiting Woman is constructed so as to appear archetypal. When joined by Juny, despite her insistence that, 'you and I, we will not be pitched into binary assignations', the Waiting Woman is further reinscribed in terms of her sexual appeal by being constructed as too old to 'ride around with boys in auto-mobiles'. Juny asks her to 'give up' waiting, to consider how she appears to others:

> Madam. The eyes have died. Though not old. Can you feel your self disappear? Can you feel your self disappear in the eyes of others? What did doubt do? It gave a clear attitude no matter how mundane. I want you to—to give up. I watched my mother. Waited, for my mother to give up. She had dreams of achieving too. But. She's no good. Please, give up, I say. Give up now.

Having asked Mo to 'give up', Juny then meets the Standing Man and 'climbs into his arms'. She distances herself from Mo by saying:

> I don't care. She's like those kind of women. They're so nice, you take advantage of them. They have no principles. You cannot offend them because they have no principles. No principle other than their own pleasure. You can say anything you want about her 'cause eventually it will be true!

Mo is given assertive lines of dialogue which lend her some measure of resistance against the 'assignations' of Juny and the Standing Man, however these do not hold sufficient power to subvert the more conservative constructions of femininity mobilised elsewhere. A conservative gender politics is referenced through Juny's reminder that it is inappropriate for an older woman to show herself to be sexually active or available and through Juny's lack of loyalty to Mo, despite having tended her whilst ill. Although it may appear misguided to make judgements about character, in a piece which so clearly eschews psychologically rounded characterisation, it is clear that Maxwell is signalling something about gender in this play, and the ambiguity of his position necessitates close scrutiny of the construction of female characters in this instance. Juny and Mo stand for essentialised versions of femininity, both young and old and in my mind the fluidity of their exchange as sexual commodities in this play means that they risk existing as archetypes. Archetypal representations of women are problematic for feminists as they invoke an essentialised, patriarchal ideal of femininity. This ideal version of femininity normalises woman's supposed proximity to nature, her predisposition towards nurturing, childbearing and rearing. For Naomi R. Goldenberg:

> If feminists do not change the assumptions of archetype or redefine the concept, there are only two options: either (1) to accept the patriarchal ideas of feminine as ultimate and unchanging and work within those or (2) to indulge in a rival search to find female archetypes, ones which can support feminist conclusions. (Goldenberg 1976: 448)

As I have established, the construction of the character of Mo, or the Waiting Woman within *Ode to the Man Who Kneels* evidences, for me, a conservative approach to gender politics. However, although I do not perceive a necessarily ironic attitude, which might enable me to overturn this reading, there are signs that Maxwell is taking a broader overview of gender than Juny or the Standing Man's construction would allow. As previously quoted, in conversation with Juny, Mo asserts simply that, '[y]ou and I, we will not be pitched into binary assignations'. Given that they are ostensibly the only women in Grid, I can only conclude that these lines represent Mo as wanting to resist the inevitable comparison of the sexual attractiveness of a younger woman with an older woman. This line belies an extra-diegetic understanding of hegemonic heteronormative gender politics, and is out of kilter with the more traditional rhetoric informing the remainder of the play. The presence of this line suggests to me that Maxwell is framing his attitude towards hegemonic gender roles by giving a character a line which informs both the fictional world of the play and the world of the production beyond. This line represents 'the intentional transmission of both information and evaluative attitude' (Hutcheon 1995: 11). Maxwell's choice of actors also provides some insight into his attitude towards roles such as Mo in *Ode*, and Alice in *People Without History*. In production the role of Mo was played by Anna Kohler; a curvaceous, strong and physically striking actor, who would perhaps not typically be cast as an archetypically attractive woman. The role of Alice was played by Tory Vazquez; who is physically slim and athletic, with a low, sonorous voice. In discussion with

LeCompte, Maxwell has outlined how his conception of Alice changed when his wife was cast in the role. He stated that initially, 'this character was very angry—very masculine, very much defying the male standards of female beauty. I think that it just became too much of a grand statement about the condition of humanity' (LeCompte 2009: 73). In response to LeCompte's question about the mutation of the role, Maxwell replied:

> [It changed when] when Brian came up with the idea to cast my wife. It had become clear that the former direction wasn't going to work. I needed to get humble with this character and bring it back to earth. How much more immediate can you get than my wife? (LeCompte 2009: 73)

Given that I have been pursuing the question of authorial attitude, it seems crucial to dwell upon Maxwell's revelation here that he felt the need to 'get humble' with a female character. Having previously dismissed a 'masculine' version of Alice as 'too much of a grand statement' it becomes possible to conceive that rather than seeking to reiterate hegemonic gender norms Maxwell is actually working *against* a constructed image of femininity. It strikes me that his move away from the ironic attitude informing his earlier pieces has resulted in, what for me, has been a troubling ambiguity of political attitude. Although his attitude towards gender may be ambiguous within the plays and the productions of *Ode* and *People Without History*, contextual information gleaned from interviews and casting decisions provides evidence to help begin to claim that his politics remain liberal rather than neo-conservative. This opacity places Maxwell in an unusual position; it distances him from avant garde peers whose work can be more readily appropriated as deconstructive or ideologically resistant. It is possible that this ambiguity arises out of what Moi has termed 'ironic undercutting' (Moi cited in Hutcheon 1995: 15).

Looking back at Maxwell's oeuvre since his early experiments with Cook County Theater Department it strikes me that the work is most accurately defined by a desire to critically represent an insider's view of America and a concomitant urge to demystify all that has become conventional about contemporary theatre practice and American cultural values. This body of work can be enjoyed on a number of levels, and I have outlined its potentially ironic nature, but for me it is most successful when interpreted as challenging the liberal humanist discourse of individualism. Maxwell demonstrates how individualism inflects, and is in turn inflected by discourses of nationality, gender, race, ethnicity and economic wealth. The myth of equal opportunity regardless of origin is exposed as Maxwell draws attention to the customarily suppressed signs of labour, training, rehearsal and preparation behind a virtuoso performance. The strain of attempting to perform well is made evident by characters rendered inarticulate by the strictures of hypermasculine speech and the expectation for the actor to confidently emote in a performative environment. Maxwell also demythologises the popular understanding that it is necessarily therapeutic to describe one's inner emotional landscape; his characters and actors are often shown to remain cruelly exposed when they do succumb to the pressure to emote. By inviting trained actors to let go of their training, and giving untrained actors challenging roles Maxwell deprives them of their learned coping mechanisms and enables audiences to catch a glimpse of human subjects rendered vulnerable as they fall short of societal expectation. Acting on stage, and acting appropriately in a wider social sphere is shown to be a high-risk enterprise shadowed by a tangible fear of failure.

Despite his critical approach to individualism I would not necessarily suggest that Maxwells' work is pessimistic. His plays and performances repeatedly feature aspirational characters whose dreams of success often stand in stark contrast to the everyday reality of their family and work life. Characters in blue-collar jobs are not necessarily disaffected or disillusioned; if they do question their situation then it is an attempt to wrangle with a new found sense of disquiet rather than to throw up their hands in despair. One of his most recent pieces, *Ads*, features a range of local participants delivering self-penned speeches testifying to a belief system. The testimonies are often set in the context of a difficult emotional situation (attending and working at a hospice; speaking as a recovered drug addict) but the figures all subscribe to an overarching belief in *something*. Contemporary American life is shown to be predicated upon an illusion of equal opportunity but the illusion is shown to be misleading rather than corrupt. The belief in the opportunity to succeed prevents his characters from becoming cynical or moribund.

In addition to demystifying the illusion of the American Dream, Maxwell also describes a world altered by transglobal capitalist forces and a super-modern drive to efficiency. However, in contradiction to Augé's theory of non-places, Maxwell brings the workers servicing the 'non-places' to the fore (suppressed in Augé's writing) and works to situate the theatre as a positive 'anthropological place' where community members come together to meet and rediscover their world anew.

Recent work by the New York City Players has revealed a drive to experiment with different media and different formats. As quoted, Maxwell has revealed that part of the mission of New York City Players is to 'try to work with new people all the time. It's a way of staying in touch with what you're doing by running it by people who aren't obliged to agree (LeCompte 2009: 73). In 2009 Maxwell did not direct his own work but rather Mendes took over the direction of *People Without History*. In 2010 in addition to creating *Ads* and developing early ideas for *Neutral Hero*, Maxwell directed *Vision Disturbance* by Christina Masciotti and wrote and directed *Das Maedchen* for Theatre Bonn. *Das Maedchen* featured experimentation with choreography as an ensemble of German and American performers improvised gestures and movement sequences against a backdrop of the projected text. Despite the change in discipline and direction it is possible to identify in this work a continued investment in the theme of emotional vulnerability; difficulties associated with both verbal and physical articulation and a concern with theatre as a symbolic meeting-place. During a post-show discussion at Bad Godesburg's Kammerspeilhaus Sibyl Kempson confessed she found the movement work in *Das Maedchen* 'very embarrassing and difficult' and as a result had to 'really pay attention to what (was) happening in the room'. The company's identification with the theatre as a meeting of minds or a space of concentration is reminiscent of what Ubersfeld has described as the socio-political function of theatre. For her, theatre promotes the opportunity to analyse hegemonic social process via onstage activity in addition to providing a model of social organisation itself. By investigating both the intra-diegetic world of his plays and the extra-diegetic environment of the theatre this book aims to provide an insight into what it might mean for an audience member to be 'in the room' with this company, this director and its very particular take on contemporary American culture.

Despite eschewing a recognisable 'style', a detailed reading of Maxwell's work as director and playwright reveals that he has an uncanny facility for identifying and denaturalising those conventions we no longer recognise to be socially constructed. Everyday patterns of speech suddenly appear strange; ignored realist theatre conventions are placed alongside post-Brechtian techniques in order to foreground their enduring influence upon the ways we watch and receive conventional theatre. By presenting a slightly off kilter version of Western liberal capitalist reality he invites his audiences to return to the proposition that convention, rather than instinct shapes their most fundamental values.

Notes

NOTES TO PREFACE

1. Telephone interview with Author 29 October 2003.
2. Email to Author 20 October 2003.
3. Email to Author 19 May 2005
4. Written by Charles Chaplin, 1936.
5. I have also encountered examples of his work on video, DVD and the company's YouTube channel.
6. 'The Turn from Postructuralism', mounted by the Centre for Research in Sex, Gender and Sexuality at Roehampton University 18 March 2009.

NOTES TO CHAPTER 1

1. *Good Samaritans*: Rosemary Allen won an award for her performance, 2005; *Drummer Wanted*: Angela Moore and Michael Schmelling won an award for Set/Lights. Maxwell also received a special citation by the OBIE committee for *House* in 1999.
2. Wessendorf describes Lehmann's re-naming of 'the current theatre-aesthetic discourse' as 'postdramatic theater' as a 'terminological upgrade' (Wessendorf 2003: 1).
3. In 2006 John O'Mahony of the *Financial Times* quizzed Maxwell about an accusation that had been aired during a post-show discussion, that *The End of Reality* was 'reactionary'. Maxwell responded that, 'I think what [the questioner] meant was that there was a kind of simplistic moral tone . . . the idea that things were better before 9/11, that kind of thing. But I didn't mind the charge of reactionary; I'm not afraid of nostalgia or tradition and pining for the past (O'Mahony 2006).
4. Richard Maxwell, *The Frame*, 2006.
5. Describing what became known as 'the culture wars', Robert M. Collins wrote that in the late 70s and 80s America experienced a, 'multifaceted struggle between different systems of moral understanding.' He distinguished between 'orthodox impulses', which felt that authority was located in 'cultural tradition, religion or conceptions of natural law' and 'progressive impulses', which 'denied such authority' and relied instead upon, 'subjective values derived from the contemporary zeitgeist' (Collins 2007: 172–173).
6. Interestingly, Gary Wilmes, a long-term Maxwell collaborator appeared in *The Girl from Monday*, Hartley's 2005 feature.
7. Interview with Author 29 October 2003.

8. Bailes illuminates that: 'The "downtown scene" in New York gestures towards what was originally a geographically informed reference (from the 1960s onwards) to the lower area of the island of Manhattan, between 14th Street and Houston and to the east of the Bowery. As a designated "scene" or style of artistic production (rather than a "place") downtown now spreads across the East River to include vibrant packets of artistic activity in parts of Brooklyn such as Williamsburg, DUMBO, Fort Greene and more recently Greenpoint and Bushwick (Bailes 2011: 159).
9. Interview with Author 29 October 2003.
10. Interview with Author 6 April 2010.
11. Zarrilli has described his approach as 'post-Stanislavski', however it is important to acknowledge that many of the discourses of Western, and American acting have been influenced by biased translations of his work. In addition, state censorship and selective appropriation of ideas by those exposed to a small proportion of Stanislavski's work presented to America during the Moscow Art Theatre's tours of 1923–1924 have contributed to only a partial understanding (Zarrilli 2009: 15). According to Hornby it was 'Diderot's application of Cartesian dualism to acting [which] laid the groundwork for performance theory for the next two centuries' (Hornby 1992: 106). The enduring influence of Diderot's eighteenth-century work has no doubt resulted in a Western reading of Stanislavski through the lens of Humanist thought, which suggests that post-Humanist approaches should be identified as post-Diderot rather than post-Stanislavski, or post-Method.
12. Email to Author, 19 May 2005.
13. Email to Author, 19 May 2005.
14. *Bill and Ted's Excellent Adventure*—Stephen Herek (1989); *Beavis and Butthead*—Mike Judge (1989).
15. Co-written with Jim Strahs.

NOTES TO CHAPTER 2

1. Acknowledged as 'the industry standard' (Gorman 2007: 237).
2. In September 2008 Maxwell discussed a draft of this chapter with me and voiced his concern that a discussion of 'Method Acting' might perhaps be seen to be outdated. He added that he had been approached by an acting student after a post-show discussion in America who picked up on his own reference to Method Acting in the talk by telling him that in his training academy, 'nobody really talks about Method anymore'.
3. Maxwell related an anecdote about his acting classes at a post-show discussion at The Pit, Barbican, London, 14 November 2006.
4. Zarrilli has noted that a 'preoccupation with emotion and the psychological has meant that most American method approaches work on "the self" and creating a character have been highly susceptible to some form of body-mind dualism. (Zarrilli 2009: 17).
5. Brian Mendes, a long-term Maxwell collaborator emphasises the fact that for him, the process of getting a play 'up and running' is never finished. (Mendes quoted in Gorman 2007).
6. Maxwell states that 'The origins of that style go back to work I was doing with the Cook County Theater Department in Chicago in the early 1990s. We were all actors trying to figure out what it was about performance that we found, as audience members, stifling—trying to throw out the rule book we had taken on. I was taught in college as an actor, essentially, to make my work convincing: to be believable and be real' (Hemming 2005).

7. Personal correspondence with Author, April 2005.
8. His essay is entitled 'Burdens of Representation' in Krasner (ed.) (2000) *Method Acting Reconsidered*.
9. Pete Simpson is a professional New York actor who regularly appears in downtown New York theatre productions.
10. I also make reference to this example in relation to Frank's performance of 'hegemonic masculinity' in Chapter 4, 'I Got Balls, See?'
11. Keanu Reeves in *Bill and Ted's Excellent Adventure* (Stephen Herek 1989); *Beavis and Butthead* as created by Mike Judge 1989.
12. Whilst I am aware that key figures such as Yvonne Rainer and Andre Antoine produced fascinating work drawing upon the skills of untrained actors and dancers I will be limiting my discussion of the deployment of amateurs and professional amateurism to the sphere of contemporary theatre.
13. Alvarez details that 'Coleridge's term "ipseity"—from the Latin ipse meaning 'he himself'—provides a useful means of accounting for the "explicit performative's attribute of self-realization"' (Alvarez 2006: 237).
14. During an interview held in July 2006 Maxwell emphasised the fact that, in his mind, exercises exploring neutrality were not necessarily designed to negate or do away with Method as a resource for actors. He pointed out that, 'the conversations I have with Brian now are like "why are you afraid of Method?" you know, what's the matter with that, what's wrong with pretending?' (Gorman 2007: 237).
15. The role of '5' or 'Marcia' was played by Marcia Hidalgo in New York and by Makeda Christodoulos during the 2006–2007 tour.
16. I also draw upon these examples to foreground a sense of Tom's being constrained by his work environment in Chapter 5 about Maxwell's use and representation of space.
17. Post-show talk at The Pit Theatre, Barbican, London, 9 November 2006.
18. Thomas Bradshaw was Playwright in Residence at the Flea Theater in 2006 and has had a number of his pieces performed in New York venues in recent years.
19. Alice Reagan describes Maxwell's characters as, 'unfamiliar creatures without skin' (Reagan 2002: 314).

NOTES TO CHAPTER 3

1. Justin Hayford recalls using this term as a title for one of his *Chicago Reader* reviews of CCTD's work, although credit for inventing the term remains ambiguous (personal email to Author, 27 April 2007). Stephanie Shaw, stated that: 'my recollection of all my reviews was that I wrote the piece and inevitably an editor at the Reader gave it a title. I think that's what happened in this case. I don't think Richard Maxwell coined the phrase. But I can't bet my life the phrase wasn't in the press materials that I handed in along with the review.' Justin Hayford worked for the *Reader* at the time, as well, so it's possible he had something to do with it (Shaw, personal email to Author 7 July 2009).
2. Maxwell won an exclusive artistic internship through Illinois State University to work with Steppenwolf Theatre in Chicago from May 1990–September 1991.
3. In addition to the four founder members, company members included, at various stages: Chris Sullivan, David Pavkovic, Lara Furniss, Jason Greenberg, Vicki Walden, Rebecca Rossen, Claire Morkin, Erica Heilman, Tony Sacre and Roberto Argentina.

4. Steppenwolf had gained a reputation for such work by realising Sam Shepard plays such as *True West* in 1980.
5. Richard Maxwell, post-show discussion event, The Barbican Pit Theatre, 9 November 2006, London.
6. Richard Maxwell, Interview with Author, New York, 15 November 2006.
7. Wilmes writes that Maxwell 'agreeably' acquiesced to his request to direct *Flight Courier Service* after he had seen the original production in New York. Maxwell was not involved in the Cook County production. Gary Wilmes 'Cook County Questions'. (personal email, 11 May 2007).
8. According to Vanden Heuvel, Derrida ascribes to the '"theological stage": recognition of the integrity of the author's vision, of authorial mastery over signs and their signifieds, and of the playwright's adherence to a conjunctive form constituted by stable constructions of character, plot, and language' (Derrida quoted in Vanden Heuvel 1991: 3).
9. Justin Hayford, "Hello from Justin Hayford". (Personal email to Author 27 April 2007).
10. Hayford has pointed out that *The Chicago Reader* is a more independent publication, whereas *The Chicago Tribune* is a large corporate daily newspaper. Justin Hayford, "Hello from Justin Hayford". (Personal email to Author 7 June 2007).
11. Justin Hayford, 'Hello from Justin Hayford'. (Personal email to Author 27 April 2007).
12. Lara Furniss 'Cook County Theater Department' (Personal email to Author 27 August 2010).
13. Doorika was founded in 1989 by Erika Yeomans and operated until 1999. Towards the end of its career they moved to New York. In 1995 the company described their work as that of a collective, "develop[ing] theater that focuses on the scoring of action and sound, elements of chance a performer's relationship to the subject matter, and the inherent associations that arise from exhaustive research specific to each piece. The synthesis of these elements renders a borderless, saturated meta-linguistic theater experience" (Maxine 2007).
14. Justin Hayford, "Hello from Justin Hayford" (Personal email to Author 27 April 2007).
15. Lin Hixson, director of Goat Island, was Furniss' sculpture adviser during her MFA at the School of the Art Institute of Chicago (1993–1994). Discussions of Furniss' work with CCTD led to Hixson attending *Clowns Plus Wrestlers*, which in turn led to several workshops between Goat Island and CCTD. Furniss states that she 'was very inspired by their work, and it influenced my approach to design, the use of space and the relationships between audience and actor' (Furniss, personal email to Author 27 August 2010).
16. Stephanie Shaw 'Passionate Indifference' (Personal email to Author 7 July 2009).
17. Brian Mendes, 'Cook County Questions' (Personal email to Author 4 May 2007).
18. Furniss recalls that, 'the first half of the show was made up of gentle movements with beautifully simple connections between actors. But by the end of the show they are like animals in a cage. The audience was placed in the round, to create an intimate setting, and I covered the floor in salt to highlight the actor's movements. The audience was unaware what the flooring was until the end, when it was so ground into the stage that clouds of dust floated up and you could taste the salt on your tongue. It was a mesmerizing performance' (Personal email to author 27 August 2010.)

19. Brian Mendes, interviewed by Author, 7 July 2006. New York.
20. Gary Wilmes 'Cook County Questions' (Personal email to Author 15 May 2007).
21. Justin Hayford, 'Hello from Justin Hayford'. (Personal email to Author 27 April 2007).
22. Company members would use their given or real names in place of character names during performance.
23. Set Designer Furniss was invited by Mendes to join CCTD as they began working on *Fable*. Her background was in Interior Design, and she was enrolled on the Masters in Sculptural Installation at the School of the Art Institute of Chicago. She collaborated with Jason Greenberg, Joe Silovsky, Christopher Furman and Monica Poplawska on *Minutes and Seconds*.
24. Furniss recalls that with *Clowns Plus Wrestlers*, 'the foundations of what a designer's role was at CCTD began to take shape. I shaped the audience and stage spaces to compliment the idea of the show and the audience experience, designed the set, helped develop the costumes and lighting . . . I sat in on every rehearsal and watched most of the performances'. (Personal email to Author 27 August 2010).
25. My suggestion that this work could be read in terms of experimentation in contemporary dance is supported by Yvonne Rainer's definition of "minimalist" dance. She states that "the display of technical virtuosity and the display of the dancer's specialized body no longer makes any sense. Dancers have been driven to search for an alternative context that allows for a more matter of fact, more concrete, more banal quality of physical being in performance, a context wherein people are engaged in actions and movements making a less spectacular demand on the body and in which skill is hard to locate". (Rainer 1996:293)
26. Brian Mendes, interview with Author, 7 July 2006, New York.
27. Although this meeting of high-art and low-culture may appear to be redolent of The Wooster Group's work in the 1990s and to represent a regularly acknowledged feature of postmodern art, I would argue that CCTD's enunciation sets out to critique esoteric forms rather than to 'resist' (Auslander 1996: 58) or 'pastiche' (Foster 1983: 116).
28. Maxwell wrote this piece after having moved to New York in 1994. He directed CCTD performers, who presented it at The Ontological Hysteric Theatre in New York and The Bop Shop, Chicago in August 1995. (Gary Wilmes, personal email to Author 11 May 2007).
29. Two teenage characters featured in *Beavis and Butthead* created by Mike Judge, 1989.
30. Bad acting and failure are discussed in relation to the performativity of gender in Chapters 1 and 3.
31. Interestingly, Mendes requested that Hayford did not review *Tosca*, as the company had come to feel uneasy about the 'size and enthusiasm of his reviews' (Furniss, personal email to Author, 27 August 2010).
32. 'Cook County Theatre Department'—Lara Furniss, (personal email to Author, 27 August 2010).
33. 'Cook County Theatre Department'—Lara Furniss, (personal email to Author, 27 August 2010).
34. The star-conveyor belt was designed and built by Gary Wilmes.
35. Richard Maxwell, "Re-wiring, Re-writing Theatre". Discussion chaired by Adrian Heathfield at The Riverside Studios, London, 18 November 2006.
36. Gary Wilmes, interviewed by Author, 6 July 2006, New York.
37. Brian Mendes, interviewed by Author, 6 July 2006, New York.

NOTES TO CHAPTER 4

1. I have designated this distinction as 'simplistic' because the differences between levels of training are perhaps not so straightforward as 'amateur' and 'professional' may suggest. For example, a number of Maxwell's long-term collaborators have performed in 'downtown' New York theatre productions for a number of years, however they may not necessarily identify as being 'trained' actors. Similarly, some colleagues do identify as having been trained, and are professional musicians or playwrights, but have little actual experience of acting under their belts. Other collaborators can be identified by the longevity of their working relationship with Maxwell, several having co-founded Cook County Theater Department with him in Chicago in the early 1990s.
2. The Barbican, London post-show discussion chaired by Dominic Cavendish, 9 November 2006.
3. Unpublished play scripts, Richard Maxwell *Drummer Wanted*, p. 8 and Richard Maxwell, *The End of Reality*, p. 11.
4. Richard Maxwell, *Showcase*, unpublished play script, p. 5.
5. Richard Maxwell, *The End of Reality*, unpublished play script, p. 13.
6. Richard Maxwell, *Ode to the Man Who Kneels*, unpublished play script, p. 1.
7. Richard Maxwell, *Ode to the Man Who Kneels*, unpublished play script, p. 5.
8. Richard Maxwell, *Drummer Wanted*, unpublished play script, p. 15.
9. Richard Maxwell, *Drummer Wanted*, unpublished play script, p. 27.
10. Richard Maxwell, *Drummer Wanted*, unpublished play script, p. 26.
11. Richard Maxwell, *The End of Reality*, unpublished play script, p. 39.
12. Richard Maxwell, *The End of Reality*, unpublished play script, p. 22.
13. Richard Maxwell, *Ode to the Man Who Kneels*, unpublished play script, p. 13.
14. Richard Maxwell, *Ode to the Man Who Kneels*, unpublished play script, p. 1.
15. Richard Maxwell, *Ode to the Man Who Kneels*, unpublished play script, p. 4.
16. Richard Maxwell, *Ode to the Man Who Kneels*, unpublished play script, p. 9. The lines were not assigned to be read aloud but to give the actor a sense-impression to convey.

NOTES TO CHAPTER 5

1. Co-written with Jim Strahs.
2. 'Concert hall slash sports facility' is a line from Father's song in Maxwell's play *House* (Maxwell 2004:125).
3. Ubersfeld's taxonomy of theatre space, represents for McAuley, an 'obligatory starting point for any theoretical reflection on the function of space in the theatre' because 'theatrical presentation of place necessarily incorporates a socio-political commentary' (McAuley 1999: 18).
4. In conversation with Elizabeth LeCompte Maxwell has discussed how his drive to work with new collaborators means that he has to 'run [his ideas] by people who aren't obliged to agree'. He provides an example in relation to his approach to the use of stage space, 'You ask somebody who's coming from a more traditional acting background "Where are we?" and they'll say, "My character is in the kitchen of a commissary. This is where the play takes place." Whereas most of the people I have worked with before will say, "We're in Liz's loft, and we're here because that's where the play is happening." . . .

How do you reconcile those two? You don't have to. You can have one foot in one and one foot in the other. But I see a lot of energy put into denying the Liz's loft part. That has never sat so well with me. You don't have to help the audience pretend we're somewhere else' (LeCompte 2009: 73).

5. At the time of writing, an excerpt from Maxwell's own production of *House* is also available to watch on You Tube.com.

6. Ben Brantley refers to the 'endearingly homemade technology' used in *Ode to the Man who Kneels* (Brantley 2007).

7. He refutes the notion that the wall is necessarily symbolic. Interviewed in 2006, Maxwell stated 'I just thought it was a cool idea. I didn't really think that . . . "oh well, what it means is that the family are without a home . . . they are forever in this Sartrean world of the rehearsal space. I think I could safely say that that's all accident, or at least unconscious"' (Gorman 2007: 241).

8. Maxwell allowed me to sit in on rehearsals in preparation for a chapter about his rehearsal processes published in *Making Contemporary Theatre: International Rehearsal Processes* edited by Jen Harvie and Andy Lavender (2010) Manchester: Manchester University Press, pp.180–201.

9. Touchstone TV and ABC Video; Series producers Hayek and Horta, 2006–2009.

10. Directed by John Badham, 1986.

11. Maxwell worked as an itern for both The Wooster Group and Richard Foreman during the early 1990s (Mufson 2004).

12. In *A Decade of Forced Entertainment* (1995), the company describe their work as follows:
    'They tried not to talk about the people who made decisions but about those people who were affected by decisions made in other times and other places. They were provincial, by choice and by accident' (Etchells 1999: 32).

13. *Showcase* was created in response to a call for new artists to 'showcase' their work and was written to be performed in one of the hotel rooms in which the showcase was located. Quotation from Maxwell *Showcase* (2003) p.4.

14. Maxwell Showcase (2003) p.4.

15. Maxwell Showcase (2003) p.5.

16. Maxwell Showcase (2003) p.3.

17. Maxwell *Good Samaritans* (2004) p. 7.

18. Maxwell *Good Samaritans* (2004) p. 12.

19. Maxwell *Good Samaritans* (2004) p. 32.

20. Maxwell *Good Samaritans* (2004) p. 25.

21. Maxwell *Good Samaritans* (2004) p. 37.

22. Maxwell (2006) *End of Reality*, p. 9.

23. Maxwell (2006) *End of Reality*, p. 43.

24. Maxwell (2006) *End of Reality*, p. 10.

25. Maxwell (2006) *End of Reality*, p. 33.

26. Maxwell (2006) *End of Reality*, p. 34.

27. Maxwell (2006) *End of Reality*, p.19.

28. Maxwell (2006) *End of Reality*, p. 43.

29. Maxwell and Strahs *Cowboys and Indians* (1998) p. 1.

30. Maxwell and Strahs *Cowboys and Indians* (1998) p. 16.

31. Maxwell and Strahs *Cowboys and Indians* (1998) p. 26.

32. Maxwell and Strahs *Cowboys and Indians* (1998) p. 27.

33. Maxwell *The Frame* (2006) p. 16.

34. Maxwell *The Frame* (2006) p. 21.

35. Maxwell *The Frame* (2006) p.16.

36. Maxwell (2007) *Ode to the Man Who Kneels*, p. 1.

37. Maxwell (2007) *Ode to the Man Who Kneels*, p .9.
38. Maxwell (2007) *Ode to the Man Who Kneels*, p. 5.
39. Maxwell (2007) *Ode to the Man Who Kneels*, p. 12.
40. Maxwell (2007) *Ode to the Man Who Kneels*, p. 1.
41. Maxwell, *Ode to the Man Who Kneels*, pp. 2 and 3.

NOTES TO CHAPTER 6

1. Richard Maxwell, *The End of Reality*, 2006
2. Interview with Richard Maxwell, 1 December 2010.
3. Richard Maxwell (2007) *Ode to the Man Who Kneels*, p. 6.
4. Richard Maxwell (2007) *Ode to the Man Who Kneels*, p. 5.

Bibliography

Agnew, John, (2002) "Introduction" in Agnew, John A. and Jonathan M. Smith (eds.) *American Place/American Space: Geographies of the Contemporary United States*. Edinburgh: Edinburgh University Press, pp. 1–18.

Agnew, John A. and Joanne Sharp (eds.) (2002) *America, Frontier Nation: From Abstract Space to Worldly Place*. Edinburgh: Edinburgh University Press.

Agnew, John A. and Jonathan M. Smith (2002) (eds.) *American Place/American Space: Geographies of the Contemporary United States*. Edinburgh: Edinburgh University Press.

Ahmed Sara, (2000) *Strange Encounters: Embodied Others in Post-Coloniality*. London and New York: Routledge.

Alvarez Natalie I. (2006) "Authenticity and the 'Divinely Amateur'. The Romantic in Richard Maxwell" in Ozieblo, Barbara and Maria Narbona-Carrion (eds.) *Codifying the National Self: Spectators, Actors and the American Dramatic Text*. Brussels: Peter Lang, pp. 233–250.

Archer, Louise, Simon Pratt and David Phillips (2001) "Working-class Men's Constructions of Masculinity and Negotiations of (Non) Participation in Higher Education" *Gender and Education* 13 (4): pp. 431–449.

Aronson, Arnold (2005) *Looking into the Abyss: Essays on Scenography*, Ann Arbor: University of Michigan Press.

Arts Beat (2010) "Under the Radar: Five Questions about Ads", January 13. Available at: http://artsbeat.blogs.nytimes.com/2010/01/13/under-the-radar-five-questions-about-ads/. Accessed 9 August 2010.

Augé, Marc (1995) *Non Places: Introduction to an Anthropology of Supermodernity*, translated by John Howe. London: Verso.

Auslander, Philip (1997) *From Acting to Performance: Essays in Modernism and Postmodernism*. London: Routledge.

Auslander, Philip (2002) "Just be Yourself: Logocentrism and Difference in Performance Theory" in Phillip B. Zarilli (ed.) *Acting (Re) Considered: a Theoretical and Practical Guide*. London: Routledge.

Bailes, Sara Jane (2000) "Moving Backwards, Forwards Remembering: Goat Island Performance Group". Available at: Goat Island website: www.goatislandperformance.org/writing.htm. Accessed 5 January 2006.

Bailes, Sara Jane (2005) "Struggling to Perform: Radical Amateurism and Forced Entertainment" *Theatre Forum International* 26 (Winter/Spring): pp. 56—65.

Bailes, Sara Jane (2010) "Elevator Repair Service—Cab Legs (1997) to Gatz (2006): Reversing the Ruins: the Power of Theatrical Misconception" in Harvie, Jen and Andy Lavender (eds.) *Making Contemporary Theatre: International Rehearsal Processes*. Manchester: Manchester University Press, pp. 81–100.

Bailes, Sara Jane (2011) *Performance Theatre and the Poetics of Failure*. Abingdon and New York: Routledge.

Barbaro, Michael (2010) "N. Y. Political Leaders' Rift Grows on Islam Center" *New York Times*, 24 August 2010. Available at: http://www.nytimes.com/2010/08/25/nyregion/25bloomberg.html?src=mv. Accessed 25 August 2010.

Baron-Cohen, Simon (2003) *The Essential Difference*. London: Penguin.

Baudrillard, Jean (1986) *America*, translated by Chris Turner. Paris: Bernard Grasset.

Beck, Denis C. "The Paradox of the Method Actor: Rethinking the Stanislavsky Legacy" in David Krasner (ed.) *Method Acting Reconsidered: Theory, Practice, Future*. Hampshire: Macmillan Press, pp. 261–282.

Bigsby, C.W.E. (2000) *Modern American Drama, 1945-2000*, Cambridge: Cambridge University Press.

Bomb Magazine (2010) "Young Jean Lee Interviewed by Richard Maxwell: Theater Interview at Mabou Mines Theater in New York City" Posted July 2010. Available at: http://www.bombsite.com/issues/999/articles/3594 Accessed 11 August 2010.

Bommer Lawrence (1996) "Many Styles Converge In 'Clowns'" *Chicago Tribune* 19 March. Available at: https://securesite.chireader.com/cgi-bin/Archive/. Accessed 10 October 2006.

Bottoms, Steven (1998) *The Theatre of Sam Shepard: States of Crisis*. Cambridge: Cambridge University Press.

Bottoms, Steve (2007) "Biochemically Stressed" in Bottoms, Steve and Matthew Goulish (eds.) *Small Acts of Repair*. London and New York: Routledge, pp. 73–78.

Bowser, Betty Ann (1998) "Off-Broadway Hit: The NewsHour with Jim Lehrer Transcript" 3 June. Available at: http://www.pbs.org/newshour/bb/entertainment/jan-june98/denver_6–3.html. Accessed 3 May 2007.

Brantley, Ben (2006) "The Banality of Violence in a Willfully Numb Universe" *New York Times* 17 January 2006. Available at: http://theater2.nytimes.com/2006/01/17/theater/reviews/17bran.html. Accessed 5 February 2006.

Brantley, Ben (2007) "The Land of the Big Sky and the Deep Inner Void" *The New York Times*, 6 November. Available at: http://theater2.nytimes.com. Accessed 10 September 2009.

Brenner, Wayne Alan (2003) "Drummer Wanted: Richard Maxwell" *The Austin Chronicle*. Available at: http://www.austinchronicle.com/issues/dispach/2003–01–1/arts_exhibitionism5.html. Accessed 15 July 2003.

Butler, Judith (1990) *Gender Trouble: Feminism and the Subversion of Identity*. New York: Routledge.

Carney, George O. (1995) (ed.) *Fast Food, Stock Cars and Rock 'n' Roll: Place and Space in American Pop Culture*. Lanham, MD: Rowman and Littlefield.

Cerrato, Laura (1993) "Postmodernism and Beckett's Aesthetics of Failure" in Buning, Marius and Lois Oppenheim (eds.) *Samuel Beckett Today/Aujourd hui*, 1993 Aesthetics of Failure/ 2nd International Beckett Symposium 1992, The Hague. Amsterdam: Rodophi Press, pp. 21–29.

Chaudhuri, Una (1995) *Staging Place: the Geography of Modern Drama*. Ann Arbor: University of Michigan Press.

Coates, Jennifer (2003) *Men Talk: Stories in the Making of Masculinities*. Oxford: Blackwell Publishing.

Cochrane, Claire (2001) "The Pervasiveness of the Commonplace: The Historian and Amateur Theatre" *Theatre Research International* 26 (3): pp. 233–242.

Collins, Robert M. (2007) *Transforming America: Politics and Culture in the Reagan Years*. New York: Columbia University Press.

Collins, Samuel (1996) "Head Out On the Highway: Anthropological Encounters with the Supermodern" *Postmodern Culture*, 7 (1). Electronic Journal available at http://pmc.iath.virginia.edu/text-only/issue.996/review-2.996

Culler, J. (1975) *Structuralist Poetics: Structuralism, Linguistics and The Study of Literature*. Oxford: Routledge and Kegan Paul.

de Beauvoir (1973) *The Second Sex*, trans E. M. Parshley, New York:Vintage.

De Certeau, Michel (1988) *The Writing of History*. New York: Columbia University Press.

Derrida, Jacques (1996) *Archive Fever: A Freudian Impression*, translated by Eric Prenowitz. Chicago: University of Chicago Press.

Donohue, Joseph (1989) "Evidence and Documentation" in Postlewait, Thomas and Bruce A. McConahie (eds.) *Interpreting the Theatrical Past: Essays in the Historiography of Performance*. Iowa City: University of Iowa Press.

Duncan, Russell and Joseph Goddard (2009) *Contemporary America*, third edition, Basingstoke: Palgrave Macmillan.

Easthope, Antony (1986) *What a Man's Gotta Do: The Masculine Myth in Popular Culture,* London: Paladin Grafton Books.

Ellis, Samantha (2005) "Numb and Number" *The Guardian* 2 March 2005. Available at: http://www.guardian.co.uk/stage/2005/mar/02/theatre4. Accessed 17 November 2005.

Engelhardt, Tom (1998) *The End of Victory Culture: Cold War America and the Disillusions of Generation*. Amherst: University of Massachusetts Press.

Etchells Tim (2003) Presentation at Live Culture Event, Tate Modern, London. 29 March 2003.

Etchells, Tim (1999) *Certain Fragments: Contemporary Performance and Forced Entertainment*, London: Routledge.

Eynat-Confino, Irene and Eva Šarmová (eds.) (2000) *Space and the Postmodern Stage*. Prague: Ekon.

Falk, Florence (1981) "Men Without Women: The Shepard Landscape" in Bonnie Marranca (ed.) *American Dreams*. New York: PAJ Publications, pp. 90–125.

Feingold, Michael (2003) "Henry IV, Square One" *The Village Voice*, October 8–14. Available at: http://www.nycplayers.org/press/view/18. Accessed 2 March 2011.

Fiske, John (1987) *Television Culture*. London: Routledge.

Foreman, Richard (1992) *Unbalancing Acts: Foundations for a Theater*, New York: Theatre Communications Group.

Foster, Hal (1983) (ed.) *Postmodern Culture*. London: Pluto Press.

Gardner, Lyn (2001) "Quiet Revolution" The Guardian, 6 September 2001. Available at: http://www.guardian.co.uk/culture/2001/sep/06/artsfeatures1/print. Accessed 6 March 2005.

Gardner, Lyn (2005) "Joe" *The Guardian*, 4 March 2005. Available at: http://www.guardian.co.uk/stage/2005/mar/04/theatre. Accessed 8 March 2005.

Gardner, Lyn (2006) "The End of Reality" *The Guardian*, 11 November 2006. Available at: http://www.guardian.co.uk/stage/2006/nov/11/theatre. Accessed 13 November 2006.

Goffman, Erving (1963) *Stigma: Notes on the Management of Spoiled Identity*. Englewood Cliffs, NJ: Prentice Hall.

Goldenberg, Naomi R. (1976) "A Feminist Critique of Jung" *Signs: Journal of Women in Culture and Society* 2 (2): pp. 443–449.

Gorman, Sarah (2005) "New Theatre Making: Richard Maxwell", *Contemporary Theatre Review*, 15(2), pp.284–288.

Gorman, Sarah (2007) "Refusing Shorthand: Richard Maxwell" *Contemporary Theatre Review* 17 (2): pp. 235–241.

Gorman, Sarah (2010) "Richard Maxwell and the New York City Players—The End of Reality (2006)—Exploring Acting" in Jen Harvie and Andy Lavender (eds.) *Making Contemporary Theatre: International Rehearsal Processes*. Manchester: Manchester University Press, pp. 180–201.

Govan, Emma, Helen Nicholson and Katie Normington (2007) *Making a Performance: Devising Histories and Contemporary Practices*. London and New York: Routledge.

Graver, David (2002) "The Actor's Bodies" in Auslander Philip (ed.) *Performance: Critical Concepts (Volume 2)*. New York and London: Routledge, pp. 221–235.

Hardison-Londré, Felicia and Daniel J. Watermeir (1998) *The History of North American Theater: from Pre-Columbian times to the Present*. New York: Continuum.

Hayford, Justin (1994) "Magical Medium: Minutes and Seconds, Cook County Theater Department" *Chicago Reader*, 18 November. Available at: https://securesite.chireader.com/cgi-bin/Archive/. Accessed 10 October 2006.

Hayford Justin (1996) "On Stage: Cook County Theater Department's Mini Puccini" *Chicago Reader*, 8 November. Available at: https://securesite.chireader.com/cgi-bin/Archive/. Accessed 10 October 2006.

Hayford, Justin (1997a) "Flight Courier Service". *Chicago Reader*, 14 November. Available at: https://securesite.chireader.com/cgi-bin/Archive/. Accessed 10 October 2006.

Hayford, Justin (1997b) "Theater Review: The Persecution of Arnold Petch" *Chicago Reader*, 14 March, p. 28.

Hemming, Sarah (2005) "More than Words: The Silent Blend in Maxwell's House" *Financial Times*, 7 March 2005. Available at: http://www.ft.com/cms/s/2/69a15934–8ead-11d9–8aae-00000e2511c8.html. Accessed 17 November 2005.

Hodge, Alison (ed.) (2000) *Twentieth Century Actor Training*. London and New York: Routledge.

Hornby, Richard (1992) *The End of Acting: A Radical View*. New York: Applause Books.

Horrocks, Roger (1994) *Masculinity in Crisis: Myths, Fantasies and Realities*. Basingstoke: Palgrave Macmillan.

Hutcheon, Linda (1995) *Irony's Edge: The Theory and Politics of Irony*. London and New York: Routledge.

Isherwood, Charles (2010) "Detailed Reflections, Verbal & Visual" *New York Times*, 14 January 2010. p. 1 and 5.

Jenkins, Janet (1993) *In the Sprit of* Fluxus. Minneapolis: Walker Art Center.

Johnson, Sally and Ulrike Hanna Meinhof (eds.) (1997) *Language and Masculinity*. Oxford: Blackwell Publishing.

Joy, Jenn (2006) "Reflections on Failure: Hooman Sharifi's We Failed to Hold this Reality in Mind" with an interview by Andre Lepecki, *The Drama Review* 50 (4): pp. 45–51.

Kear, Adrian (2005) "Troublesome Amateurs: Theatre, Ethics and the Labour of Mimesis" *Performance Research* 10 (1): pp. 26–46.

Kelsey, John (2008) "Richard Maxwell" *Bomb Magazine* 105 (Fall 2008). Available at: http://bombsite.com/issues/105/articles/3183. Accessed 11 August 2010.

Kimmel, Michael S. (1987) *Changing Men: New Directions in Research on Men and Masculinity*. Newbury Park, CA: SAGE.

King, Bruce (1991) *Contemporary American Theatre*. Hampshire: Macmillan.

Kirby, Michael (2002) "On Acting and Non-Acting" in Zarilli, Phillip B. (ed.) *Acting (Re) Considered: A Theoretical and Practical Guide*. London: Routledge.

Klein, Naomi (2007) "The Age of Disaster Capitalism" *The Guardian*, 10 September. Available at: http://www.guardian.co.uk/world/2007/sep/10/usa.terrorism. Accessed 20 October 2007.

Kobialka Michal (2002) "Historical Archives, Events and Facts: History Writing as Fragmentary Performance", *Performance Research* 7 (4): pp. 3–11.

Kozloff, Sarah (1992) "Narrative Theory and Television" in R. C. Allen (ed.) *Channels of Discourse, Reassembled*. London: Routledge, pp. 67–95.

Krasner David (2000a) *Method Acting Reconsidered: Theory, Practice, Future*, Hampshire: Macmillan Press.

Krasner David (2000b) "Strasberg, Adler and Meisner: Method Acting" in Hodge, Alison (ed.) *Twentieth Century Actor Training*. London andand New York: Routledge, pp. 129–150.

Lehmann, Hans-Thies (2006) *Postdramatic Theatre*, translated by Karen Jürs-Munby. Abingdon and New York: Routledge.

LeCompte, Elizabeth (2009) "Grist for Society: An Interview with the Playwright" *American Theatre*, September: pp. 72–73.

Letzler Cole, Susan (2001) "Sam Shepard in Rehearsal: Curse of the Starving Class" in *Playwrights in Rehearsal: The Seduction of Company*, by Susan Letzler Cole. New York: Routledge, pp. 1–25.

Leyland, Matthew (2004) "The Unbelievable Truth" *Sight and Sound* Issue XIV, pp. 78–99.

Lyotard, J. F. (1979) *The Postmodern Condition: A Report on Knowledge*, translated by G. Bennington and B. Massumi. Manchester: Manchester University Press.

Mangan, Michael (2003) *Staging Masculinities: History, Gender, Performance*. Basingstoke: Palgrave Macmillan.

Marks, Peter (1999) 'Theater Review: Drone on the Range: Adventures in the Mild, Mild West' the *New York Times*. Available at: http://www.nytimes.com/1999/04/06/theater/theater-review-drone-on-the-range-adventures-in-the-mild-mild-west.html?scp=1andsq=Drone+on+the+Range%3A+Adventures+in+the+Mild%2C+Mild+Westandst=nyt. Accessed 8 September 2009.

Marranca, Bonnie (1981) *American Dreams*. New York: PAJ Publications.

Marranca, Bonnie (2002) "PerformanceContemporary: Interview with Richard Maxwell" 17 December 2002, Location One, New York. Available at: http://www.location1.org/mediab/artist.php#m. Accessed 20 August 2003.

Marranca, Bonnie (2003) "The Wooster Group: A Dictionary of Ideas" *PAJ: A Journal of Performance and Art* 74: pp. 1–18.

Mason, Jeffrey D. (1999) "Introduction: American Stages" in Jeffrey D. Mason and J. Ellen Gainer (eds.) *Performing America: Cultural Nationalism in American Theater*. Ann Arbor: University of Michigan Press.

Mauro, Lucia (2002) "Richard Maxwell, The Boxer" Stage Persona: *PerformInk Online*. Available at: http://www.performink.com/Archives/stagepersonae/2002/MaxwellRichard.html. Accessed 14 November 2003.

Maxine Magazine (1995) "Girl Talking with Doorika", interview in *Maxine* magazine. Available at: http://members.core.com/~anthill/doorika.html. Accessed 16 April 2007.

Maxwell, Richard (2001) *Drummer Wanted*, unpublished script purchased from NYCP.

Maxwell, Richard (2003) *Showcase*, unpublished script purchased from NYCP.

Maxwell, Richard (2004a) *Good Samaritans*, unpublished script purchased from NYCP.

Maxwell, Richard (2004b) *Plays 1996–2000*, New York: Theatre Communications Group.

Maxwell, Richard (2006) *End of Reality*, unpublished script purchased from NYCP.

Maxwell, Richard (2006) *The Frame*, unpublished script, provided by author.

Maxwell, Richard (2007) *Ode to the Man Who Kneels*, unpublished script from www.nycplayers.org. Accessed 5 July 2008.

Maxwell, Richard (2009) "People Without History" *American Theatre*, September: pp. 74–80.

Maxwell, Richard (2010) *Das Maedchen (The Girl Torn Between the Days)*, Theater Bonn.

Maxwell, Richard and Brian Mendes (2006) "Talk Karaoke" *Contemporary Theatre Review* 16 (3): pp. 348–354.

Maxwell, Richard and Jim Strahs (1998) *Cowboys and Indians*, unpublished script, provided by author.

McAuley, Gay (1999) *Space in Performance: Making Meaning in the Theatre.* Ann Arbor: University of Michigan Press.

McDonnell, Bill (2005) "The Politics of Historiography—Towards an Ethics of Representation" *Research in Drama Education* 10 (2): pp. 127–138.

McKinley, Jesse (2006) "Playwright's Trademark is Deadpan. Now He Wants to Tweak It" *New York Times*, 18 January 2006. Available at: http://www. nytimes.com/2006/01/18/theater/newsandfeatures/18maxw.html?_r=1andscp= 1andsq=trademark+is+deadpanandst=nyt. Accessed 18 January 2006.

McNulty, Charles (2003) "Bitch Slapped by Shakespeare" *The Village Voice*, September, pp. 24–30. Available at: http://www.villagevoice.com/issues/0339/ mcunlty.php. Accessed 27 November 2004.

McTeague, James H. (1994) *Playwrights and Acting: Acting Methodologies for Brecht, Pinter, and Shepard.* Westport Connecticut: Greenwood Press, pp. 105–127.

Meštrović, Stjepan G. (1997) *Postemotional Society*, London: SAGE.

Mermikides, Alex (2002) "Forced Entertainment—The Travels (2002)" in Harvie, Jen and Andy Lavender (eds.) *Making Contemporary Theatre: International Rehearsal Processes.* Manchester: Manchester University Press, pp. 101–120.

Mogen, David, Mark Busby and Paul Bryant, (eds.) (1989) *The Frontier Experience and the American Dream: Essays on American Literature.* College Station: Texas AandM University Press.

Moore, Steve. (2003) "Flicking the Switch: Toggling between the Real and Artificial with Richard Maxwell." Interview with Steve Moore *Austin Chronicle* 19 September 2003. Available at: www.nycplayers.org. Accessed 10 January 2004.

Mufson, Daniel (2004) "The Burden of Irony, the Onus of Cool: The Wooster Group's Influence on Cannon Company and Richard Maxwell" in Johan Callens (ed.) *The Wooster Group and Its Traditions.* Brussels: Peter Lang, pp. 263–273.

Norris, Christopher (1995) "Versions of Apocalypse: Kant, Derrida, Foucault" in Bull, Malcolm (ed.) *Apocalypse Theory and the Ends of the World.* Oxford: Blackwell Publishers, pp. 227—249.

O'Mahony, John (2006) "Theatre's Thoroughly Reluctant Firebrand" *Financial Times*, 30 October 2006. Available at: http://www.ft.com/cms/s/0/3aea53c8–67bb-11db-8ea5-0000779e2340.html. Accessed 20 June 2009.

O. States, Bert (2002) "Phenomenology of the Actor" in Phillip B. Zarilli (ed.) *Acting (Re) Considered: a Theoretical and Practical Guide.* London: Routledge.

Oswald, Sally (2006) "House Lights: Richard Maxwell's Early Plays" *PAJ* 82: pp. 105–110.

Ozieblo, Barbara (2006) "Codifying the National Self: Spectators, Actors and the American Dramatic Text" in Ozieblo, Barbara and Maria Narbona-Carrion (eds.) *Codifying the National Self: Spectators, Actors and the American Dramatic Text.* Brussels: Peter Lang, pp. 12–19.

Ozieblo, B and M. Narbona-Carrion (eds.) (2006) *Codifying the National Self: Spectators, Actors and the American Dramatic Text.* Brussels: Peter Lang, pp. 11–20.

Perks, Robert and Alistair Thomson (eds.) (1998) *The Oral History Reader.* London: Routledge.

Pleck Joseph H. (1983) *The Myth of Masculinity.* Cambridge: MIT Press.

Pogrebin, Robin (2000) "A Playwright who Creates People not Roles" *New York Times*, 25 September 2000. Available at: http://select.nytimes.com/search/ restricted/article? Accessed 4 January 2007.

Postlewait Thomas and Bruce A. McConachie (1989) *Interpreting the Theatrical Past: Essays in the Historiography of Performance.* Iowa City: University of Iowa Press.

Quick, Andrew (2007) *The Wooster Group Workbook.* New York: Routledge.

Quirke, Kieran (2005) "Joe" *The Metro*, 7 March 2005, p. 23.

Rainer, Yvonne (1996) "A Quasi-Survey of Some of the 'Minimalist' Tendencies in the Quantitatively Minimal Dance Activity Midst the Plethora, or an Analysis of Trio A". In Huxley, Michael and Noel Witts (eds.) *The Twentieth Century Performance Reader.* London: Routledge.

Rayner, Alice (1994) *To Act, To Do, To Perform: Drama and the Phenomenology of Action.* Ann Arbor: University of Michigan Press.

Reagan, Alice (2002) "Performance Review: Drummer Wanted" *Theatre Journal* 54 (2): pp. 314–315.

Ridout, Nicholas (2006) *Stage Fright: Animals and Other Theatrical Problems.* Cambridge: Cambridge University Press.

Román, David (2005) *Performance in America: Contemporary U. S. Culture and the Performing Arts,* Durham and London: Duke University Press.

Rotundo, E. Anthony (1993) *American Manhood: Transformations in Masculinity from the Revolution to the Modern Era.* New York: Basic Books.

Sandman, Jenny (2009) "A Curtain Up Review: People without History" *Curtain Up Internet Theater Magazine.* Available at: http://www.curtainup.com/peoplewithouthistory.html. Accessed 23 September 2009.

Savran, David (1989) *Breaking the Rules: Wooster Group,* New York Theatre Communications Group.

Savran, David (1991) "New Realism: Mamet, Mann and Nelson" in King, Bruce (ed.) *Contemporary American Theatre.* Hampshire: Macmillan.

Sayre, H. M (1989) *The Object of Performance.* Chicago: University of Chicago Press.

Sellar, Tom (2010) "The City's Best (And Not So Best) Progressive Theater" *Village Voice.* Available at: http://www.villagevoice.com/2010–01–05/theater/the-city-s-best-and-not-so-best-progressive-theater/. Accessed 6 October 2010.

Sennett, Richard (2004) "The Age of Anxiety" *The Guardian*, 23 October 2004. Available at: http://www.guardian.co.uk/books/2004/oct/23/usa.politics. Accessed 11 May 2005.

Shimakawa, Karen (2007) "Young Jean Lee's Ugly Feelings about Race and Gender: Stuplime Animation in Songs of the Dragons Flying to Heaven" in *Women and Performance* 17 (1): pp. 89–102.

Soloski, Alexis (2002) "Theater Reviews: Joe" *Time Out New York*, 12–19 September 2002. Available at: http://www.nycplayers.org/reviews/02_TONY_091202.html. Accessed 23 June 2007.

Stinespring, Louise, "Just be Yourself: Derrida Difference and the Meisner Technique" in David Krasner (ed.) *Method Acting Reconsidered: Theory, Practice, Future.* Basingstoke: Macmillan Press, pp. 97–109.

Swettenham, Neal (2008) "The Actor's Problem: Performing the Plays of Richard Foreman" *New Theatre Quarterly* 24 (1): pp. 65—74.

Turner, Cathy (2004) "Palimpsests or Potential Space? Finding a Vocabulary for Site-Specific Performance" *New Theatre Quarterly* 20 (4): pp. 373–390.

Ubersfeld, Anne (1996) *Termes Cles de l'Analyse du Theatre.* Paris: Seuil.

Vanden Heuvel (2004) "L.S.D (Let's Say Deconstruction!) Narrating Emergence in American Alternative Avant-Garde Theatre History", in Johans Callens (ed.) *The Wooster Group and Its Traditions.* Brussels, Peter Lang.

Verk Produksjoner: Video montage from Verk Produksjoner's production of *House* in Oslo, March 2005. Available at: http://www.youtube.com/watch?v=7wc1OanFK9w. Accessed 8 November 2008.

Vonnegut, Kurt (2000) "You Can Go Home Again." In Skrebneski, Victor (ed.) *Steppenwolf: Twenty-Five Years of an Actor's Theater*. Illinois: Sourcebooks Inc.

Vorlicky, Robert H. (1999) "Marking Change, Marking America: Contemporary Performance and Men's Autobiographical Selves", in J. D. Mason and J. Ellen Gainer (eds.) *Performing America: Cultural Nationalism in American Theater*: Ann Arbor: University of Michigan Press, pp. 193–209.

Walsh, Brian (2004) "Shallow Hal, Chipper Bob: Mood Swinging at the Next Wave" *PAJ* 26 (2): pp. 103–109.

Warren, Donald (1998) "'Study of MARs—Middle American Radicals' quoted in Sally Robinson, 'Unyoung, Unpoor, Unblack': John Updike and the Construction of Middle American Masculinity" *Modern Fiction Studies* 44 (2): pp. 331–363.

Wehle, Philippa (2001) "Rich Maxwell: Dramatising the Mundane" *Theatre Forum* 18 (Winter/Spring): pp. 3–8.

Wehle, Phillippa (2007) "Lost in Translation, or why French-language plays are not often seen on American stages" *Yale French Studies* No. 112. pp. 157–170.

Wellman, Mac (2006) "Preface" in Wellman, Mac and Young Jean Lee eds. *An Anthology of New Theater from Downtown New York*. Minneapolis: University of Minnesota Press.

Welton Martin (2005) "Once More with Feeling" *Performance Research* 10 (1): pp. 100–112.

Wessendorf, Markus (2001) "The (Un)settled Space of Richard Maxwell's House" *Modern Drama* 44 (4): pp. 437–457.

Wessendorf, Markus (2003) "The Postdramatic Theatre of Richard Maxwell." Available at: http://www2.hawaii.edu/~wessendo/Maxwell.htm. Accessed 15 February 2006.

Westgate, J. Chris (2005) "Negotiating the American West in Sam Shepards' Family Plays" *Modern Drama* 48 (4): pp. 726–743.

White, Mimi (1992) *Tele-Advising: Therapeutic Discourse in American Television*. Chapel Hill and London: University of North Carolina Press.

Windschuttle, Keith (1998) "Foucault as Historian" *Critical Review of International Social and Political Philosophy*, Vol. 1, No. 2, Summer 1998, pp. 5–35. Available at http://www.sydneyline.com/foucault%20as%20historian.htm. Accessed 20 January 2007.

Wise, Sophie (1999) "What I like about Hal Hartley, or rather, What Hal Hartley Likes about Me: The Performance of the Spectator" in Lesley Stern and George Kouvaros eds. *Falling for You: Essays on Cinema and Performance*. Sydney: Power Institute, pp. 245–275.

Zarrilli, Phillip B. (ed.) (2002) *Acting (Re) Considered: A Theoretical and Practical Guide*. London: Routledge.

Zarrilli, Phillip B. (2009) *Psychophysical Acting: An Intercultural Approach After Stanislavski*. London: Routledge.

Zinn, Howard (1996) *A People's History of the United States from 1492 to the Present*, second edition. Harlow: Pearson Education Ltd.

Index

A

Acting, xiv, xviii, 2–3, 19, 20, 22, 23, 25, 28, 50–51, 56, 61, 65, 67, 73, 77, 79, 94, 119, 122, 129; bad, 18, 22, 30–49, 62; deadpan style (*see* deadpan); industrial, 23; method (*see* Method Acting); neutral (*see* neutrality); postdramatic (*see* postdramatic theatre)

actors: 11–13, non-actors, 19, 64; untrained, 2–3, 10–12, 27, 34, 39, 42–43, 47–49, 68, 72–73, 129. *See also* non-professional actors, amateur actors

agency, xvi, 39–40, 53, 72–73, 90; illusion of, 4–5, 22–23, 29, 117

Agnew, John, 4–5, 7, 28, 104, 109–116

Allen, Rosemary, 18–19, 97, 106–107, 131n1. *See also* Hurley, Kevin

Alvarez, Natalie, xiv-xv, 25, 43–44, 73, 96, 133n13

amateur actors, 26, 42–44, 47, 65, 72, 76–77

amateurism, 18, 48, 73–75; radical, 42–43; professional, 25

America, xvii-xviii, 3–10, 15, 17, 20, 26–29, 32, 93, 101–102, 104, 109, 112, 115, 128

American, xv, xviii, 3–10, 13–18, 20, 22–23, 24–28, 61, 64, 93, 102, 110–111, 115–116, 129; acting, 36–37; culture, xviii, 1, 3, 5, 8, 15, 29, 64, 112–113, 130; frontier; 28, 104, 109, 112; life, 88, 129; literature, 109, 111; male, 9, 15, 27, 71, 89–90; people, 3, 9, 109–110; speech, 10, 120, 123; theatre, 13, 73, 94; values,

3–4, 7–8, 13, 110. *See also* American Dream

American Dream, xviii, 4, 6, 22–23, 28, 93, 104, 109–110, 112, 115–116, 117, 129

anthropological space, 91; place, 27, 93–94, 103, 105, 107, 116, 129

anti-hegemonic, 117

anti-humanism, xv, xviii, 15, 17, 33, 41, 120. *See also* humanism

anti-intellectual, 26

Aronson, Arnold, 19, 99–100. *See also* homemade

Asperger's syndrome, 83. *See also* Baron-Cohen, Simon; autism

aspiration, 5, 24, 30, 39–40, 68, 84, 106, 107–108, 113, 115, 129

Augé, Marc, 27–28, 93–94, 97, 101–105, 107, 129. *See also* non-place; anthropological space

Auslander, Philip, 32, 135n27

authenticity, 12, 17–18, 19, 43, 47, 64, 74–75, 118

autism, 70, 77, 83–84, 88

autonomy, 30, 32, 33–35, 39, 48–49, 67, 92–93, 99

avant-garde, 2–3, 16–18, 54, 60, 61, 99

B

Bailes, Sara Jane, xvi, 18, 24–25, 42–43, 96, 132n8

Barbican, the, xv, 40, 43–44

Baron-Cohen, Simon, 70, 76–77, 83–84, 88

Barthes, Roland, xvii, 17

Baudrillard, Jean, 27–28, 101–102, 104

Beavis and Butthead, 26, 41, 61

Beckett, Samuel, 2–3

Bel, Jerome, 17
belief, 15, 29, 33, 34, 44, 46, 76, 129;
    systems, 7, 9, 25,129
Bill and Ted, 26
blue-collar workers, 4, 9, 28–29, 30,
    38, 67, 100, 102, 115–116, 120,
    129. *See also* class
Bottoms, Steve, 14–15, 20–21, 22
Bradshaw, Thomas, 13, 17, 44–48, 73,
    120–121; character of Tom in
    EOR, 84, 85, 88, 107–108
Brantley, Ben, 12–13, 30, 61–62
Brecht, Bertolt, 2, 11, 28–29, 99, 130
representation, burden of, 36. *See also*
    David Wiles
Bush, George W., 3, 8, 54
Butler, Judith, 31, 33–34, 70, 72, 74,
    76, 90

C

capitalism, 7, 102; liberal, 7; multina-
    tional, 4, 29
casting, 1, 35, 38, 44, 70, 74, 122, 128
CCTD. *See* Cook County Theater
    Department
Chaudhuri, Una, 4, 91, 93, 97,
    101–102
Chicago Reader, the, 54, 57
Chicago Tribune, the, 54
civic pride, 109, 115
class, xviii, 3–4, 7, 22–23, 25, 27, 29,
    30, 31, 34, 38–39, 64, 69–70,
    72–73, 74, 76, 89–90, 102, 115,
    120; blue-collar (*see* blue-collar
    worker); middle, 6–7, 25, 70–71,
    75, 120, 121; middle America,
    xv, 70–71; upper, 110; working,
    xvi, 14, 25, 69, 70, 72, 74, 75,
    76, 89–90, 115–116
Clinton, Bill, 8
Coates, Jen, xviii, 26, 70–71, 88, 89
Cold War, the, 109
Collins, Robert M., 8, 26–27, 88–89,
    131n5
Collins, Samuel, 103
continuity, 25–26, 52, 53, 54, 57, 61,
    66, 67–68, 96
Cook County Theater Department: 1,
    3, 11, 25–26, 35, 50–58, 61–68,
    128–129; *Clowns Plus Wrestlers*,
    25, 55, 57, 59, 65; *Elimination*,
    55–56; *Fable*, 25, 55; *Minutes
    and Seconds*, xi, 25, 55, 57–60,
    62, 65; *Nothing and Advertising*;

25, 55, 57, 59, 61, 65; *Swing
    Your Lady*, 51, 54, 56–57, 60,
    62, 64; *Tosca*, xi, 55, 62, 63
cool, 16–17, 82, 118, 119
coping mechanisms, 20, 22, 129
cowboy, 5, 15, 28, 77, 86–88, 93,
    110–111,112, 114–115, 125
crisis, 9, 14, 25, 26, 27, 69–70, 88–89,
    91
Culler, Jonathan, 95

D

dance, 20, 58, 59; postmodern dance,
    2; minimalist dance, 57–58. *See
    also* Yvonne Rainer
de Beauvoir, Simone, 72
De Certeau, Michel, 51- 53
deadpan, 10–12, 25, 31, 35–36, 61–62,
    119
deconstruction, xviii, 16–17, 51, 61,
    62–63, 124; deconstructive, 2,
    10, 17, 20, 32–33, 67–68, 100,
    125, 128
Democratic and Republican, 4, 5
denegation, 92–93, 96, 97, 100, 101,
    116. *See also* Ubersfeld
Derrida, Jacques, 17, 52–53 or 52, 53,
    68, 95
devised theatre, 52, 55–56
diegetic, 65, 74, 96; extra, 1–2, 31, 47,
    96, 116, 117, 127,130; intra,
    31, 47, 73, 130. *See also* non-
    diegetic
directing, 10, 15, 27, 63–64, 70
downtown New York, 2, 13–14,
    16–17, 31, 42, 69, 73, 118, 119,
    124, 132n8
Duncan, Russell, 5–8, 13

E

Easthope, Anthony, 27
Elevator Repair Service, 13–14, 15, 17,
    18
emotion, 7, 8, 10, 11, 12–13, 15,
    23–24, 32, 36, 37, 66, 71,
    73–74, 75, 80, 84, 86–88, 118,
    132n4; emoting, 25, 26, 30,
    35–36, 38 79, 128–129; post-
    emotional, xviii, 69
emotional landscape, 77, 79, 84, 129
empathy, 5, 19, 69, 70, 71, 83, 88, 89,
    126
engendered, 27, 72, 93, 107
Etchells, Tim, xvi, 13, 21–22, 25

extreme male brain, the, 83. *See also* female brain

F

failure, xvii, 14, 18, 20–22, 36, 39, 44, 62, 63, 65, 66, 67, 69, 70, 72, 74–75, 76, 77, 83, 89, 129
Falk, Florence, 87–88
female brain, 83
femininity, 75, 126–127, 128
feminism, xviii, 70, 75
Fletcher, Jim, 23, 42, 45–47, 85, 106, 113, 121
Fluxus, 55, 57
Forced Entertainment, xiv, xvi, 2, 11, 17, 19, 21–22, 102; *Marathon Lexicon*, 22, *Portrait*, 22
Foreman, Richard, 2, 11, 13, 16, 18–20, 32, 92, 99–100
Foucault, Michel, 17, 33
found text, 57–58, 62, 67
freedom, 4 5–6, 30, 111, 115
freewill, 34, 48–49
Frontier, the, 7, 16, 28, 87, 109–110, 111, 112, 113, 115
Furniss, Lara, xix, 52, 55, 58–60, 63, 134n15, 134n18, 135nn23–24

G

Gardner, Lyn, 10
Gender, xv, xviii, 17, 22–23, 28–29, 38–39, 69–70, 72–77, 88–90, 120, 126–128. *See also* engendered
Gleason, Kate, 3, 50, 52, 55, 68
global: capitalist society, 115; commerce, 7; concerns, 24; enterprise, 102; market forces, xvi, 7; transglobal, 102, 129
Goat Island, xiv, xvi, 17, 20–21, 55–56
Goddard, Joseph, 5–8, 13. *See also* Duncan, Russell

H

Hartley, Hal, 11–13, 15–16
Hayford, Justin, 54–55, 57, 61–63, 67, 133n1, 134n10, 135n31
hegemony, 17; hegemonic, 2, 20, 29, 37, 72–73, 75, 77, 90, 93, 100, 127–128, 130; hegemonic discourse, 17; post-hegemonic, 109, 112. *See also* anti-hegemonic
Hemming, Sarah, 10, 62, 64
hermeneutic, 27, 91, 95–96, 97, 100, 116

hero, 9, 10, 108, 112, 129; heroic, 15; heroism, 15
heterosexist, 31, 33, 76
high-risk, 65, 129
historiography, 28–29, 53, 117
homemade, 18, 99
homophobic, 122–123
honesty, xiv, 6–7, 28, 122–124
Hornby, Richard, 32, 36–38, 132n11
Horrocks, Roger, 70–71, 88
humanism, 1–2, 21
humour, xiv, 8, 60, 125
Hurley, Kevin, 18–19, 97, 105–107
Hutcheon, Linda, 117–120, 124, 127
hypermasculine, xv, 9, 26–27, 77, 85, 86, 87, 128–129; hypermasculinity, 76, 77–78, 84, 88

I

ideology, xviii, 4–5, 6, 17, 22–23, 31, 37, 77, 95, 100, 109, 113
inarticulacy, xvi, 128–129
individualism, 3, 4–5, 7, 128–129
intellectual, xiv-xv, xvii, 14–15, 23, 60, 61, 67, 88, 118; over-intellectualized, 23. *See also* anti-intellectual
ipseity and alterity, 43
irony, 8, 17, 28, 64, 75, 87, 88, 124, 125; as mode of discourse, 117–118; transideological, 119. *See also* Hutcheon, Linda

J

Jackson Turner, Frederick, 28, 109
Jesurun, John, 11

K

Kear, Adrian, 25, 42–43, 48
Kempson, Sibyl, 13, 17, 24, 42, 46, 62, 73, 130
Kimmel, Michael S., 75–76, 89, 118
Klein, Naomi, xiv, 7, 9
Krasner, David, 34–35, 36–39, 48–49

L

Lacan, Jacques, 17
LeCompte, Ellen, xi, 40
LeCompte, Liz, 10, 124–125, 127–128, 129, 136–137n4
Lecoq, Jacques, 26, 42
Lee, Young Jean, 13–14, 16–17, 47, 69
Lehmann, Thomas, 2, 118
liberal, 4, 6, 21, 28–29, 69, 121, 123, 128, 130. *See also* non-liberal

liberal capitalism. *See* Capitalism
live: enactment, 74; event; 74; liveness,
    21–22; medium, 21; perfor-
    mance, 18, 36; theatre, 73. *See
    also* performance
Loft, the, 54–55
Lone Twin, 17
losers, 38, 47, 62, 107

M

machismo, 15, 87; macho, 41, 45–46,
    61, 78, 81
Mamet, David, 4, 14–16, 38
Mangan, Michael, 70, 75, 89
manifest destiny, 109
Marranca, Bonnie, 13–14, 30, 33, 51,
    56, 64, 99
masculinity, xv, xviii, 1, 11, 14, 16,
    26–27, 69–78, 84, 87, 88, 117,
    123, 125
masking-up, 26, 71
mastery, 14, 43, 64
Maxwell, Richard: xiii-xviii, 1–37,
    38–39, 41–52, 54–56, 60–85,87–
    105, 107, 109–113, 115–125,
    127–130; *Ads*, 7–8, 10–11, 119,
    129; *Billings*, 3, 26, 51, 67,
    77–78, 80–81, 93, 103, 120;
    Boxing 2000, 8, 26, 30, 39, 51,
    66, 77–79, 82, 102, 119, 122;
    Burger King, 6, 52, 103, 108;
    Burlesque, 3, 51, 55, 57, 59, 61,
    65, 68; *Caveman*, 77–78, 80–81,
    125; *Cowboys and Indians*,
    5, 28, 93, 110, 112, 114–115;
    Darkness of this Reading, the,
    10; *Das Maedchen*, xviii,10, 28,
    120, 122–123, 125, 129–130,
    Drummer Wanted, xv, 1, 8, 18,
    24, 30, 39–40, 45–46, 78, 81,
    83, 88, 97–98, 100, 119; *End of
    Reality, the*, xiii, xv, 8–10, 24,
    26,28, 30, 44, 46–47, 50, 62,
    67, 73, 77–80, 84, 93, 97–98,
    107, 120, 122, 124, 131n3; *Feud
    Other, the*, 10; *Flight Courier Ser-
    vice*, 51–52, 55, 103. *See* CCTD
    shows; *Frame, the*, xiv, 5, 28, 93,
    110–112, 114–115; *Good Samar-
    itans*, 1, 18, 93, 97–98, 105;
    Henry IV (Part 1) Shakespeare,
    xv, xvii, 43, 52, 73, 118. *See* also
    Shakespeare; *House*, 1, 26, 28,
    30–31, 39, 51, 61, 66, 80, 87,
    91, 96–97, 102, 119, 125; *Joe*,
    51, 66, 73, 88, 99, *Neutral Hero*,
    10, 129; *Ode to the Man Who
    Kneels*, xi, xviii, 5, 8, 26, 28, 77,
    80,84–85, 93, 110, 113–115,
    125, 127; *People Without His-
    tory*, xviii, 28, 52, 87, 123–125,
    127–129; *Portrait*, 22; *Showcase*,
    xv, 26, 28, 79, 93, 104, 106–108;
    Showy Lady Slipper, 77, 80, 119;
    Ute Mnos Vs Crazy Liquors,
    122; *I'm Feeling So Emotional*,
    24; *Showtunes*, 24
McAuley, Gay, 91–93, 95–100, 116,
    136n3
McDonaldization, 7
McDonalds, 6–7
Mendes, Brian, xvi, 3, 11, 23–24, 42,
    47, 50, 51, 54, 56, 60, 62–63,
    65, 68, 73–74, 79, 99, 113, 119,
    129,132n5
Mermikides, Alex, 21–22
Mestrovic, Stjepan, 7–8, 69
meta-theatrical, 2, 61, 71, 89
Method Acting, method acting, 1,
    20, 22–23, 31–32, 35–37, 39,
    43–44, 89
Middle Class, 6, 25, 70–71, 75,
    120–121
mimetic, anti-mimetic, 18, 31, 36
mind/body dualism, 23, 37
MSRI paradigm, 75–76, 83
Mufson, Daniel, 118
music; 10, 14–15, 24–25, 39, 42, 51,
    54, 59, 65–67, 78, 95, 115, 120
mythologies, 4–6, 15, 26–29, 77, 86,
    93, 109–112, 115, 126, 128–
    129.

N

narrative: 2, 12, 15–16, 35, 39–40,
    56–57, 61, 65, 67,71,88,94,
    117, 122; linear realist narrative,
    66, 92; narrative closure, 17,
    67,95
national identities, 4–6, 109
Nature Theatre of Oklahoma, 13,
    16–17
neighborhood, 85, 108
neutrality, 11, 17, 25–26, 71, 102
New England Self, California Self, 26,
    88
non-diegetic, 65
non-liberal, 124

Non-place, 27–28, 93, 97, 101–104,
        107, 117, 129
non-professional actors, 2, 11,42, 44

O
Obama, Barack, 8
Ontological Hysteric Theater, 3, 19
opportunity, xvi, 1, 5, 8, 28–30, 39,
        44, 66, 70, 72, 77, 93, 104,
        109–110, 112, 115–116, 120,
        128–130; land of, 34
Ozieblo, Barbara, 9

P
Park Place, New York, 8, 106
patriarchy, patriarchal, xviii, 124, 127
Performance Art, 2, 32, 55, 57, 94
performance, xvi-xviii, 2, 7, 10–12,
        16–18, 20–22, 24, 26, 30–31,
        34–37, 40–43, 47, 49, 51–52,
        54–55, 57, 59, 61–69, 71–79,
        82, 89–98, 100, 119–129,
        132n6; Performance Studies,
        32–33. *See* Performance Art.
performativity, 11–12, 22, 70, 72, 76, 89
Phelan, Peggy, 21
philanthropy, 7, 103, 113, 115
Pleck, Joseph H.75–77, 83, 89
Pogrebin, Robin, 10, 30, 34, 42, 48,
        61, 73
postcolonialism, xvi, 9
postdramatic theatre, 2, 95, 118
post-hegemonic culture, 109
posthumanism, 9, 20–22, 120
postmodern, xvi, 2, 8–9, 16–17, 59, 94,
        118. *See* also supermodernity.
postmodernism; 93
post-structuralist, xiv, xvii-xviii, 12,
        16–17, 37, 41, 95
presence, 4–5,12, 17–18, 24–26, 28,
        36, 38, 64, 66, 72, 74, 76, 85,
        95, 110, 119, 127
Protestant, 27, 88
Puritan Work- Ethic, 7, 29,
proxemics, 33, 74
psychophysical, 23–24

Q
quotidian, 9, 16, 24–25, 55, 60, 65–66,
        94

R
race, xviii, 4, 8, 16–17, 30–31, 34, 39,
        44, 69–70, 76, 12–122, 128

racism, 121–122
Rainer, Yvonne, 59, 135n25
realist: 2, 17, 25, 27, 44, 71, 91–93,
        95–97, 100, 105, 116–117, 124,
        130; realism, xviii, 10, 12–13,
        27, 33, 37, 55, 96, 100; New
        Realism, 13; hyperrealism13;
        super-realism14; the New Real-
        ists, 13–14
rehearsal: xiii-xiv, xvi, 18, 21–22,
        24, 27–28, 34, 52, 54–55, 63,
        66–68, 71, 75, 92–93, 96–100,
        116, 121–122, 128; rehearsal
        aesthetic, 18, 63, 92–93, 96,
        100, 116
Ridout, Nicholas, 18
Rimini Protokoll, 17
Rotundo, E. Anthony, 70, 88–89
rupture, 27, 51–54, 67

S
Savran, David, 14–15, 22, 56
scenic place, 100, 101. *See* stage space.
secondhand, 99
self-determination, 35, 40. *See* also
        agency.
self-esteem, 8, 108, 115
self-reflexivity, xiv, 52–53, 71, 123
September 11th, 9/11, 9
sexism, 120–122, 124
Shakespeare, William, xv, 43–44, 52,
        57, 73, 118
Shaw, Stephanie, 55
Shepard, Sam, 4, 6, 14–16, 87, 101, 115
shorthand, xvii, 11, 25
Smith, Jonathan M. 28, 109, 113
Social mobility, xviii, 3–6, 64, 93, 110,
        115–116
Social geography, xv, 28
solipsism, 8, 37, 88
Soloski, Alexis, 10–11, 73–74
song, 8, 22, 24–25, 41, 54, 59, 61,
        65–66, 86, 94, 107, 113, 114,
        117, 120
stage space, 91–92, 96–97, 116, 136n4.
        See also scenic place.
Stanislavski, Constantin, 20, 36–37
Steppenwolf Theater, 3, 50, 51, 55
style, 10–12, 18, 23, 25–26, 30–32, 35,
        37, 41, 50–51, 61–62, 64, 67,
        71, 73, 94, 111, 119, 130
subaltern subjects, 9, 28
subversion, 18, 55, 97, 98–99, 117,
        119, 122, 126

supermodernity, 27–28, 102–104, 107, 116, 129. *See* also postmodernism.

T

task 20–21, 23–25, 31–32, 34–35, 41–43, 48, 63, 65–68, 72, 74–75, 89, 124
Taxonomy of Spatial Function, 91–92. *See* also Ubersfeld.
The Wooster Group, 17, 22–23, 31, 33, 36–37, 76, 78, 112, 119–120, 135n27
theatre: xiii-xviii, 1–2, 10–11, 13–14, 18, 20–22, 24–26, 29–31, 35, 37, 39, 43–44, 48, 50–52, 54–57, 59. 61, 68–73, 75, 89, 91–96, 98, 99, 100, 102, 116, 118, 119, 128–130; deconstructive theatre, 2, 10, 17, 32–33, 67, 100, 125, 128; devised theatre, 20, 52, 55, 65; experimental theatre, 13, 16–17, 28–29, 42, 52, 57, 60–61, 71, 92, 95,117; postdramatic theatre, 2, 95, 118; theatre as a place of socio-political commentary, 4, 16–17, 27, 29, 116, 136n3
theological 2, 52, 68
Therapeutic Culture, Therapeutic Attitude, 7–8, 26, 29, 70, 80, 84, 88–90, 129
trademark, 11, 61, 119

U

ubermarionettes, 38
Ubersfeld, Anne, 91–93, 96–97, 100, 116, 130, 136n3
United States Constitution, 4, 6, 116
utilitarian, 23, 67, 71, 92, 98, 105, 126

V

Vazquez, Tory, 127
Verfremdungseffekt, 2, 93
Verk Produksjoner, 91, 94–95
vernacular, argot, xviii, 6, 11, 26, 27, 34, 44–45, 47, 61, 64, 66, 81–82, 85, 103, 111, 120
Victoria, 17
Victory Culture, xviii, 104, 109
Vietnam 6, 109
viewing convention,31, 95–96, 100
virtuosity, 12, 17, 43, 59, 64
Vorlicky, Bob, 26, 70, 74–75, 89
vulnerability, 4, 8, 21, 26, 46–48, 62, 64, 66, 69, 77, 86–87, 117, 120, 130

W

Watergate, 6
Wehle, Phillipa, xv, xvii, 3, 8, 10, 42, 48
Wellman, Mac, 13, 14
Wessendorf, Markus, 24, 31, 38, 47, 62, 66, 94, 97, 99, 115
West, the; western: xv, xvii, xviii, 5, 7, 23, 29, 39, 43, 51, 69, 88–89, 102, 123,130, 132n11; Mid West, 13–14; Frontier/Wild, 15, 28, 86–87, 93, 109–112, 115
Western Liberal Capitalism, 7, 29, 130
Wiles, David, 36
Wilmes, Gary, 3, 42, 50–51, 54–56, 59–64, 68, 131n6, 134n7
Working Class, xvi, 14, 25, 69–76, 89–90, 115. *See* also class,
working poor, the, 104, 116

Z

Zarrilli, Phillip B. 23, 32